San Francisco
Bay Area & Wine Country

Selection of

356 Restaurants

& **60** Hotels

2007
1ᵉ edition

Manufacture française des pneumatiques Michelin
Société en commandite par actions au capital de 304 000 000 EUR
Place des Carmes-Déchaux – 63000 Clermont-Ferrand (France)
R.C.S. Clermont-Fd B 855 200 507

No part of this publication may be reproduced in any form
without the prior permission of the publisher.

© **Michelin et Cie, Propriétaires-éditeurs**
Dépot légal Octobre 2006

Made in Canada

Published in 2006

Please send your comments to:

Michelin North America, Inc.
Travel Publications
One Parkway South – Greenville, SC 29615 USA
TEL: 1-800-423-0485
FAX: 1-800-378-7471
www.michelintravel.com
michelin.guides@us.michelin.com

Dear reader

As successor to the late Édouard Michelin, whose unflagging support made it possible to introduce the Michelin Guide collection in North America, I am thrilled to launch our first Michelin Guide for San Francisco. Our teams have made every effort to produce a selection that does full justice to the rich diversity of the restaurant and hotel scene in San Francisco and the Bay Area.

The Michelin Guide provides a comprehensive selection and rating, in all categories of comfort and prices. As part of our meticulous and highly confidential evaluation process, Michelin inspectors—American and European—conducted anonymous visits to restaurants and hotels in San Francisco and the Bay Area. Michelin's inspectors are the eyes and ears of the customers, and thus their anonymity is key to ensure that they receive the same treatment as any other guest. The decision to award a star is a collective one, based on the consensus of all inspectors who have visited a particular establishment.

Our company's two founders, Édouard and André Michelin, published the first Michelin Guide in 1900, to provide motorists with practical information about where they could service and repair their cars, and find quality accommodations and a good meal. The star-rating system for outstanding restaurants was introduced in 1926. The same system is used for our present American selections.

I sincerely hope that the Michelin Guide San Francisco and the Bay Area 2007 will become your favorite guide to the region's restaurants and hotels. On behalf of all our Michelin employees, let me wish you the very best enjoyment in your San Francisco dining and hotel experiences.

Michel Rollier
Chief Executive Officer, Michelin

Table of contents

Table of contents

Table of contents

How to use this Guide

Hotels classified according to comfort
(more pleasant if in red)

🏠 Comfortable enough

🏠 Comfortable

🏢 Very comfortable

🏢 Top class comfort

🏛 Luxury in the traditional style

Map References
(Hotels)

Mini/Maxi Prices
prices do not include the various taxes

Hotel symbols
149
rooms No. of rooms and suites
 ♿ Wheelchair access
 Exercise room
 Spa
 Swimming pool
 Equipped conference room

Star for good food
❀ to ❀❀❀

Restaurant symbols
 Cash only
 ♿ Wheelchair access
 Garden or terrace dining
 Brunch
 A particularly interesting wine list
 Jacket required
 Valet parking

San Francisco areas or neighborhoods
Each area is color coded...
■ San Francisco City
■ East of San Francisco
■ North of San Francisco
■ South of San Francisco
■ Wine Country

The Hotel

s20
359 Colombus Ave.
Phone: 555-867-5309
Fax: 555-867-5400
Web: www.thehotel.com
Prices: rooms: $395 - $645 • suites: $850 - $1,300 • restaurants: **$$**

149 Rooms
2 Suites

Wine Country Napa Valley

Perch ❀❀

Seafood

001
43 E. 38th St.
Phone: 333-900-8877
Fax: 333-980-1212
Web: www.perch.us
Prices: $$$$

Open daily 9am - midnight
Closed Christmas Day

Castro Cole Valley

The city's special-occasion spot for more than 40 years, the restaurant now operates under the auspices of chef and owner Bill Smith. It's no wonder that his restaurant, with its romantic main dining room lighted with 900 custom candles, and set with Limoges china and Louis XVI-style furnishings, is prized for an enchanting evening out.

In this sanctuary of classic French cuisine, you can choose your own dishes within the framework of a three-, four-, or five-course prix-fixe menu. Although it constantly changes, the selection includes a long list of French favorites (peppered filet mignon with braised endive, boneless quail stuffed with ris de veau, Grand Marnier soufflé), many interpreted with California products. For non-meat eaters, a vegetarian tasting menu is always an option.

On the wine list, you'll discover an excellent selection of French varietals, including Riesling and Gewürztraminer from the chef's native Alsace region, as well as white Burgundy and red Bordeaux.

Restaurants classified according to comfort
(more pleasant if in red)

※ **Comfortable enough**

※※ **Comfortable**

※※※ **Very comfortable**

※※※※ **Top class comfort**

※※※※※ **Luxury in the traditional style**

Name, address and information about the establishment

Map References (Restaurants)

Inspectors' favorites for good value

Price classification (Restaurants)

⊂⊃	under $25
$$	$25 to $40
$$$	$40 to $60
$$$$	over $60

San Francisco

Antica Osteria ⊕

Italian ※※

n°2 2 Market St.

Phone: 555-855-2222
Fax: 555-855-4700
Web: www.anticarestaurant.com
Prices: $$$

Tue - Thu 11am - 10pm
Fri - Sun 11am - midnight
Closed Mon

Meat lovers, rejoice! The Brazilian concept at this restaurant means that for one set price, you can eat all you want. A variety of meats (pork loin, ribs, top sirloin of beef, sausage, chicken) is cooked on skewers over an open fire and brought straight to your table by a waiter clad in gaucho garb. They'll keep bringing food until you tell them to stop. A small sign placed on your table will inform the staff of the state of your appetite: turn up the green side, *sim por favor* ("yes, please, I want more") or the red side, *nao obrigado* ("no thanks, I'm full").

To go with all that tasty meat, there's a salad bar, a buffet of side dishes, and your choice of dessert. Wine racks and Brazilian landscape paintings embellish the colorful dining space.

Boros

American ※

croft Way (bet. College & Piedmont Aves.)

Thu - Tue 11am - 10:30pm
Closed Wed & January 3 - 15

star at this Mediterranean meze house, where low
casual, convivial atmosphere add to the appeal. The
ng room with its bright walls and inlaid-tile tables
ne for sharing meze (the menu lists over 20 different
h homemade yogurt with cucumber and garlic to
pe leaves to pan-fried cubes of calf's liver. Most of
come from Turkey, but there are Greek and Lebanese
ems like char-grilled octopus and hummus.

of small plates doesn't float your boat, there's also
of daily specials, including meat kebabs and grilled
aiter will fill you in on the delightful desserts, such as
d kadayif filled with almonds, pistachios and honey.

ancisco

Appetizers
*Fantine of Ahi Tuna,
Moroccan Spiced Lemon
Confit, Fresh Herbs

Trio of Cold Foie'un Foie
Gras: Orange Terrine, Aspic
Poached Truffle Torchon

Sesame-crusted Hamachi, Yuzu
Shiso, Shiitake Mushroom
Salad*

Entrées
*White Sturgeon en papillote,
Cabbage, Tarbais Beans

Smoked Duck and Razor Clam

Brandt-roasted Halibut,
English Peas, Bacon and
Lettuce, Poultry Jus

Turf & Surf: Roasted Veal
Sirloin, Braised Langoustine,
Salsify, Gratin, Truffle
Hollandaise*

Desserts
*Chocolate Comparison:
Gianduja Bonbon,
Marshmallow and Fudge,
White Sherbet, Ice Cream

Coffee Mousse Bar, Dark
Chocolate Tuies, Frangipan
Cream

Coconut Truffle, Exotic Fruit
and Chocolate Pearls*

Sample menu for starred restaurants

A brief history of San Francisco

Why do so many San Franciscans walk around smiling? Is it the food? The air? The yoga studios? Ask any of them, and they'll be happy to tell you: they live in the best, most beautiful city in the world.

While this 49-square-mile city, with its iconic cable cars, precipitous hills and stunning views of San Francisco Bay, is awe-inspiring, to truly experience the city, you must sample its varied culinary styles. From North Beach cioppino to Dungeness crab and from sourdough bread to Chardonnay and Cabernet Sauvignon, the cuisine of the San Francisco area reflects the bounty of the bay, the fertile farmland, and the nearby vineyards, as well as the diverse population.

The Golden Gate – For more than two centuries, explorers sailed right past the "Golden Gate," as the narrow, fog-cloaked entrance of San Francisco Bay came to be called. The entrance was finally discovered in 1769 by an overland scouting party from Mexico, then under Spanish rule. More Spaniards soon arrived, building a small fort called the Presidio and a Catholic missionary outpost, Mission Dolores.

The Spanish mandate was to colonize the land and pacify the natives, but the soil was poor and the natives were reluctant converts. By the time Mexico won its independence in 1821 and gave the natives land of their own, it was too late. Demoralized, the tribes surrendered their shares to the powerful ranching families known as the *Californios*.

Noe, De Haro, Bernal, Vallejo; many streets, neighborhoods and towns in the Bay Area were

Cable car on Stockton Street

Brigitta L. House/MICHELIN

named after the Spanish *rancheros*, who prospered for about 25 years selling tallow and hides to visiting ships. Gradually a scrappy village—Yerba Buena (Spanish for "good herb")—took root on the tip of San Francisco Peninsula. In 1846 California became part of the United States. Yerba Buena's name was changed to San Francisco the following year.

Forty-Niners – In 1848 San Francisco had a population of 800, one school, one newspaper and a barely realized street grid. Then gold was discovered at Sutter's Mill near Sacramento. By 1849, 90,000 hungry prospectors—called "forty-niners"—had arrived to chase their fortunes.

Grog shops, brothels, flophouses, gambling halls and opium dens were rife, as were, perhaps surprisingly, opera houses and theaters. The 1859 discovery of the Comstock Lode, a fabulously rich vein of silver in Nevada, brought a second wave of prosperity and a rash of new construction, from world-class hotels to Golden Gate Park.

The Big One – On the morning of April 18, 1906, natural disaster struck in the form of a massive earthquake on the San Andreas Fault. By noon, 52 fires were burning throughout the city, devouring 514 blocks and leaving 250,000 people homeless. Yet a determined spirit prevailed and the rebuilding began almost before the smoke had cleared.

San Francisco Comes of Age – Over the next fifty years, San Francisco developed its contemporary character. In the 1920s and 1930s its progressivism came to the fore as unions won major gains for workers, despite the Great Depression. Later the city opened its arms to the "outcasts" of mainstream society—from the disaffected Beat poets of the 1950s to idealistic flower children of the 1960s. Gay liberation and feminism took hold in the 1970s and are still powerful forces in the city today.

But the city also has a business-minded side. As computer companies flourished in the 1990s, city coffers bulged. Forward-thinking politicians wisely spent money refurbishing historic buildings, including City Hall and the Opera House, and putting up stunning new ones, such as the Museum of Modern Art. Hundreds of Internet start-ups set up shop in warehouses south of Market (SoMa), an area now home to museums and restaurants. Today the city claims 790,000 residents, whose numbers are bolstered by 16 million visitors each year.

Both visitors and locals revel in the Bay Area's thousands of restaurants (there are more than 3,300 in the city alone). In keeping with San Franciscans' health-conscious attitude, many of the city's eateries emphasize fresh, local organic products, prepared simply to highlight their natural goodness.

Bon appétit!

A brief history of San Francisco

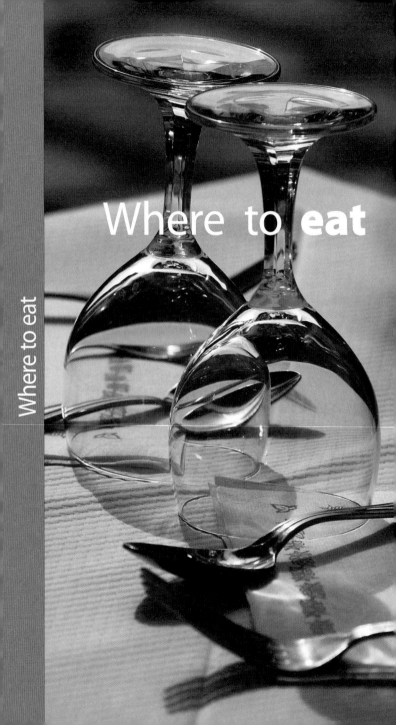

Where to **eat**

Alphabetical list of Restaurants

A

A. Sabella's	✗✗✗	130
Absinthe	✗✗	42
À Côté	✗	178
Acquerello	✿ ✗✗✗	108
Adagia	✗✗	178
Ajanta	✗	179
Albona	✗✗	130
Alexander's Steakhouse	✗✗✗	222
All Seasons Cafe	✗✗	260
Amber India	✗	222
Ame	✗✗✗	160
Americano	✗✗	160
Ana Mandara	✗✗✗	131
Anchor Oyster Bar	✗	32
Angèle	✗✗	260
Anjou	✗✗	60
Annalien	✗	261
Aperto	✗	92
Applewood	✗✗	288
Aqua	✿✿ ✗✗✗	52
Arcadia	✗✗✗	223
Asia de Cuba	✗✗	60
A 16	☺ ✗✗	78
Auberge du Soleil	✿ ✗✗✗	250
Azie	✗✗	161
Aziza	✗✗	146

B

bacar	✗✗	161
Bacco	✗✗	32
Balboa Cafe	✗✗	78
Barndiva	✗	288
Bar Crudo	✗	61
Bar Tartine	☺ ✗	92
Bay Wolf	☺ ✗✗	179
Betelnut Pejiu Wu	☺ ✗	79
Bistro Aix	✗	79
Bistro 350	✗✗	93
Bistro Boudin	✗	131
Bistro Don Giovanni	✗✗	261
Bistro Elan	✗	223
Bistro Jeanty	✿ ✗✗	252
Bistro Ralph	✗	289
Bistro V	✗✗	289
Bix	✗✗	132
Blowfish Sushi	✗	93

Blue Plate	✗	94
Boca	✗✗	200
Bocadillos	✗	61
Boon Fly Café	✗	262
Bouchon	✿ ✗✗	254
Boulevard	✿ ✗✗	156
Bounty Hunter	✗	262
Brannan's Grill	✗✗	263
Brazen Head (The)	✗	80
Brix	✗✗	263
Buckeye Roadhouse	✗✗	200
Bungalow 44	✗✗	201
Burgermeister	✗	33
Burma Superstar	✗	146
Bushi-Tei	✿ ✗✗	74

C

Café Chez Maman	✗	94
Cafe Citti	✗	298
Café de la Presse	✗	62
Café Fanny	✗	180
Cafe Gibraltar	☺ ✗✗	224
Café Gratitude	✗	95
Café Jacqueline	✗	132
Cafe La Haye	✗✗	298
Cafe Marcella	✗✗	224
Caffè Verbena	✗✗	180
Campton Place	✗✗✗	62
C & L Steakhouse	✗✗✗	116
Cantankerous Fish	✗✗	225
Canteen	✗	116
Celadon	✗	264
César	✗	181
Chapeau!	✗✗	147
Charanga	✗	95
Chaya Brasserie	✗✗	162
Chenery Park	✗✗	33
Chez Nous	✗	80
Chez Panisse	✿ ✗✗	176
Chez Papa	✗	96
Chez TJ	✿ ✗✗✗	220
Chow	✗	34
Cindy's Backstreet Kitchen	✗✗	264
Circolo	✗✗	96
Citizen Cake	✗	42
Citron	✗	181
Clementine	☺ ✗✗	147

Where to eat

Restaurants by Cuisine type

Afghan

Helmand (The)	135

American

Balboa Cafe	78
Bistro Boudin	131
Bix	132
Blue Plate	94
Bounty Hunter	262
Brannan's Grill	263
Buckeye Roadhouse	200
Bungalow 44	201
Burgermeister	33
C & L Steakhouse	116
Chenery Park	33
Chow	34
Cindy's Backstreet Kitchen	264
Cuvée	266
Deuce	299
Foothill Cafe	267
Hayes Street Grill	43
Home	36
Lark Creek Inn	205
Liberty Cafe & Bakery	100
Market	268
Maverick	101
Myth	139
rnm	46
Sauce	46
Taylor's Automatic Refresher	274
Wolf House	302
Woodward's Garden	105
zazu	294
Zin	294

Asian

Azie	161
Betelnut Pejiu Wu	79
Crustacean	117

Bakery

Café Fanny	180
Tartine Bakery	104

Basque

Iluna Basque	136
Piperade	140

Brazilian

Espetus Churrascaria	43

Burmese

Burma Superstar	146
Nan Yang	186

Californian

Adagia	178
All Seasons Cafe	260
Americano	160
Applewood	288
Auberge du Soleil	250
bacar	161
Bar Tartine	92
Bay Wolf	179
Bistro Elan	223
Bistro Ralph	289
Boon Fly Café	262
Boulevard	156
Brix	263
Canteen	116
Chez Panisse	176
Citizen Cake	42
Domaine Chandon	266
downtown	182
Dry Creek Kitchen	282
El Dorado Kitchen	300
Farmhouse Inn and Restaurant	284
1550 Hyde Cafe and Wine Bar	117
Foreign Cinema	98
Fork	202
Fournou's Ovens	118
Glen Ellen Inn	300
Hawthorne Lane	163
Hurley's	267
Jardinière	44
John Ash and Co.	290
Julia's Kitchen	268
Manka's Inverness Lodge	207
N.V.	270
Napa Valley Grill	270
Navio	231
Nopa	45
Olema Inn	208
Olivia	187
Oola	166
PlumpJack Cafe	85
Sent Sovi	235
Simmer	211
Slow Club	103
Spago Palo Alto	237

Chapeau!	147
Chez Papa	96
Clementine	147
Emile's	226
Fleur de Lys	56
Fringale	162
Garçon	98
Grand Cafe	64
Jeanty at Jack's	65
K & L Bistro	286
La Folie	110
La Provence	99
La Rose Bistro	185
La Suite	164
Le Charm	165
Left Bank	206
Le Papillon	230
Mirepoix	291
Plumed Horse (The)	234
South Park Cafe	168
Zazie	39

Fusion

Asia de Cuba	60
Bushi-Tei	74
Chaya Brasserie	162
Pomelo	151

Gastropub

Brazen Head (The)	80

Greek

Kokkari Estiatorio	136

Indian

Ajanta	179
Amber India	222
Dosa	97
Gaylord	203
Indian Oven	44
Junnoon	229
Lotus of India	206

International

Sonoma-Meritâge Martini Oyster Bar and Grill	301
Wappo Bar Bistro	275

Italian

Acquerello	108
Albona	130
Aperto	92
A 16	78
Bacco	32
Bistro Don Giovanni	261
Cafe Citti	298
Caffè Verbena	180
Cook St. Helena	265
Cucina	201
Delfina	97
Della Santina's	299
Dopo	182
Fior d'Italia	133
Florio	81
Frantoio	203
Incanto	37
L'Osteria del Forno	137
Mixx Enoteca Luigi	291
North Beach Restaurant	139
Oliveto	187
Osteria	232
Palio d'Asti	67
Piazza D'Angelo	209
Piazza Italia	233
Poggio	210
Posticino	272
Quince	76
Rose Pistola	140
Santi	292
Sociale	86
Tommaso's	142
Trattoria Contadina	142
Trattoria La Siciliana	191
Tra Vigne	274
Vivande	87

Japanese

Blowfish Sushi	93
Deep Sushi	34
Ebisu	148
Grandeho's Kamekyo	134
Hana	290
Kabuto	148
Kiji	99
Kirala	184
Koo	150
Kyo-ya	164
Maki	83
Medicine Eatstation	66
Mifune	84
O Chamé	186
Ozumo	167
Sanraku	69
Sebo	47
Shabu-Sen	86
Sushi Bistro	152
Sushi Groove	122
Sushi Ran	198
Tokyo Go Go	104
Uzen	191
Zushi Puzzle	87

Restaurants by Cuisine type

Latin American

Mediterranean

Mexican

Middle Eastern

Moroccan

Persian

Peruvian

Pizza

Seafood

Spanish

Steakhouse

Thai

Turkish

Vegetarian

Vietnamese

After 100 years of reviewing restaurants, we've still kept our figure.

We've gained something important from a century of evaluating restaurants and hotels: trust. Our professionally trained inspectors anonymously rate quality, service, and atmosphere so you get the real story. To learn more, visit michelintravel.com.

MICHELIN
A better way forward

Starred Restaurants

Within the selection we offer you, some restaurants deserve to be highlighted for their particularly good cuisine. When giving one, two or three Michelin stars, there are a number of things that we judge, including the quality of the ingredients, the technical skill and flair that goes into their preparation, the blend and clarity of flavors, and the balance of the menu. Just as important is the ability to produce excellent cooking time and again. We make as many visits as we need, so that our readers can be sure of quality and consistency.

A two- or three-star restaurant has to offer something very special in its cuisine; a real element of creativity, originality or "personality" that sets it apart from the rest. Three stars – our highest award – are given to the very best restaurants, where the whole dining experience is superb.

Cuisine in any style, modern or traditional, may be eligible for a star. Because we apply the same independent standards everywhere, the awards have become benchmarks of reliability and excellence in over 20 European countries. This is particularly true in France, where we have awarded stars for almost 80 years, and where the expression "Now that's real three-star quality!" has entered into the language.

The awarding of a star is based solely on the quality of the cuisine.

Exceptional cuisine, worth a special journey

One always eats here extremely well, often superbly. Distinctive dishes are precisely executed, using superlative ingredients.

		page
French Laundry (The)	XXXX	248

Excellent cuisine, worth a detour

Skillfully and carefully crafted dishes of outstanding quality.

		page
Aqua	XXX	52
Cyrus	XXXX	280
Manresa	XXX	218
Michael Mina	XXXX	54

A very good restaurant in its category

A place offering cuisine prepared to a consistently high standard.

		page			page
Acquerello	XXX	108	Fleur de Lys	XXX	56
Auberge du Soleil	XXX	250	Gary Danko	XXX	128
Bistro Jeanty	XX	252	K & L Bistro	X	286
Bouchon	XX	254	La Folie	XXX	110
Boulevard	XX	156	La Toque	XXX	256
Bushi-Tei	XX	74	Masa's	XXXX	112
Chez Panisse	XX	176	Quince	XXX	76
Chez TJ	XXX	220	Range	XX	90
Dry Creek Kitchen	XXX	282	Ritz-Carlton Dining Room	XXXX	114
Farmhouse Inn			Rubicon	XX	58
and Restaurant	XXX	284	Sushi Ran	X	198
Fifth Floor	XXXX	158	Terra	XX	258

Bib gourmand

This symbol indicates our inspectors' favorites for good value. For $35 or less, you can enjoy two courses and a glass of wine or a dessert (not including tax or gratuity).

Bon appétit!

A 16	✗✗	78	Mamacita	✗	84
Bar Tartine	✗	92	Mirepoix	✗	291
Bay Wolf	✗✗	179	Olivia	✗	187
Betelnut Pejiu Wu	✗	79	Pauline's Pizza	✗	102
Cafe Gibraltar	✗✗	224	Posticino	✗	272
Clementine	✗✗	147	rnm	✗	46
Cook St. Helena	✗	265	Santi	✗✗	292
Cuvée	✗✗	266	Sauce	✗✗	46
Delfina	✗	97	Slanted Door (The)	✗✗	70
El Dorado Kitchen	✗✗	300	Slow Club	✗	103
Foothill Cafe	✗✗	267	South Park Cafe	✗	168
Gaylord	✗✗	203	Tablespoon	✗✗	122
Greens	✗	82	Tartine Bakery	✗	104
Insalata's	✗✗	204	Tokyo Go Go	✗	104
Junnoon	✗✗	229	Tommaso's	✗	142
Koi Palace	✗	229	2223	✗	38
Kokkari Estiatorio	✗✗	136	Universal Cafe	✗	105
Koo	✗	150	Yank Sing	✗✗	170
Le Charm	✗	165	Zuzu	✗	276

Where to eat

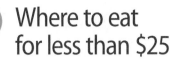

Where to eat for less than $25

Where to have brunch

© Robert Holmes

San Jose, Santana Row

Where to have a late dinner

Restaurants taking last orders after 10:30pm at least four nights a week.

© Robert Holmes

Eating out in Sausalito

San Francisco
City

Alamo Square

Castro District
Cole Valley, Haight-Ashbury, Noe Valley

Epicenter of gay San Francisco, the Castro *(bounded roughly by Market, 22nd, Douglass and Church Sts.)* hums with energy night and day along its central commercial corridor, **Castro Street**. This thoroughfare is also home to the 1922 **Castro Theatre,** San Francisco's grandest movie palace, along with a plethora of bookstores, bars, shops and cafes. It's hard to find any spot in the district where you can't see at least one rainbow flag, the universal symbol of gay pride.

The neighborhood took on its present character in the 1970s, when enterprising gay designers began purchasing the Castro's 19th-century Victorians at rock-bottom prices and fixing them up. In 1977 residents succeeded in electing one of their own, **Harvey Milk,** to the city's Board of Supervisors. Slain by fellow supervisor Dan White the following year, Milk remains a revered figure for being the first openly gay elected official in U.S. history.

Noe Valley – Once land used for cattle ranching and sheep grazing, the Victorian cottage-lined streets of neighboring Noe Valley are now largely populated by the stroller set. The area's colorful commercial thoroughfare, **24th Street** overflows with designer-clothing shops, bookstores and wine merchants.

Haight-Ashbury – Although more than three decades have passed since the Human Be-In and the Summer of Love, a 1960s countercultural ethos still clings to the Haight (as it's known), centered on Haight Street between Central Avenue and Stanyan Street, just west of the Castro.

Brigitta L. House/MICHELIN

Vintage boutiques, Haight-Ashbury

The stretch of Haight Street between Central Avenue and Stanyan Street, known as "the Upper Haight," is packed with thrift stores, vintage boutiques and coffeehouses, most of which cater to hip twenty-somethings.

Near the southwest corner of Golden Gate Park, **Cole Valley** is a quiet upscale enclave known for its family-run bakeries, good restaurants and gourmet food shops.

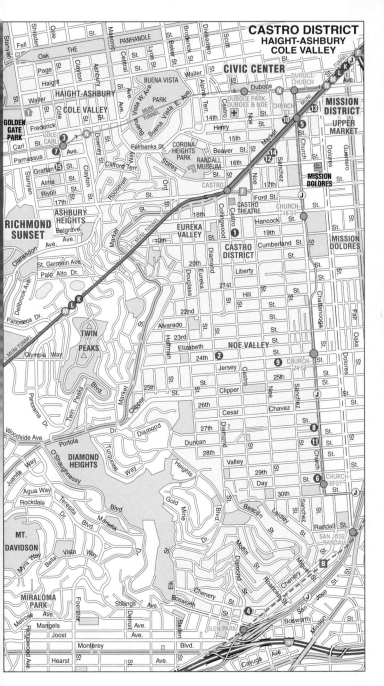

Anchor Oyster Bar

001

Seafood ✗

579 Castro St. (bet. 18th & 19th Sts.)

Phone:	415-431-3990	Mon – Fri 11:30am - 10pm
Fax:	N/A	Sat noon - 10pm
Web:	N/A	Sun 4pm - 9:30pm
Prices:	$$	Closed major holidays

Looking for luxury in the Castro? You've come to the wrong place. On the other hand, if you're looking for wonderfully fresh shellfish, Anchor Oyster Bar is the place to go. Since 1977, this tiny, no-frills oyster bar has packed in bivalve lovers like sardines.

What it lacks in atmosphere (the eatery holds a smattering of stainless-steel tables and a long, white-marble counter; you have to walk through the little kitchen to access the restrooms), it more than makes up for with the quality of its seafood. Oysters on the half-shell, steamed clams and mussels, and seafood salads are complemented by an array of fresh fish listed on a board above the bar. Who needs flashy décor when you can have seafood this good?

Bacco

002

Italian ✗✗

737 Diamond St. (bet. Elizabeth & 24th Sts.)

Phone:	415-282-4969	Mon – Sat 5:30pm - 10pm
Fax:	415-282-1315	Sun 5pm - 9:30pm
Web:	www.baccosf.com	
Prices:	$$	

This Noe Valley trattoria draws diners from around the city to its warm gold-toned dining room. Tile floors, arched openings and Italian ceramics lend a Tuscan feel to the space, while the quiet neighborhood creates a Victorian charm.

Since the restaurant opened in 1993, chef/owner Vincenzo Cucco has been dishing up honest Italian fare, enhanced by a good choice of nightly specials. If stuffed pan-seared calamari, homemade pappardelle topped with Bolognese sauce and fresh ricotta, and milk-fed veal stew with cipolline, peas, carrots and soft polenta make your mouth water, and moderate prices appeal to your pocketbook, you've come to the right place. The short wine list focuses on Italian varietals, classified by price.

Burgermeister

A m e r i c a n ✗

86 Carl St. (at Cole St.)

Phone:	415-566-1274	Open daily 11am - 10pm
Fax:	415-566-2259	
Web:	www.burgermeistersf.com	
Prices:	⬭⬭	

In health-conscious San Francisco, you might be reluctant to admit that you're craving a good old-fashioned burger. Happily, this no-frills Cole Valley burger joint can accommodate you. Since this is the City by the Bay, the beef at Burgermeister comes from Marin County's Niman Ranch, where it is raised humanely without hormones or antibiotics, and the land is treated as a sustainable resource. Expect startlingly flavorful meat, perfectly grilled and served on a warm sesame-seed bun. And since this is California, there are, of course, several veggie burgers on the menu, including a vegan incarnation.

If you can't make it to Cole Valley, you'll find other locations in North Beach *(759 Columbus Ave.)* and in the Castro district *(138 Church St.)*.

Chenery Park

004

A m e r i c a n ✗✗

683 Chenery St. (at Diamond St.)

Phone:	415-337-8537	Mon – Thu 5:30pm - 9:30pm
Fax:	415-337-0390	Fri – Sat 5:30pm - 10pm
Web:	www.chenerypark.com	Sun 5:30pm - 9pm
Prices:	$$	

Richard Rosen and Gaines Dobbins worked together at L'Avenue and Boulevard before partnering in their own venture in 2000. Located in the relatively unknown neighborhood of Glen Park, south of Noe Valley, Chenery Park highlights small plates, entrées and daily specials (come Monday for fried chicken, Friday for sautéed crab cakes), all at moderate prices.

Fresh flowers, sage-colored walls, and bold abstract paintings by local artist Joe Novak decorate the contemporary dining space, which is divided into a main floor and an upstairs mezzanine. From dry-aged New York sirloin to spicy seafood gumbo, the menu zeros in on the best of regional American cuisine.

Every Tuesday is Family Night, when the restaurant rolls out a separate menu designed just for kids.

San Francisco City Castro

Chow

American ✕

005

215 Church St. (at Market St.)

Phone: 415-552-2469
Fax: 415-552-8629
Web: N/A
Prices: ✆✆

Mon – Thu 11am - 11pm
Fri 11am - midnight
Sat 10am - midnight
Sun 10am - 11pm
Closed Thanksgiving & Christmas Day

Chow bills its menu as American, but when they say "American," they mean melting pot. From wontons to wood-fired pizzas and Thai-style noodles to home-style pork chops, this upper Market eatery features eclectic dishes to please almost any palate. Located right on the streetcar line, Chow attracts locals with its casual vibe, tasty cuisine and low prices. The menu follows the seasons, and desserts like the warm ginger cake, creamy cheesecake and pecan pie are made fresh daily. Added features? A kids' menu, and a peaceful outdoor patio.

Chow doesn't take reservations, but call right before you come, and they'll add your name to the waiting list. Sister, Park Chow, in the Sunset district *(1240 Ninth Ave.)* serves the same menu.

Deep Sushi

Japanese ✕

006

1740 Church St. (bet. Day & 29th Sts.)

Phone: 415-970-3337
Fax: 415-970-0551
Web: www.deepsushi-sf.com
Prices: $$

Mon – Sat 6pm - 11pm
Closed Sun

If you know where to go, Noe Valley can get pretty lively. Take Deep Sushi, for example. It's hidden away on a quiet street with no visible sign, but behind its windowed façade, this joint can really jump. The sushi bar in front is the place to be, where young chefs create original rolls with evocative names like Dragon Breath (spicy crab topped with unagi, avocado and spicy sauce), Sunkissed (smoked salmon, sun-dried tomato and cream cheese) and Yellow Fever (ei, imago, grilled scallion and tobiko).

If you're looking for a place to have a glass of sake or a cocktail before your meal, head back to the bar, an animated atmosphere for starters (try the Katsuo tataki, seared Hawaiian bonito with ponzu sauce, or the romi-romi salmon).

EOS

Contemporary Asian ✗

901 Cole St. (at Carl St.)

Phone:	415-566-3063	Sun – Thu 5:30pm - 10pm
Fax:	415-566-2663	Fri – Sat 5:30pm - 11pm
Web:	www.eossf.com	
Prices:	$$	

The first decision you'll have to make at this Cole Valley corner restaurant and bar (near Haight Ashbury) is whether to eat in the celadon-green dining room, or at the seductive wine bar next door.

If you choose the former, plan to order several small plates and share them around the table. Spicy pan-fried Chinese long beans, Madras curry potato cakes with purple plum chutney, cod steamed in sake-soy broth in a clay pot, and tea-smoked Peking duck breast with ginger-quince compote typify the selections on the monthly changing menu.

If you prefer to dine in the wine bar, you'll have access to the same menu, plus a longer list of wines—which you can order by the glass, the taste, or the flight.

Eric's

008

Chinese ✗

1500 Church St. (at 27th St.)

Phone:	415-282-0919	Sun – Thu 11am - 9pm
Fax:	415-282-9989	Fri – Sat 11am - 9:30pm
Web:	N/A	
Prices:	ᗧ	

At lunch, it's almost impossible to find a better deal than the bargain prices offered at this Noe Valley Chinese restaurant. For around $6, you can have the soup of the day, a generous entrée, fresh fruit and green tea. That's a meal that will leave both your appetite and your wallet satisfied. At dinner, prices go up a bit, but they're still quite attractive. Hunan and Mandarin recipes rule the menu, which lists dishes like Eric's spicy eggplant, Hunan fish (battered rock cod in a sweet sauce), spicy smoked pork, and five-taste chicken.

Orchids and carved-wood screens adorn the simple dining room, where you can expect efficient and speedy service. Eric's doesn't take reservations, so go prepared to wait in line.

Fresca

Peruvian

3945 24th St. (bet. Noe & Sanchez Sts.)

Phone:	415-695-0549
Fax:	415-695-0384
Web:	www.frescasf.com
Prices:	$$

Sun – Thu 11am - 3pm & 5pm - 10pm
Fri – Sat 11am - 10pm

San Franciscans get a taste of Peru's piquant cuisine at this family-owned restaurant. What started out as a Peruvian fast-food place founded by Lima native Jose Calvo-Perez in the West Portal district *(24 W. Portal Ave.)* has mushroomed to include two sit-down restaurants *(the other is at 2114 Fillmore St.)*.

Fresca's Noe Valley outpost focuses on a ceviche bar, where Peruvian black ceviche (calamari, scallops and prawns in squid-ink lime juice with salsa criolla) and ceviche cocotuna (yellowfin tuna with ginger, lime-infused coconut water and Andean corn) play starring roles. Elsewhere on the menu, American ingredients meet Peruvian recipes in dishes like *arroz con mariscos* (a version of seafood paella), and *lomo saltado* (strips of beef tenderloin with onion, tomato and cilantro).

Home

American

2100 Market St. (at Church St.)

Phone:	415-503-0333
Fax:	N/A
Web:	www.home-sf.com
Prices:	$$

Mon – Thu 5pm - 10pm
Fri 5pm - 11pm
Sat 10am - 2pm & 5pm - 11pm
Sun 10am - 2pm & 5pm - 10pm

You'll find all the comforts of home at this popular Castro hangout. White walls frame red banquettes and large windows open onto busy Market Street, while an enclosed patio provides a charming place to spend a cool San Francisco evening (it's heated in winter). The kitchen puts a California spin on comfort-food classics such as Niman Ranch meatloaf, macaroni and cheese, and Mrs. Cleaver's tuna casserole topped with toasted bread crumbs. Indeed, you almost expect June herself to emerge from the kitchen in her neatly pressed shirtwaist. In lieu of Mrs. Cleaver, the pastry chef concocts some wonderful old-fashioned desserts, notably the banana bread pudding.

A second location in Cow Hollow *(2032 Union St.)* insures that you're never too far from Home.

Incanto

011

1550 Church St. (at Duncan St.)

Phone:	415-641-4500	Wed – Mon 5:30pm - 10pm
Fax:	415-641-4546	Closed Tue
Web:	www.incanto.biz	
Prices:	$$	

Decked out with handcrafted stone, antique woodwork and 16th-century Latin parchments, Incanto is a restaurant with a conscience. Besides supporting sustainable agriculture, the Noe Valley eatery adds a partial service charge of 5% to every bill in order to share tips with the unsung heroes of the kitchen.

The great thing about food made from sustainably grown products is that it tastes better. You can't go wrong with entrées like milk-braised pork shoulder with escarole and creamy polenta, or handkerchief pasta topped with rustic pork ragu. Beyond the 170-bottle wine list, you can order vino by the half-liter, the 2.5-ounce pour, and more than 20 choices by the glass. Feeling adventurous? Try the Mystery Flight, designed to test your palate with three select Italian wines.

Lime

Contemporary ⚔

012

2247 Market St. (bet. Noe & Sanchez Sts.)

Phone:	415-621-5256	Mon – Thu 5pm - midnight
Fax:	415-621-5504	Fri – Sat 5pm - 1am
Web:	www.lime-sf.com	Sun 10:30am - midnight
Prices:	⊜	

Half cocktail bar, half restaurant, Lime wows with its psychedelic 1960s décor by designer Craige Walters. Plexiglass ceilings, pink mirrors, and a white-marble, sushi-style bar flanked by low lime-green seats all contribute to the oh-so-hip vibe.

The comely cast at the bar sipping house-infused vodka and vanilla mojitos is ready to party, buoyed up by the blaring DJ-orchestrated tunes. Meanwhile, diners seated at immaculate white oval tables and in curving leather banquettes split inexpensive small plates of flavorful globally inspired fare: zucchini frites with basil aioli, ricotta gnocchi with shiitake mushrooms, tandoori chicken skewers, and Moroccan lamb chops.

The kitchen stays open until midnight to keep the party going.

Mecca

Contemporary

2029 Market St. (bet. Dolores & 14th Sts.)

Phone:	415-621-7000	Mon – Sat 5pm - 11pm
Fax:	415-621-7094	Sun noon - 11pm
Web:	www.sfmecca.com	
Prices:	$$$	

Mecca abounds with nightclub flair, from the circular bar in the middle room of this 5,000-square-foot industrial-chic space—where Castro's cool stay to drink, socialize and people-watch—to the sleek dining room with its crystal chandelier and spot-lit black-and-white photographs, well-spaced tables and cozy curving booths. An urban mix of tunes, spun by a DJ six nights a week, sets the party mood.

In summer 2006, a new chef took over the kitchen and fashioned a fresh menu using regional American ingredients; Hudson Valley foie gras, andouille sausage, wild Petral sole and Fulton Valley chicken are just a sampling of what you might find on your plate. Each week, the chef goes down-home with a three-course Southern Sunday Supper; it's a steal at just under $30.

2223

Contemporary

2223 Market St. (bet. Noe & Sanchez Sts.)

Phone:	415-431-0692	Mon – Thu 5:30pm - 9:30pm
Fax:	415-865-0836	Fri – Sat 5:30pm - 11pm
Web:	www.2223restaurant.com	Sun 10:30am - 2:30pm & 5:30pm - 9:30pm
Prices:	$$	

Dinner at 2223 starts with a warm welcome from the smiling hostess who greets you at the entrance. Then, you can proceed to the lively bar for a drink, or go directly to your table in the attractive honey-colored dining room, with its wood floor and high-backed caramel-colored leather banquettes.

Here, chef/owner Melinda Randolph puts her twist on contemporary American recipes, adding a pinch of Californian, a dash of French, and a soupçon of Asian accents. Availability of market-fresh ingredients dictates the flavorful dishes on the frequently changing menu. If it's offered on the dessert menu, try the Granny Smith apple galette, a crisp puff-pastry turnover served warm with vanilla ice cream, huckleberry compote and maple-glazed walnuts. Locals love the Sunday brunch.

San Francisco City Castro

Zazie

015

941 Cole St. (bet. Carl St. & Parnassus Ave.)

Phone:	415-564-5332	Mon – Fri 8am - 9:30pm
Fax:	N/A	Sat – Sun 9am - 10pm
Web:	www.zaziesf.com	
Prices:	☙	

Named for the Louis Malle film *Zazie dans le Métro*, this Cole Valley neighborhood bistro keeps residents' hunger at bay all day by serving breakfast, lunch and dinner. Start your day with lemon ricotta pancakes, challah French toast or poached eggs Monaco (with prosciutto and tomatoes). At lunch, choose among soups and salads (the popular salade Niçoise even has a vegetarian version without tuna and eggs), sandwiches and plats du jour; in the evening, stick-to-your-ribs fare such as chicken sauté Grand-Mère, herb-crusted sole, and lamb chops au vin cater to heartier appetitites.

The dining room's sunny yellow walls are hung with French art posters, but the garden patio is the clear preference in warm weather.

San Francisco City Castro

Civic Center
Hayes Valley, Lower Haight, Tenderloin

The only remnant of a 1905 plan to remake San Francisco according to the principles of the City Beautiful movement—replete with wide boulevards and grand monuments—Civic Center is home to San Francisco's magnificent City Hall, as well as several of the city's grandest performance spaces and cultural institutions including the War Memorial Opera House, Davies Symphony Hall, the gleaming granite San Francisco Public Library, and the stellar Asian Art Museum.

In 1945 Civic Center played a significant role in world history. From April to June of that year the United Nations convened in the War Memorial Opera House, and the UN Charter was signed in the Herbst Theatre. That said, it's not much of a neighborhood—its huge buildings and vast plazas *(bounded by Market St., Van Ness Ave. and Golden Gate Ave.)* didn't leave much room for residential development. Instead, to the dismay of city officials, Civic Center has become a magnet for the city's homeless population. Hopes are high that the recent completion of an 18-story eco-friendly federal office building *(7th and Mission Sts.)*, combined with more effective social-service programs, will help revitalize the area.

San Francisco's "town center" has one life during the day, when government offices are in full swing, and another at night, when concert goers flock to the area's popular restaurants and theaters.

The Tenderloin – To the north of Civic Center is an area bounded by Geary, Jones, Mission and Van Ness streets with a long, perilous reputation. Dubbed "The Tenderloin" (a reference to bygone days when policemen were paid more to cover the dangerous streets and thus could afford more expensive cuts of meat), this area is the most urban neighborhood within the city, home to a sliding-scale population. Here, the adventurous visitor will find culinary styles as diverse as the residents.

Hayes Valley – Just a few blocks west of Civic Center, Hayes Valley—centered on Hayes Street between Franklin and Laguna streets—is a great place to eat and shop if you're in the area, with a number of funky upscale boutiques and a dozen restaurants serving everything from

City Hall

sushi to coq au vin. Most restaurants require reservations between 6pm and 7:30pm, peak hours for pre-performance dinners.

Bordering Hayes Valley on the west, the **Lower Haight**, as the area of Haight Ashbury between Divisadero and Webster streets is called, appeals to a young crowd with its alternative nightclub scene.

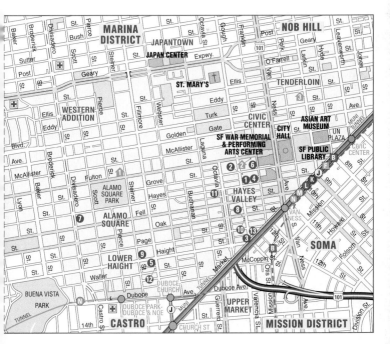

Absinthe

French ✗✗

001

398 Hayes St. (at Gough St.)

Phone:	415-551-1590
Fax:	415-252-2386
Web:	www.absinthe.com
Prices:	$$$

Tue – Thu 11:30am - midnight
Fri 11:30am - 2am
Sat 11am - 2am
Sun 11am - 10pm
Closed Mon

Although absinthe—the toxic anise-flavored liqueur so popular with avant-garde poets and painters in mid-19th-century France—was officially banned in 1915, its spirit hovers in this Belle Époque-style French brasserie. Here, vintage absinthe posters and walls of banquettes inset with small oval mirrors bespeak a bygone era. In the second dining room, a fresco depicts the *fée verte*, or "green muse," as absinthe was once known.

Most of the dishes on the changing menu are inspired by French recipes like onion soup gratinée, duck pâté, coq au vin and cassoulet. Oyster lovers can choose from a bounty of selections from both the east and west coasts. The more than 300 bottles on the global wine list come thanks to the restaurant's partnership with Arlequin Wine Merchant next door.

Citizen Cake

Californian ✗

002

399 Grove St. (at Gough St.)

Phone:	415-861-2228
Fax:	415-861-0565
Web:	www.citizencake.com
Prices:	$$

Tue – Fri 8am - 10pm
Sat 10am - 10pm
Sun 10am - 5pm
Closed Mon & January 1 - 8

"Let them eat cake" is good advice, especially when the cake in question comes from pastry chef Elizabeth Falkner's patisserie. Opened in 1997 in SoMa, Citizen Cake moved to its present location, mere steps away from the War Memorial Opera House and the Davies Symphony Hall, in 2000.

While Falkner's place is well known for its take-away cakes and breads, it's also open for breakfast, lunch and dinner. It's worth lingering in the high-ceilinged dining room for the likes of pork osso buco with rapini tops and cheddar grits, and tagliatelle tossed with escarole, pine nuts and currants. Don't even think about skipping dessert here. Sweets may have punny names like Back in the Apple Again, Scarborough Pear, and Je Ne Sais Quoise, but their flavors don't fool around.

Espetus Churrascaria

003

Brazilian ✗

1686 Market St. (at Gough St.)

Phone: 415-552-8792
Fax: 415-552-8793
Web: www.espetus.com
Prices: $$

Open daily 11:30am - 3pm & 5pm - 10pm
Closed Thanksgiving & Christmas Day

&

Meat lovers, rejoice! The Brazilian concept at Espetus (the name means "skewer") means that for one set price, you can eat all you want. A variety of meats (pork loin, ribs, top sirloin of beef, sausage, chicken) is cooked on skewers over an open fire and brought straight to your table by a waiter clad in gaucho garb. They'll keep bringing food until you tell them to stop. A small sign placed on your table will inform the staff of the state of your appetite: turn up the green side, *sim por favor* ("yes, please, I want more") or the red side, *nao obrigado* ("no thanks, I'm full").

To go with all that tasty meat, there's a salad bar, a buffet of side dishes, and your choice of dessert. Wine racks and Brazilian landscape paintings embellish the colorful dining space.

Hayes Street Grill

004

American ✗✗

324 Hayes St. (bet. Franklin & Gough Sts.)

Phone: 415-863-5545
Fax: 415-863-1873
Web: www.hayesstreetgrill.com
Prices: $$$

Mon – Thu 11:30am - 2pm & 5pm - 9:30pm
Fri 11:30am - 2pm & 5pm - 10:30pm
Sat 5:30pm -10:30pm
Sun 5pm - 8:30pm

&

A Civic Center institution, Hayes Street Grill opened in 1979 as a partnership between Richard Sander and food critic Patricia Unterman, author of the *San Francisco Food Lover's Guide*. At lunchtime the grill is popular with government types, while at night music fans dine here before catching a performance at the War Memorial Opera House or the Davies Symphony Hall, just steps away at San Francisco's Performing Arts Center.

The menu changes daily, depending on what is fresh at the market (Unterman was one of the founders of the Ferry Plaza Farmers Market), and concentrates on seafood from nearby waters, such as harpoon-caught Ventura swordfish, Half Moon Bay petrale sole, or Monterey Bay sardines. Grilled fish comes with your choice of sauce on the side.

San Francisco City Civic Center

Indian Oven

 005

Indian

233 Fillmore St. (bet. Haight & Waller Sts.)

Phone: 415-626-1628
Fax: 415-553-3259
Web: www.indianovensf.com
Prices: 💰💰

Open daily 5pm - 11pm

Since it opened in 1987, Indian Oven has repeatedly won the locals' vote for the city's best Indian restaurant. The Lower Haight establishment is perpetually packed, and for good reason.

For starters, there's the tasty North Indian cuisine. Dishes like *Bengan pakoras* (eggplant dipped in chickpea batter and fried), tandoori prawns, and lamb *pasanda* (cooked in a sauce made from yogurt, cream and ground cashews) begin with fresh ingredients and end with happy customers who keep coming back for more. Vegetarian specialties, including naan that can be served plain or stuffed with fruit and nuts, are sure to please non-meat eaters.

Prompt service and the ability to have a full meal for less than $25 are two more reasons to dine here. Ask for a seat in the intimate second-floor dining room.

Jardinière

006

Californian

300 Grove St. (at Franklin St.)

Phone: 415-861-5555
Fax: 415-861-5580
Web: www.jardiniere.com
Prices: $$$$

Sun – Wed 5pm - 10pm
Thu – Sat 5pm - 10:30pm

The owner of Jardinière, acclaimed chef Traci Des Jardins has been having a love affair with the land since she was a girl on a farm in California's San Joachin Valley. Her commitment to recycling, eco-friendly farming and sustainable seafood assures that only the best-quality ingredients appear on your plate. House-made charcuterie, Wolf Ranch quail with foraged mushrooms, and duck confit with marinated Le Puy lentils reflect the French accents in Des Jardins' changing à la carte and six-course tasting menus. A selection of delectable cheeses will tempt you to add another course to your meal.

Inside this landmark, a block from the Opera House, Pat Kuleto sets the stage for celebration with a golden dome in the shape of an inverted champagne glass that hovers above the oval bar.

Nopa

007

Californian ✗

560 Divisadero St. (at Hayes St.)

Phone:	415-864-8643	Open daily 6pm - 1am
Fax:	N/A	Closed July 4
Web:	www.nopasf.com	
Prices:	$$	

♿

Over the years, this building on the corner of Divisadero and Hayes housed a laundromat before being reborn as a restaurant in April 2006. Located a block west of Alamo Square in Western Addition, Nopa is an acronym for North of the Panhandle. Three alumni from Chow in the Castro, chef Laurence Jossel, Allyson Woodman and Jeff Hanak, combined forces to open this buzzing loft-like establishment, decorated with an urban mural by local artist Brian Barneclo.

What the chef calls "urban rustic" food translates into stylish riffs on Cal-Med recipes (spring vegetable tagine with lemon yogurt, flatbread of asparagus, arugula and prosciutto, Mediterranean fish stew). Nopa doesn't accept advance reservations, but you can call starting at 5pm for same-day dining.

paul k

008

Mediterranean ✗✗

199 Gough St. (at Oak St.)

Phone:	415-552-7132	Tue – Thu 5pm - 10pm
Fax:	415-552-9810	Fri – Sat 5pm - 11pm
Web:	www.paulkrestaurant.com	Sun 5pm - 9:30pm
Prices:	$$	Closed Mon

In 1999, when Paul Kavouksorian sold Picnix, the sandwich-and-salad place he had operated in the Presidio for 16 years, he moved to Hayes Valley to open this intimate neighborhood eatery. True to the owner's Armenian heritage, paul k blends exotic touches of the Middle East into its Mediterranean-accented fare. The likes of duck breast rubbed with Syrian spices, grilled Prime ribeye peppered with chili harissa, and, for dessert, sesame Napoleon with mascarpone, dried cherries and apricots fill the small, weekly changing menu.

A short but good selection of wines are whimsically classified under such headings as "pensive red beauties that blossom with our food," and "perfumed whites you can dabble behind your ears."

San Francisco City Civic Center

rnm ☺

American ✕

009

598 Haight St. (at Steiner St.)

Phone:	415-551-7900	Tue – Thu 5:30pm - 10pm
Fax:	415-551-7901	Fri – Sat 5:30pm - 11pm
Web:	www.rnmrestaurant.com	Closed Sun & Mon
Prices:	$$	

Opened in 2002, rnm is one sexy "neighborhood joint," as the restaurant bills itself. The interior is blanketed in a sleek, urbane décor, replete with deep earthy colors, aluminum mesh curtains and modern bistro furniture. There's a flat-screen TV behind the bar, and a few stools afford a close-up view of the action in the open kitchen. Upstairs, the mezzanine exudes a lounge-like atmosphere.

On the menu, small and large plates mean meals can be catered to individual appetites. Justine Miner's creative California fare expresses delightful touches of Italy and France in dishes like white-corn chowder with morels, and pan-roasted duck breast with cherry gastrique and English pea and mint risotto. Come before 7pm (Tuesday to Saturday) for the bargain three-course fixed-price menu.

Sauce ☺

American ✕✕

010

131 Gough St. (bet. Oak & Page Sts.)

Phone:	415-252-1369	Open daily 5pm - 2am
Fax:	415-252-7588	
Web:	www.saucesf.com	
Prices:	$$	

A California twist distinguishes home-style American fare at this Hayes Valley newcomer. Roasted chicken mac 'n' cheese, for example, is made with hand-rolled papardelle in a creamy four-cheese sauce topped with shredded chicken and blanched asparagus. Bacon-wrapped meatloaf and oatmeal stout fish 'n' chips will sate your appetite before or after (the restaurant serves 'til midnight) a performance at the Civic Center complex. For dessert, the PB&J (pan-seared sponge cake layered with homemade strawberry preserves, Frangelico peanut butter and vanilla ice cream) will leave you lamenting the fact that Mom never thought up such a delicious combination.

Modern décor, in shades of brown and yellow with a minimum of bric-a-brac, won't distract you from the hearty portions on your plate.

Sebo

011

517 Hayes St. (at Octavia St.)

Phone:	415-864-2122	Tue – Sat 6pm - 10:30pm
Fax:	N/A	Closed Sun & Mon
Web:	N/A	
Prices:	$$	

A recent addition to Hayes Valley's renaissance, Sebo will appeal to those who appreciate impeccably fresh and delicately flavored sushi. Don't be put off by the fact that Sebo's owners are American; dishes here represent those you would find at a traditional Japanese sushi house (there's no California roll on this menu).

You'll feel like you're in a friend's kitchen when you pull up a chair at the open, inviting sushi bar at the back of the room. This is the place to be if you want to order the omakase chef's tasting (it's only served at the sushi bar). Some of the best seasonal fish available appears on the concise menu, which also lists its waters of origin. Unique nigiri selections include giant clams, and maki rolls like maguro with lemon, avocado, kaiware, sea salt and sesame oil.

Thep Phanom

Thai ✗✗

012

400 Waller St. (at Fillmore St.)

Phone:	415-431-2526	Open daily 5:30pm - 10:30pm
Fax:	N/A	
Web:	www.thepphanom.com	
Prices:	$$	

This Thai restaurant in the Lower Haight has been a hit since it opened in 1986. Thep Phanom bills itself as serving "authentic Thai cuisine," and it doesn't fall short of its mark. Chef/owner Pathama Parikanont proudly uses fresh ingredients such as coconut milk, lemongrass, ginger, basil, chiles and curry powder, which infuse his cooking with the sometimes delicate, sometimes fiery tastes and fragrances typical of well-prepared Thai cuisine. With 99 different dishes on the menu, there's something to appeal to most every palate, and the prices are reasonable, to boot.

Asian knick-knacks and Thai paintings color the surroundings in the small dining room.

San Francisco City Civic Center

Zuni Café

013

1658 Market St. (bet. Franklin & Gough Sts.)

Phone:	415-552-2522
Fax:	415-552-9149
Web:	N/A
Prices:	$$$

Tue – Sat 11:30am - midnight
Sun 11am - 11pm
Closed Mon

Informal and elegant with its quirky dining spaces, copper-topped bar, and floor-to-ceiling windows peering out on Market Street, Zuni Café occupies a high place in San Francisco's gastronomic landscape. Chef/owner Judy Rodgers, who trained at Chez Panisse, has been overseeing the kitchen here for 26 years. The constantly changing list of Mediterranean dishes reflects her love of southern France and Italy.

Although the menu choices turn over frequently, regulars still clamor for the signature roasted chicken for two served with warm Tuscan-style bread salad, as well as the house-ground hamburgers and the thin-crust brick-oven-baked pizzas. Then there's the oyster and shellfish bar, not to mention house-cured meats. Late lunch and dinner menus accommodate those with unusual schedules.

San Francisco City Civic Center

Financial District
Union Square

Contrary to its laid-back image, San Francisco does have a bustling business district. On weekdays, cars, buses, streetcars, pedestrians, and pierced and tattooed bicycle messengers clog the streets of the triangle bounded by Kearny, Jackson and Market streets. Lines snake out the doors of the better take-out sandwich shops and salad bars, and expense-account restaurants do a brisk lunch business. At night, though, the area is practically deserted.

A Bit of History – The 1906 earthquake and fire destroyed this district, which was almost entirely built on landfill in the years following the Gold Rush, but it was largely reconstructed by 1909. Many of the new buildings were done in the Classical style; in the 1920s the first skyscrapers started going up. By the 1970s, after the **Transamerica Pyramid** *(600 Montgomery St.)* was erected, preservationists were starting to panic and strict limitations were placed on the height and bulk of new buildings. Since then most new construction has gone up south of Market Street.

The waterfront promenade known as the **Embarcadero** ("boarding place" in Spanish), has been reborn in recent years as a park paved with sidewalks and lined with palms. It is here, inside the soaring central arcade of the renovated 1898 **Ferry Building** *(at Market St.)* that you'll find the **Ferry Building Marketplace**, a showcase for artisan cheeses, gelato, exotic teas and handmade chocolates. The Saturday market, held on the rear plaza overlooking the bay *(8am–2pm)*, abounds with organic produce, mouth-watering baked goods, fresh pasta and more.

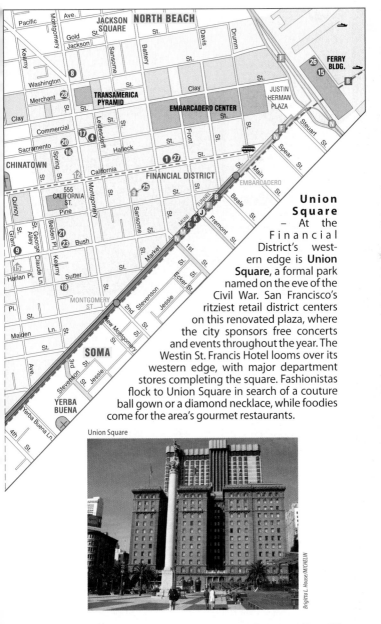

Union Square – At the Financial District's western edge is **Union Square**, a formal park named on the eve of the Civil War. San Francisco's ritziest retail district centers on this renovated plaza, where the city sponsors free concerts and events throughout the year. The Westin St. Francis Hotel looms over its western edge, with major department stores completing the square. Fashionistas flock to Union Square in search of a couture ball gown or a diamond necklace, while foodies come for the area's gourmet restaurants.

Union Square

Brigitta L. House/MICHELIN

Aqua ❀❀

001

Seafood 🍴🍴🍴

252 California St. (bet. Battery & Front Sts.)

Phone:	415-956-9662	Mon – Fri 11:30am - 2pm
Fax:	415-956-5229	& 5:30pm - 10:30pm
Web:	www.aqua-sf.com	Sat 5:30pm - 10:30pm
Prices:	$$$$	Sun 5:30pm - 9:30pm

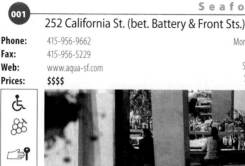

Aqua/Marleen Severijn

Whether to celebrate a special occasion, impress a date, or entertain a business colleague, a meal in this sophisticated 120-seat restaurant will change the way you think about seafood.

Chef Laurent Manrique grew up in the Gascony region of France and learned to cook at his grandmother's auberge. His resume includes time in the kitchens at Taillevent and Toit de Passy in Paris, Peacock Alley (at the Waldorf-Astoria) and Gertrude's in New York City, as well as Campton Place in San Francisco. Manrique's cuisine is a pure expression of the finest ingredients. It's not easy to improve on a perfect piece of fish, but the chef manages to do it in seasonal compositions such as Aqua's signature Ahi tuna tartare, and flawlessly cooked Alaskan black cod accompanied by thin slices of delicately smoked bacon and glazed carrots.

To round out your repast, the superb wine list presents some 500 bottles from California, France, Italy and Spain, and includes house labels created in partnership with California winemakers. The dining space abounds with artful flower arrangements, adding colorful focal points to the room's muted tones.

Appetizers

Tartare of Ahi Tuna, Moroccan Spices, Lemon Confit, Fresh Herbs

Trio of Cold Artisan Foie Gras: Orange Terrine, Syrah Poached, Truffled Torchon

Sesame-crusted Hamachi, Yuzu, Shiso, Shiitake Mushroom Salad

Entrées

White Sturgeon en papillote, Cabbage, Tarbais Beans, Smoked Duck and Razor Clams

Brioche-crusted Halibut, English Peas, Bacon and Lettuce, Poultry Jus

"Surf & Turf": Roasted Veal Sirloin, Poached Langoustine, Salsify Gratin, Truffle Hollandaise

Desserts

Chocolate Composition: Gianduja Bonbons, Marshmallow and Fudge, White-chocolate Ice Cream

Coffee Mousse Bar, Dark Chocolate Sauce, Havana Cream

Coconut Soufflé, Exotic Fruit and Chocolate Pearls

SEAFOOD

Michael Mina ✿ ✿

002

335 Powell St. (bet. Geary & Post Sts.)

Phone:	415-397-9222	Open daily 5:30pm – 10pm
Fax:	415-397-9220	Closed major holidays
Web:	www.michaelmina.net	
Prices:	$$$$	

Michael Mina/Eric Laignel

Perched on a corner of Union Square, the venerable St. Francis Hotel *(see hotel listings)* makes a fittingly elegant nest for Michael Mina. The luxurious dining room off the hotel's lobby tacitly demands that the well-heeled clientele dress for dinner, while neutral tones realize a soothing backdrop for imposing columns that soar up to the high ceiling, Murano glass light fixtures, and large arched windows covered with Roman shades.

Celebrated chef Michael Mina, formerly of San Francisco's Aqua and Charles Nob Hill, designs his menu in trios. Colors and flavors marry in novel combinations on the three-course prix-fixe menu. For each dish, preparations are presented in threes based on the main ingredient. Seared diver scallops, for example, could come with Meyer lemon and Osetra caviar, with butternut squash and black truffle, and with scarlet beets and Maine lobster. Dessert brings more triads. If you choose "citrus," you might find grapefruit ginger pie, Meyer lemon cheesecake, and a Key lime Napoleon gracing your plate.

Attentive service dovetails with the luxe surroundings, and the sommelier gives good advice about the voluminous wine list, while respecting diners' budgets.

Appetizers

Ahi Tuna Tartare with Scotch Bonnet Pepper, Bosc Pear and Sesame Oil

Roasted Foie Gras Torchon with Crimson Rhubarb, Star Anise, Maui Gold Pineapple, Vanilla, Seckel Pear and Port Wine

Seared Diver Scallops with Marinated Scallops, Meyer Lemon, Osetra Caviar, Sweet Yellow Corn, Black Truffle, Scarlet Beet, and Maine Lobster

Entrées

Maine Lobster Pot Pie with Brandied Lobster Cream and Seasonal Vegetables

Olive-Oil-poached Rack of Lamb with Ricotta Tortellini, Watercress, Zucchini, Anchovy, Sweet 100 Tomato, Pine Nuts, Garlic, Niçoise Olives, Parsley and Pearl Onions

Kobe Beef Rib Roast – Braised Zabaton, with Artichoke, Roasted Garlic, Morel Mushroom Jus, Wasabi Chickpea, Radish, Teriyaki, Horseradish Fingerling, Caramelized Onions and Worcestershire

Desserts

Root-Beer Float with warm Chocolate Chip Cookies

Chocolate-Peanut Butter Pudding Cake with a Shake, Banana Bread Pudding, Banana Pot de Crème, Devil's Food Cake and a Caramel Sundae

Berry Shortcake Ice-Cream Sundae with Raspberry, Devonshire Ice Cream, Blueberry, Crème-Fraîche Sherbet, Strawberry, and Milk-Chocolate Mousse

Fleur de Lys

003

French 🍴🍴🍴

777 Sutter St. (bet. Jones & Taylor Sts.)

Phone:	415-673-7779	Mon – Thu 6pm - 9:30pm
Fax:	415-673-4619	Fri 5:30pm - 10pm
Web:	www.fleurdelyssf.com	Sat 5pm - 10pm
Prices:	$$$$	Closed Sun

Fleur de Lys

San Francisco's special-occasion spot for more than 40 years, Fleur de Lys now operates under the auspices of French-born chef and owner Hubert Keller. It's no wonder that his restaurant, with its romantic main dining room tented with 900 yards of custom-printed fabric, and set with Limoges china and Louis XVI-style furnishings, is prized for an enchanting evening out.

In this sanctuary of classic French cuisine, you can choose your own dishes within the framework of a three-, four-, or five-course prix-fixe menu. Although it constantly changes, the selection includes a long list of French favorites (peppered filet mignon with braised endive, boneless quail stuffed with ris de veau, Grand Marnier soufflé), many interpreted with California products. For non-meat eaters, a vegetarian tasting menu is always an option.

On the wine list, you'll discover an excellent selection of French varietals, including Riesling and Gewürztraminer from the chef's native Alsace region, as well as white Burgundy and red Bordeaux.

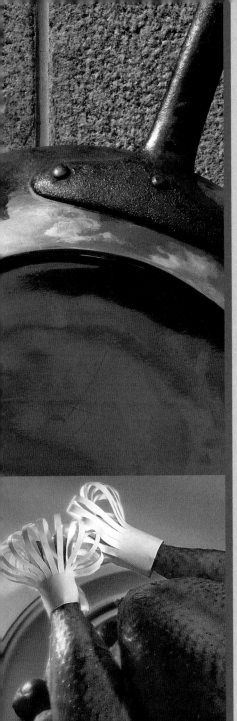

Appetizers

*Maine Lobster and Truffle
Cappuccino, Fingerling Potato
and Leek with Corn, Lobster
and Black-Pepper Skillet Bread*

*White and Green Asparagus
salad, dressed with a Cream
of Salsify with Black Truffles
and Aged Xérès Vinegar, topped
with Foie Gras and Pistachio
"Marble"*

*Untraditional Ahi Tuna Tartare
topped with Oxtail Consommé
"en gelée" with Golden Brown
Panisses*

Entrées

*Sea Bass with Black Trumpet
Mushroom Crust, Warm Cabbage
and Bacon Salad, Watermelon
Radish and Riesling Sauce*

*Roasted Colorado Lamb Loin and
Braised Lamb Cheek Cannelloni
with Lapsang Souchong Smoked
Tea-infused Lamb Reduction and
Vanilla Oil*

*Roasted Squab Breast Filled with
Foie Gras and Truffles with a
Ravioli of Squab Leg Confit and
Sauternes-Ginger Sauce*

Desserts

*Caramel Banana Cream Tart
with delicate Praline Fondant
and Pina Colada Frozen Tower*

*Bittersweet Chocolate Mousse
presented with an Apple-Brioche
Sandwich and a warm Dark-
Chocolate Doughnut cooled off
with Black- and White-Chocolate
Sorbets*

*Saffron Crème Brûlée with
Frozen Rhubarb Yogurt and
Chocolate Shooter with Dark-
rum Sabayon*

Rubicon ❀

Contemporary 🍴🍴

004

558 Sacramento St. (bet. Montgomery & Sansome Sts.)

Phone:	415-434-4100	Mon – Tue 5:30pm - 10pm
Fax:	415-421-7648	Wed 11:30am - 1:30pm & 5:30pm - 10pm
Web:	www.sfrubicon.com	Thu – Sat 5:30pm - 10pm
Prices:	$$$	Closed Sun

Rubicon

Part of Drew Nieporent's Myriad Restaurant Group (which includes such renowned New York City establishments as Tribeca Grill, Montrachet, and Nobu), Rubicon has been a hit with San Francisco diners since it opened in 1994. It's little wonder why. In addition to Nieporent, Rubicon boasts an all-star cast of co-owners including actors Robert DeNiro and Robin Williams (a local resident) and film director Francis Ford Coppola.

Against a sober backdrop of polished cherry wood and bright white walls embellished with paintings by Robert DeNiro Sr., chef Stuart Brioza presents a contemporary menu based on fresh, seasonal products simply cooked to preserve the essence of each ingredient. Sautéed skate wing might be perfectly paired with a fragrant purée of blueberries; black truffle gnocchi napped with fontina fondue, or squab breasts smoked over fruitwood and served with mustard greens, dried fruit and foie gras; it all depends on what the chef finds at the Ferry Building Market each day.

Master sommelier Larry Stone oversees the award-winning script of 1,600 bottles, on which California, Burgundy and Rhône vintages make special appearances.

Appetizers

Crispy Spiced Quail with Tart Onions, Lemon Confit and Basil

Rolled Yellowfin Tuna with Black Trumpets, Foie Gras and Oxtail Glaze

Caramelized Garlic Soup with Dungeness Crab, Prosciutto and Chardonnay Vinegar

Entrées

Sauté of Local Petrale Sole with Baby Artichoke, Olives, Meyer Lemon and Potato Mousseline

Paprika-spiced Cloverdale Rabbit with Asparagus, Black Olive, Stinging Nettle and Pepitas

Almond-crusted Loin of Lamb with Cauliflower, Medjool Dates, Sesame and Grain Mustard

Desserts

Aged Sardinian Pecorino and Walnut Cake with Roasted Clementines and Arbequina Olive-Oil Ice Cream

Warm Chocolate Pecan Crêpes with Brown-Butter-poached Figs and Szechuan Pepper Sabayon

Caramelized Mascarpone Custard with Lime-Passionfruit Caramel and Mango Granita

Anjou

005

44 Campton Pl. (bet. Grant & Stockton Sts.)

Phone:	415-392-5373	Tue – Sat 11:30am - 2pm & 6pm - 10pm
Fax:	N/A	Closed Sun & Mon
Web:	www.anjou-sf.com	
Prices:	$$	

Located on a little side street around the corner from Campton Place hotel, Anjou takes its name from the native region of its chef and owner, Pierre Morin. You'll recognize the restaurant by its cheery yellow-and-white-striped awning and by the vintage blue Citroën parked in front. Inside, exposed brick and brass accent the bistro décor, and black-and-white photographs of France ornament the walls.

Chef Pierre has a way with bistro recipes, *bien sûr*, serving duck-leg confit with wild mushrooms and frisée, marrying calf's liver with applewood-smoked bacon and onions, and wrapping California sea bass in a mushroom crêpe. The two-course Express Menu is the way to go for a quick lunch. And as a finale, what could be more à propos than warm Anjou pears in Cointreau sabayon?

Asia de Cuba

006

495 Geary St. (at Taylor St.)

Phone:	415-929-2300	Sun – Wed 11:30am - 2:30pm
Fax:	415-929-2377	& 5:30pm - 10:30pm
Web:	www.clifthotel.com	Thu – Sat 11:30am - 2:30pm
Prices:	$$$$	& 5:30pm - 11:30pm

Looking for a place to party? Head for the Clift Hotel *(see hotel listings)* near Union Square. Inside the sleek wonderland designed by Philippe Starck, you'll find Asia de Cuba. The San Francisco setting of Jeffrey Chodorow's successful restaurant concept attracts the young and the hip to its nightclub ambience. Glamour gleams in the floor-length velvet drapes, moody lighting from Murano-glass lamps, and a cross-shaped communal table fashioned from Venetian glass.

Fusing Asian and Latin cuisines, the food captures your palate as the décor does your eye. Tunapica, for instance, combines tuna tartare with Spanish olives, black currants, almonds and coconut, all tossed in soy-lime vinaigrette. Bring friends for sharing; the servings are nearly as big as the prices.

Bar Crudo

007

603 Bush St. (at Stockton St.)

Phone: 415-956-0396
Fax: 415-563-7539
Web: www.barcrudo.com
Prices: $$

Mon – Thu 6pm - 10:30pm
Fri – Sat 6pm - 11pm
Closed Sun & major holidays

Think of Bar Crudo as your neighborhood raw bar. Sure, it's located above the Stockton Tunnel on a rather unappealing block, but twin brothers Mike (the chef) and Tim (the manager) Selvera have hit on a winning concept here. Crudo (raw fish), shellfish (oysters on the half-shell, Gulf prawns, Maine lobster and Dungeness crab), and cold food are the mainstays of the menu. A few hot dishes are offered too, including the creamy seafood chowder, chock-full of clams, mussels, squid and shrimp (but no desserts). A short list of wines and a good selection of Belgian beers make fitting accompaniments.

The place is tiny, about 30 seats, and tables bunch together on the mezzanine-like second level; the ground level holds two small zinc counters where you can pull up a stool, if you prefer.

Bocadillos

008

710 Montgomery St. (at Washington St.)

Phone: 415-982-2622
Fax: 415-982-0177
Web: www.bocasf.com
Prices: ෙ

Mon – Fri 7am - 11pm
Sat 5pm - 11pm
Closed Sun

♿

Spanish for "little sandwiches," Bocadillos is chef Gerald Hirigoyen's (also of Piperade) contribution to the tapas craze. Small plates star at dinner, prepared in a variety of ways: *a la plancha* (prawns with garlic flakes and lemon confit), marinated (tai snapper ceviche), roasted (baby back ribs with honey and sherry glaze), to name a few. If you're in an offal mood, order tripe basquaise or pigs trotters from the "Innard Circle."

The restaurant is open non-stop all day on weekdays. Drop in at noon (they don't take reservations) for one of the signature bocadillos, such as 18-month-aged Serrano ham with tomato rub, or Catalan sausage with arugula and shaved Manchego.

In the dining room, votive-like lights reflect off bright painted-brick walls, bathing guests in a sultry glow.

San Francisco City Financial District

Café de la Presse

009

French ✗

352 Grant Ave. (at Bush St.)

Phone:	415-398-2680	Mon – Thu 11:30am - 2:30pm & 5:30pm - 9pm
Fax:	415-249-0916	Fri – Sun 11:30am - 2:30pm & 5:30pm - 10pm
Web:	www.cafedelapresse.com	
Prices:	$$	

Located on a busy corner across from the Chinatown gate and adjacent to the Triton Hotel, Café de la Presse is now run by the same group that owns Aqua and C&L Steakhouse. Step inside and you're enveloped in a true bistro scene, complete with wood parquet floors, Belle Époque light fixtures, a horseshoe-shaped bar, and a newsstand that sells international newspapers.

Grab a copy of *Le Monde* and take a seat at one of the round, marble bistro tables. Don't read French? Immerse yourself in the trendy fashion and lifestyle videos shown on the two flat-screen monitors. Thanks to the savoir faire of the French chef and his team, country pâté, salade frisée, monkfish à la Marseillaise, lamb casserole, and scrumptious praline profiteroles are sure to titillate your taste buds. *Bon appétit!*

Campton Place

010

Contemporary ✗✗✗

340 Stockton St. (bet. Post & Sutter Sts.)

Phone:	415-955-5555	Sun – Thu 11:30am - 2pm & 5:30pm - 9pm
Fax:	415-955-5559	Fri 11:30am - 2pm & 5:30pm - 9:30pm
Web:	www.camptonplace.com	Sat noon- 2pm & 5:30pm - 9:30pm
Prices:	$$$$	

You'll be swathed in soft lighting and hues of cream, gold and cocoa in this formal dining room, located off the lobby of Union Square's swank Campton Place hotel. Clean lines characterize this space, the centerpiece of which is a fanciful blown-glass flower suspended from the ceiling. Along the walls, framed collages add sparks of color.

While the décor hits its mark, the kitchen floundered in a state of transition at the beginning of 2006, after chef Daniel Humm left. The current menu presents a choice of three or four courses from the à la carte list, or a multicourse chef's tasting that incorporates products like Hama Hama River oysters, artisan foie gras, beef from Four Story Hills Farms, and a wonderful selection of artisanal cheeses.

Colibrí

011

438 Geary St (bet. Mason & Taylor Sts.)

Phone:	415-440-2737	Mon – Thu 11:30am - 2:30pm & 4pm - 11pm
Fax:	415-440-0866	Fri 11:30am - 2:30pm & 4pm - midnight
Web:	www.colibrimexicanbistro.com	Sat 10am - 2:30pm & 4pm - midnight
Prices:	$$	Sun 10am - 2:30pm & 4pm - 11pm

The soul of colonial Mexico lives in this pretty cantina, where gold and terra-cotta paints color the walls, circular wooden chandeliers hang overhead, and wrought-iron details provide authentic accents.

Despite its convenient location across the street from the Curran and Geary theaters, Colibrí is more than just a place for a pre-show bite. You'll want to linger in this warm environment, to sip a margarita, savor a Mexican wine, or sample some of the 100 tequilas on the lengthy beverage list. And, of course, you'll need some tapas to accompany that drink. The list ranges from crispy handmade *tostadas de tinga* to traditional mole poblano.

If you are trying to catch a show, however, the menu helpfully indicates those dishes with a short preparation time.

Cortez

012

550 Geary St. (bet. Jones & Taylor Sts.)

Phone:	415-292-6360	Sun – Thu 5pm - 10pm
Fax:	415-673-7080	Fri – Sat 5pm - 11pm
Web:	www.cortezrestaurant.com	
Prices:	$$	

You'll immediately sense the bold spirit of this establishment, named for the Spanish explorer Hernando Cortez. Designed by Michael Brennan, the restaurant fits seamlessly into the sleekly contemporary Hotel Adagio *(see Financial District hotel listings)*, where you'll find the restaurant just off the lobby. In the long, narrow dining space, multicolored orb light fixtures seem to float above the boisterous room, and illuminated geometric panels behind the bar recall the work of Dutch artist Piet Mondrian.

The adventurous Mediterranean fare at Cortez explores the small-plate concept by offering combinations (katafi-crusted crab cake with tarragon aioli and citrus-marinated cabbage, or smoked trout on frisée, with apples avocado and warm fingerling potatoes) that are sized for sharing.

San Francisco City Financial District

San Francisco City **Financial District**

Farallon

013

Seafood ✗✗✗

450 Post St. (bet. Mason & Powell Sts.)

Phone:	415-956-6969	Mon – Thu 5:30pm - 10pm
Fax:	415-834-1234	Fri – Sat 5:30pm - 11pm
Web:	www.farallonrestaurant.com	Sun 5pm - 10pm
Prices:	$$$	

An undersea theme swims through Pat Kuleto's capricious design at Farallon, where flamboyant blown-glass jellyfish chandeliers hover over tables in the Jelly Bar, huge sea urchin fixtures light the Pool Room, and curving booths nestle in the Nautilus Room. Opened in 1997 in a historic building near Union Square, Farallon is named for the group of islands that lie off the coast of San Francisco.

The design presents a perfect backdrop for chef/owner Mark Franz's "coastal cuisine"; the chef's team plumbs the seas—and supports sustainable fishing practices—for fresh additions to the daily changing menu. Pacific halibut, Dungeness crab, Columbia River sturgeon, North Atlantic black mussels, and New Zealand John Dory are just a few examples of what you might catch.

Grand Cafe

014

French ✗✗

501 Geary St. (at Taylor St.)

Phone:	415-292-0101	Mon – Thu 11:30am - 2:30pm & 5:30pm - 10pm
Fax:	415-292-0150	Fri 11:30am - 2:30pm & 5:30pm - 11pm
Web:	www.grandcafe-sf.com	Sat 8am - 2:30pm & 5:30pm - 11pm
Prices:	$$	Sun 9am - 2:30pm & 5:30pm - 10pm

Grand is as grand does, and there's no doubt that the name fits the setting in the case of this uplifting brasserie. Part of the Hotel Monaco (see hotel listings), the Grand Cafe occupies an elegantly restored turn-of-the-20th-century ballroom, adorned in Art Deco splendor with 30-foot ceilings, soaring columns, sparkling chandeliers, leafy palms, and a mosaic floor.

From the open kitchen comes a wide range of French bistro dishes, kicked up with California flair. Skate wing, for instance, is served with sunchokes, brown butter and caperberries; roasted breast of Petaluma chicken comes with mashed potatoes and braising greens; and grilled hanger steak is accompanied by truffle fries.

The cherry wood bar at the adjoining Petite Café is a popular spot for a cocktail or a pre-theater bite.

Hog Island Oyster Co.

Seafood ✗

015

1 Ferry Building (at The Embarcadero)

Phone:	415-391-7117	Mon – Fri 11:30am - 8pm
Fax:	415-391-7118	Sat – Sun 11am - 6pm
Web:	www.hogislandoysters.com	
Prices:	$$	

You'll go hog-wild—or oyster wild—for the mollusks served at this little U-shaped black-marble counter in the Ferry Building. Seated on the high stools, you'll enjoy a view of the bay as you slurp down the freshest oysters in the city.

Most of the oysters here are harvested daily at the company's farm in Tomales Bay, about 45 miles north of San Francisco (others are flown in from Washington State and British Columbia). The concise menu changes daily to feature the best of the season, but Tomales Bay sweetwaters get the popular vote. There are no raw deals here, only sweet ones, like a flight of sake with kumamotos, or a glass of Pinot Blanc with Snow Creek oysters from Washington state.

If you want your shellfish to go, place your order in advance and bring your own cooler.

Jeanty at Jack's

French ✗✗

016

615 Sacramento St. (bet. Kearny & Montgomery Sts.)

Phone:	415-693-0941	Mon – Fri 11am - 10pm
Fax:	415-693-0947	Sat – Sun 5pm - 10pm
Web:	www.jeantyatjacks.com	
Prices:	$$$	

A San Francisco staple since 1864, Jack's has been reborn with the help of French chef and current proprietor, Philippe Jeanty. The arrival of Jeanty's restaurant in the Financial District means that fans won't have to go to Bistro Jeanty in Yountville to enjoy the chef's excellent brasserie fare.

Carefully restored in Belle Époque style, the restaurant offers dining on four levels, including an open mezzanine over the bar area (the second floor is reserved for private dining). Redwood paneling, a black and white tile floor, bistro chairs and antique French posters lend an authentic character to the ground-floor dining room. On the menu, starters such as foie gras au torchon, escargots and rabbit terrine share space with classic entrées, coq au vin, steak tartare, and cassoulet.

Les Amis

568 Sacramento St. (bet. Montgomery & Sansome Sts.)

Phone:	415-291-9145	Mon – Fri 11:30am - 2:30pm & 5:30pm - 10pm
Fax:	415-291-9146	Sat 5:30pm - 10pm
Web:	www.lesamissf.com	Closed Sun
Prices:	$$$	

In the spirit of friendship, take a loved one to Les Amis. This newcomer opened its big red doors in an old Financial District firehouse at the end of 2005, taking the space most recently occupied by Zare. Now comfortable banquettes that curve at the end line the long walls of the sober room.

The same team that runs Plouf and B44 operates Les Amis, with chef Thomas Weibull at the helm. Known for his Cal-French food at Plouf, Weibull weaves Mediterranean threads through his menu of kicked-up French cuisine, stuffing grilled squid with chorizo purée, and encasing halibut with a crust of piccholine olives and almonds.

Although the heart of the seductive wine list lies in France, there's a good choice of local vintages, too.

Medicine Eatstation

161 Sutter St. (bet. Kearny & Montgomery Sts.)

Phone:	415-677-4405	Mon – Thu 11:30am - 2:30pm & 5:30pm - 9pm
Fax:	415-677-4406	Fri – Sat 11:30am - 2:30pm & 5:30pm - 10pm
Web:	www.medicinerestaurant.com	Closed Sun
Prices:	$$	

The third level of Crocker Galleria is where you'll find this serene vegetarian restaurant, where the mottos "Loving kindness to your body" and "Simple food for jaded palates" are posted at the entrance. Although the philosophy echoes the Zen Buddhist sentiment that "food is medicine," you won't need a spoonful of sugar to make this "medicine" go down.

New-shojin cuisine (as it's called here) is more than good for you; it's fresh and flavorful, too. Take the signature medicine roll: nine-grain rice is wrapped around a tasty combination of avocado, sour plum, nori, carrot, shiso leaf, spicy sprouts and flax seed. Yuzu or green-tea shaved ice will prove the perfect sweet to wrap up your meal.

Note that a 17% tip is automatically included in your check; no additional tipping is accepted.

San Francisco City **Financial District**

Millennium

019

Vegetarian ✗✗

580 Geary St. (at Jones St.)

Phone:	415-345-3900
Fax:	415-345-3941
Web:	www.millenniumrestaurant.com
Prices:	$$

Sun – Thu 5:30pm - 9:30pm
Fri – Sat 5:30pm - 10pm

The Savoy Hotel houses this well-known vegetarian restaurant. Chef Eric Tucker, who was part of the founding team, is passionate about healthy food. A graduate of the National Gourmet Institute for Food and Health in New York City, Tucker follows three simple rules when it comes to his sophisticated cuisine: it must be fresh and flavorful, it must use only organic ingredients and support local farmers, and it must never use genetically modified foods.

The result? Market-fresh products expressed in such globally inspired dishes as grilled abalone mushroom paella, Balinese salt-and-pepper-crusted oyster mushrooms, and truffled white bean cassoulet. Following suit, the wine list breaks down into organic, vegan, and selections that use biodynamic production techniques.

Palio d'Asti

020

Italian ✗✗

640 Sacramento St. (bet. Kearny & Montgomery Sts.)

Phone:	415-395-9800
Fax:	415-362-6002
Web:	www.paliodasti.com
Prices:	$$$

Mon – Fri 11:30am - 2:30pm & 5:30pm - 9pm
Closed Sat & Sun

Opened by Gianni Fassio in 1990, Palio d'Asti pays tribute to the medieval bareback horse race run each year since the 13th century in the triangular piazza of the Italian town of Asti. Bright Palio flags hang from the ceiling of the large dining room, where you can watch chefs in the glass-enclosed kitchen. Stately concrete columns may suggest the stone buildings of yore, but there's nothing Old World about the atmosphere, which bustles with Financial District business types.

Authentic cuisine looks to different regions of Italy, depending on the season. In fall and winter, chef/owner Daniel Scherotter plays up the food of Piemonte, Emilia Romagna and Tuscany. Rome and Umbria come to the fore in spring, while the southern accents of Sicily and Naples flavor the summer menu.

San Francisco City Financial District

Plouf

021

Seafood ✗

40 Belden Pl. (bet. Bush & Pine Sts.)

Phone:	415-986-6491	Mon – Thu 11:30am - 3pm & 5:30pm - 10pm
Fax:	415-986-6492	Fri 11:30am - 3pm & 5:30pm - 11pm
Web:	www.ploufsf.com	Sat 5:30pm - 11pm
Prices:	$$	Closed Sun

In French, plouf is the sound that a stone makes when it drops into the water, and it makes an appropriate name for a restaurant whose angle is seafood with a French accent.

Don't spend too much time fishing around the menu. Go straight for the house specialty, steamed mussels and steamed clams. Both are offered in a variety of preparations (marinière, provençale, bretonne), the mussels paired with crispy fries. Other main course offerings include excellent bouillabaisse and *fruits de mer* (wine-braised Atlantic monkfish, Ahi tuna au poivre, grilled Arctic char) fresh from the market. To add to the seashore ambience, waiters are dressed in blue-and-white-striped shirts, and the walls are decorated with large trophy fish.

Postrio

022

Contemporary ✗✗✗

545 Post St. (bet. Mason & Taylor Sts.)

Phone:	415-776-7825	Sun – Wed 5:30pm - 10pm
Fax:	415-776-6702	Thu – Sat 5:30pm - 10:30pm
Web:	www.postrio.com	
Prices:	$$$$	

Opened in 1989 in the Prescott Hotel *(see hotel listings)* near Union Square, Postrio was Wolfgang Puck's first restaurant outside Southern California. Pat Kuleto gets the credit for the elegant design of the three-level space, where a sweeping staircase leads from the casual grill down to the main dining room dressed with modern art and egg-shaped light fixtures wrapped by "ribbons" of copper strips.

Wolfgang Puck's stamp is on creative nightly changing fare such as spiced lamb crepinette with golden raisins, sweet-chile-glazed halibut and a coconut ice-cream sandwich, well executed by Puck protégés and brothers Mitchell and Steven Rosenthal (also of Town Hall in nearby SoMa).

Don't let the 700 selections on the global wine list intimidate you; bottles start at $25.

Sam's Grill & Seafood

Seafood ✗✗

023

374 Bush St. (bet. Kearny & Montgomery Sts.)

Phone: 415-421-0594
Fax: 415-421-2632
Web: N/A
Prices: $$

Mon – Fri 11am - 9pm
Closed Sat & Sun

This masculine, wood-paneled saloon-style grill room has entertained the city's prominent businessmen since it opened as M.B. Moraghan and Sons in the open-air California Market in 1867. In its current incarnation, Sam's still draws movers and shakers, who pack the tables at lunch (reservations highly recommended). Hours accommodate a Financial District clientele who go home early and eat at home on weekends.

Salads piled high with crab, prawns, or bay shrimp; fried calamari and seafood cocktails; and seafood pastas share menu space with the charcoal-broiled fresh catch and a lengthy list of shellfish. If it's privacy you seek for those contract negotiations, request one of the 13 discreet alcoves that foster seclusion with curtain "doors" and buzzers to summon the waiter.

Sanraku

Japanese ✗

024

704 Sutter St. (at Taylor St.)

Phone: 415-771-0803
Fax: 415-771-0893
Web: www.sanraku.com
Prices:

Mon – Sat 11am - 10pm
Sun 4pm - 10pm

Simplicity is the keynote of this Japanese restaurant, where white walls and blond wood tables form the backdrop for tasty sushi and sashimi as well as rice and noodles. A mix of Asian and American diners frequent this minimalist establishment for traditional Japanese cuisine at prices that won't overwhelm their budgets.

By far, the best deal at lunch or dinner is the combination meal. For less than $25 at dinner, you have a wide choice among sushi, sashimi, teriyaki and tempura. A bowl of fresh miso soup will start you off, and green-tea ice cream makes a refreshing finale.

If you're in SoMa, check out Sanraku's sister restaurant at Metreon (4th and Mission Sts.), where video gamers meet sushi lovers in an airy space overlooking Yerba Buena Gardens.

Silks

025

222 Sansome St. (bet. California & Pine Sts.)

Phone:	415-986-2020	Mon 11:30am - 2pm
Fax:	415-986-5667	Tue – Fri 11:30am - 2pm & 6pm - 9pm
Web:	www.silksdining.com	Sat 6pm - 9pm
Prices:	$$$$	Closed Sun

The sleek Mandarin Oriental Hotel hides a discreet dining room on its second floor. A perfect place for a power lunch or a quiet dinner, Silks reflects the journey of Marco Polo along the Silk Road to China with its hand-painted silk chandeliers, Asian artifacts, and persimmon silk draperies.

Silks' contemporary cuisine combines global influences and pan-Asian flair, as in panko-crusted Dungeness crab croquette with yuzu aioli, and mirin soy-marinated King salmon with black forbidden rice. Choose à la carte at lunch; for dinner you'll have a choice between a three- or four-course prix-fixe tasting menu.

A reasonably priced wine list enumerates more than 350 labels, which, like the food at Silks, includes selections from around the world.

The Slanted Door

026

1 Ferry Building (at The Embarcadero)

Phone:	415-861-8032	Sun – Thu 11am - 2:30pm & 5:30pm - 10pm
Fax:	415-861-8329	Fri – Sat 11am - 2:30pm & 5:30pm - 10:30pm
Web:	www.slanteddoor.com	
Prices:	$$	

When Chef/owner Charles Phan fled Vietnam with his family in 1975, little did he dream that one day he would own one of San Francisco's most popular restaurants. Phan and his family emigrated to San Francisco's Mission District, where the first Slanted Door opened in 1995. Its popularity slowly grew, and the restaurant moved in 2005 to bigger digs in the Ferry Building. Its current glass-walled space boasts great views of the Bay Bridge, and a terrace for alfresco dining.

Phan interprets traditional Vietnamese recipes using regional American ingredients. *Pho bo*, a Vietnamese beef soup, is made here with Niman Ranch London broil, and cellophane noodles are topped with Dungeness crab meat. Designed specifically to complement the food, the wine list focuses on Rieslings, both fruity and dry.

Tadich Grill

027

240 California St. (bet. Battery & Front Sts.)

Phone: 415-391-1849
Fax: N/A
Web: N/A
Prices: $$

Mon – Fri 11am - 9:30pm
Sat 11:30am - 9:30pm
Closed Sun

If you're looking for a restaurant that always pans out, Tadich Grill is a good prospect. A San Francisco institution since the Gold Rush days, the grill has long been a family-run operation. The precursor to this wood-paneled room with its original plaster ceiling was a coffee stand on Long Wharf, started in 1849 by three Croatian immigrants.

You'll find no trendy presentations here. Instead, the menu cites timeless specialties such as oysters Rockefeller, cioppino, and Hangtown Fry (a frittata made with oysters and bacon)—a recipe that dates back to the West Coast's rough-and-tumble days. Fresh fish comes charcoal broiled, pan-fried, sautéed, deep-fried or baked *en casserole*. Carnivores will rejoice in the selection of meats, from chicken to filet mignon.

Tommy Toy's

028

655 Montgomery St. (bet. Clay & Washington Sts.)

Phone: 415-397-4888
Fax: 415-397-0469
Web: www.tommytoys.com
Prices: $$$

Mon – Fri 11:30am - 2:30pm
& 5:30pm - 9:30pm
Sat – Sun 5:30pm - 9:30pm

Favored by movers and shakers since 1986, Tommy Toy's Financial District stalwart is fit for royalty—the Ching Dynasty's Empress Dowager, to be exact. Antique tapestries and ceramics, hand-silvered mirrors, etched-glass and silk draperies bring the opulence of Imperial China to life in the luxurious dining room.

Toy bills his food as "haute cuisine Chinoise," a hint at the fusion of French technique and Chinese recipes that prevails in the kitchen. At midday, business types go for the Executive Luncheon, five courses for under $25. In the evening, Toy's six-course Signature Dinner starts with minced squab "Imperial" in iceberg lettuce petals, then moves on to seafood bisque, whole Maine lobster, Peking duck and wok-charred medallions of beef before ending sweetly with peach mousse.

San Francisco City Financial District

Marina District
Cow Hollow, Pacific Heights, Japantown

Pacific Heights

Brigitta L. House/MICHELIN

Extending from Pacific Heights to the northern waterfront, the Marina is a popular neighborhood for young, wealthy professionals. Visit on a sunny weekend and you'll see why: **Union Street** and **Chestnut Street** are both chock-a-block with chi-chi boutiques, spas, bars and wonderful restaurants. Outdoorsy types love to bike or jog west along Marina Green past Crissy Field to the Golden Gate Bridge and beyond.

The marshy inlet where the Marina District now lies remained untouched until **The Presidio** was established as an outpost by the Spanish in 1776. For the mud flats, sand dunes and marshes between Black Point and The Presidio, development came more slowly. At the beginning of the 19th century, dairy farms covered the southern hills and valleys—now known as Cow Hollow.

By 1913, 600 acres were filled in with sand and debris from the 1906 earthquake, creating a flat site upon which to build the Panama-Pacific International Exposition of 1915. Only the reconstructed **Palace of Fine Arts** *(Baker and Beach Sts.)* remains today. At the close of the fair, residential streets sprang up, choice homes were built, and the area soon gained a reputation as a desirable middle-class address. In 1989, the Loma Prieta quake proved disastrous for the Marina District. Unstable ground liquefied, homes collapsed and dozens of buildings were damaged. With the wounds from that earthquake now healed, the Marina District retains its affluence.

Along a high east-west ridge between Van Ness Avenue and The Presidio sits **Pacific Heights,** a neighborhood synonymous with wealth. Great for strolling, eating and shopping, this tony residential

enclave holds some of the city's finest (and biggest) 20th-century mansions and loveliest views. (Bear in mind that streets in this area ascend and descend abruptly, sometimes as much as 100 feet in one block.) **Fillmore Street** between Bush and Jackson streets contains some unique shops as well as good cafes and restaurants.

Japantown – At the south end of Pacific Heights, in a part of the city known as the Western Addition, Japantown abounds with Japanese architecture and culture. At its heart is a pagoda-crowned five-building complex of shops, sushi bars, theaters, and hotels called Japan Center. You'll have your choice of Japanese and Asian specialties at the restaurants here.

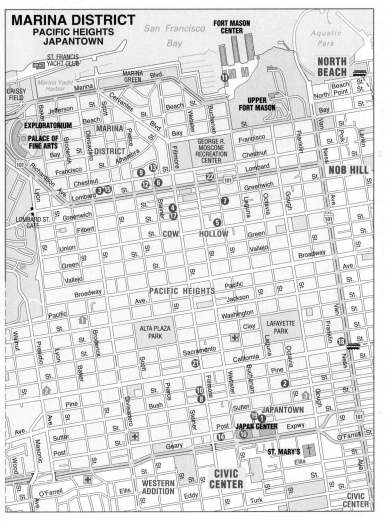

Bushi-Tei ✿

Fusion ✕✕

001

1638 Post St. (bet. Buchanan & Laguna Sts.)

Phone:	415-440-4959	Tue – Thu & Sun 5:30pm - 10:30pm
Fax:	415-440-4030	Fri – Sat 5:30pm - 11:30pm
Web:	www.bushi-tei.com	Closed Mon
Prices:	$$$	

♿

Bushi-Tei

For upscale dining in Japantown, head to Bushi-Tei. Here elements of the past (wood panels removed from an 1863 house during the demolition of Nagano, Japan) meld with modern-day design in the original décor. Running through the center of the room, the communal table of half wood, half glass is lit by votive candles and strewn with polished black river stones. Upstairs, seating on the tiny glassed-in mezzanine accommodates three tables for two.

Seiji "Waka" Wakabayashi returned from opening two restaurants in Dallas (and running Ondine in Sausalito before that) to launch Bushi-Tei in late 2005 with owner Takumi Matsuba. Dishes like fluke and golden beet carpaccio with mizuna and raspberry-ume sauce, and grilled Sonoma lamb chops with Satsuma yams, haricot vert and wasabi-port sauce express Wakabayashi's talent for fusing California products with French techniques and Japanese flair.

Patrons are carefully looked after by a pleasant, professional staff, who offer good advice about the food and wine choices. Ask them about chef Waka's omakase menu.

San Francisco City **Marina District**

Appetizers

Confit of Quail, Jamón Serrano, poached Quail Egg, Almond and Kumquat Compote

Fluke and Golden Beet Carpaccio, Mizuna, and Raspberry Ume Sauce

Miso-marinated Kobe Beef, Peppercress, Camembert, Sesame Brioche and Lemon-Pepper Oil

Entrées

Seared rare Bluefin Tuna Belly, Celery Root Purée, Bean Sprouts and Lime-Herb Sea Salt

Pan-roasted Sonoma Duck Breast, Spinach, Mascarpone-Mustard and Dried Chutney

Grilled Sonoma Lamb Chop, Satsuma Yam, Haricots Verts, Wasabi-Port Sauce

Desserts

Flourless Chocolate Soufflé Cake with Roasted Strawberry and Organic Milk Ice Cream

Apple Dumpling with French Vanilla Ice Cream and Caramel Sauce

Fromage Blanc, Fresh Fruit Mélange and Spearmint Coulis

Quince ✿

Italian 🍴🍴🍴

002

1701 Octavia St. (at Bush St.)

Phone: 415-775-8500
Fax: 415-775-8501
Web: www.quincerestaurant.com
Prices: $$$

Mon – Thu 5:30pm - 10pm
Fri – Sun 5pm - 10:30pm

Nory Ezo Suzuki

Unless it's in season, you won't find the restaurant's namesake tart fruit on the menu. Chef Michael Tusk, an alumnus of Chez Panisse and Oliveto who owns Quince with his wife, Lindsay, passionately sources only sublimely fresh seasonal products from his carefully researched network of producers.

After college, Tusk traded his art history degree for a course in the culinary arts at New York's Culinary Institute of America. His travels in Europe introduced him to the rustic fare of southern France and Italy; it is from these regions that he draws his inspiration. The chef updates Italian recipes nightly by filling cannelloni with Dungeness crab, Bloomsdale spinach and Meyer lemon; tossing maccaroncello with black truffle and foie gras sauce; and pairing Roman oxtails with clove, celery, and potato purée. Of course, a stellar meal deserves a stellar wine, and Quince's collection of local and European labels is a match for any dish here.

Service is pleasant and professional in this 1872 Pacific Heights mansion, once the Octavia Street Apothecary. Venetian chandeliers light an elegant room lined with burgundy velvet banquettes and art photographs of—you guessed it—quinces.

Appetizers

Raviolo of Bellwether
Farms Ricotta Cheese
with White Truffles

Fairview Gardens
White Asparagus with
Uovo Fritto, Pancetta
and Brown Butter

Porcini Mushrooms
Four Ways: Mousse,
Fried, Grilled and
Conserva

Entrées

Paine Farm Squab
Roasted in Salt Crust
with Cardoon Sformato
and Extra Vecchio
Balsamico

Agnolotti dal plin

Laughing Stock Farm
Pork Loin, Rib and
Stuffed Foot with
Morel Mushrooms
and Fava Beans

Desserts

Quince Crostata with
Nocino Ice Cream

Passion Fruit Soufflé

Torrone and Dark-
Chocolate Ice-Cream
Terrine

A 16 🐷

003

Italian ✗✗

2355 Chestnut St. (bet. Divisadero & Scott Sts.)

Phone: 415-771-2216
Fax: 415-771-2221
Web: www.a16sf.com
Prices: $$

Sun – Tue 5pm - 10pm
Wed – Thu 11:30am - 2:30pm & 5pm - 10pm
Fri 11:30am - 2:30pm & 5pm - 11pm
Sat 5pm - 11pm
Closed major holidays

You won't have to navigate the autostrada that runs between Naples and Bari to enjoy the cooking of southern Italy. The eponymous restaurant that mingles with tony shops on Chestnut Street will bring Neapolitan specialties to you—just look for the route sign over the door.

At lunch, chef/partner Nate Appleman whips up authentically thin, crispy pizzas, their crusts blistered from the wood-fired oven. Dinner brings a tantalizing choice of house-cured salamis, pastas, and entrées such as house-made lamb sausage with salsa verde, and roasted young chicken with wild arugula and lemon.

Partner and wine director Shelley Lindgren has assembled a long list of wines, which brings little-known Southern Italian producers to the fore. Some 40 selections are available by the glass or carafe.

Balboa Cafe

004

American ✗✗

3199 Fillmore St. (at Greenwich St.)

Phone: 415-921-3944
Fax: 415-921-3957
Web: www.balboacafe.com
Prices: $$

Mon – Fri 11:30am - 10pm
Sat – Sun 9am - 10pm

This neighborhood stalwart has been around since 1914. Its clubby atmosphere, enhanced by wood-paneled walls, antique light fixtures and a long wooden bar—a lively setting in which to sip a martini or a single-malt scotch—has changed little over the years. On the menu of American fare, you'll find everything from Dungeness crab cakes to Hoffman Farms organic chicken and a pasta offering that changes daily.

Go Saturday or Sunday for the weekend brunch, a favorite with the Cow Hollow crowd. They serve all the classics, from eggs Benedict and corned beef hash to buttermilk pancakes and French toast. Of course, the signature Balboa burger, served on a crusty baguette with house-made pickles and fries, is available any time of day.

Betelnut Pejiu Wu ☻

A s i a n ✗

2030 Union St. (bet. Buchanan & Webster Sts.)

Phone:	415-929-8855	Sun – Thu 11:30am - 11pm
Fax:	415-929-8894	Fri – Sat 11:30am - midnight
Web:	www.betelnutrestaurant.com	
Prices:	$$	

Modeled after a traditional Southeast Asian *pejiu wu*, or beer house, Betelnut specializes in fresh regional Asian "street food" served in a British Colonial ambience enhanced by swirling bamboo fans and an eclectic collection of art. The blazing-red bar attracts a young following for "deluxe drinks," house brews and sake flights, while the crowd in the dining room spans the generations.

From China and Malaysia to Thailand and Korea, the exotic flavors of the Orient will fill your plate. At Betelnut, named for the areca nut (traditionally wrapped in a betel leaf and chewed for its caffeine-like kick), wok-seared galanga beef, "bien pow" firecracker chicken, and Malaysian curry laska can fire up your palate—all the better to temper your taste buds with a mug of cold beer.

Bistro Aix

F r e n c h ✗

3340 Steiner St. (bet. Chestnut & Lombard Sts.)

Phone:	415-202-0100	Mon – Thu 6pm - 10pm
Fax:	415-202-0153	Fri – Sat 6pm - 11pm
Web:	www.bistroaix.com	Sun 5:30pm - 9:30pm
Prices:	$$	

Bistro Aix is the kind of place you wish you had in your neighborhood. It's a comfortable, unpretentious little restaurant that puts its money where your mouth is. True to his claim of serving "affordable, freshly prepared meals," chef Jonathan Beard prepares everything daily on the premises, and offers a two-course prix-fixe menu (Sunday to Thursday from 6pm to 8pm) for under $20.

Inspired by the sun-soaked South of France, the cuisine at Aix runs to crispy roasted duck leg with arugula, grilled lamb steak with potato gratin, and house-cured salmon with dill cream. The wine list, which tours the major growing regions of Europe and ends up in California, cites more than 20 selections by the glass.

Check out the pleasant heated patio out back.

San Francisco City Marina District

The Brazen Head

Gastropub ✗

007

3166 Buchanan St. (at Greenwich St.)

Phone:	415-921-7600	Open daily 4pm - 2am
Fax:	415-921-0164	
Web:	www.brazenheadsf.com	
Prices:	$$	

You won't find a sign announcing this little pub in the Marina district, so watch for the green awning at the corner of Buchanan and Greenwich streets. Neighbors would prefer to keep Brazen Head a secret, but it seems the word is out. When you walk through the door, you'll discover what they've been trying to hide. Regulars jam this lively bar, which doesn't accept reservations or credit cards. Rustic and full of character—and characters—the dimly lit interior is made cozy by wood paneling and exposed wood beams.

Gastropub fare runs the gamut from the signature Angus pepper steak, which has been on the menu since 1980, to more exotic dishes like chicken satay with spicy peanut sauce. Count on warm, efficient service.

The downside? Parking isn't easy to find in this trendy area.

Chez Nous

Mediterranean ✗

008

1911 Fillmore St. (bet. Bush & Pine Sts.)

Phone:	415-441-8044	Sun – Thu 11am - 3pm & 6pm - 10pm
Fax:	415-441-7910	Fri – Sat 11am - 3pm & 6pm - 11pm
Web:	N/A	
Prices:	⊜⊚	

Pacific Heights residents can count themselves fortunate to have a neighborhood restaurant like Chez Nous. This petite bistro bustles with diners sitting close together at zinc-topped tables in the long, narrow room. Small plates here span the Mediterranean region through Spain, France, Italy and Northern Africa. Blue-nosed sea bass with Meyer lemon-Mandarin vinaigrette, goat cheese terrine with huckleberry sauce, pommes frites with harissa aioli, and grilled lamb chops with couscous and lavender sea salt will leave your mouth watering for more. A blackboard announces the plat du jour.

Although Chez Nous has changed their no-reservations policy, they do take only a limited number of reservations. Steel yourself for a wait if you're not lucky enough to snag one.

Dragon Well

Chinese ✗

2142 Chestnut St. (bet. Pierce & Steiner Sts.)

Phone:	415-474-6888
Fax:	415-775-9888
Web:	www.dragonwell.com
Prices:	⬮⬮

Open daily 11:30am - 10pm

Opened on a lively street in the heart of the Marina in 1998, Dragon Well is a friendly dragon, indeed. This is an inexpensive neighborhood place, where you can pop in for a healthy meal, or take your food to go. Clean lines characterize the simple dining space with its rows of tables lining the long walls, while clean flavors mark the fresh, honest cuisine.

From the kitchen come time-honored Chinese recipes (hot and sour soup, Mongolian beef, Kung Pao chicken) as well as more contemporary preparations (tea-smoked duck with hoisin sauce, lemongrass chicken, Hong Kong noodles). The choice of entrées is extensive, but if you have a sweet tooth, you may be disappointed by the lack of desserts on the menu.

Florio

Italian ✗✗

1915 Fillmore St. (bet. Bush & Pine Sts.)

Phone:	415-775-4300
Fax:	415-775-4343
Web:	www.floriosf.com
Prices:	$$

Sun – Tue 5:30pm - 10pm
Wed 5:30pm - 10:30pm
Thu – Sat 5:30pm - 11pm

Florio's Left Bank look will charm you with its bistro chairs, cozy banquettes, black-and-white photos and open kitchen. The cuisine comes mostly from Italy, though a few French recipes (wilted frisée salad, steak frites, crème caramel) pepper the menu. The food at Florio is not meant to wow you. Instead, founders Doug Biederbeck (of Bix) and Joseph Graham envisioned this elegant spot as a place to enjoy simple food, smiling service and good company. Dig into seasonal fare like Tuscan fish stew, sweetbread saltimbocca, and house-made pappardelle with braised Sonoma rabbit.

The well-balanced wine list, which includes limited-production European vintages, is complemented by a lengthy liquor selection running the gamut from pastis to armagnac.

Greens 😊

Vegetarian ✗

011

Building A, Fort Mason Center

Phone:	415-771-6222	Mon 5:30pm - 9pm
Fax:	415-771-3472	Tue – Sat noon - 2:30pm & 5:30pm - 9pm
Web:	www.greensrestaurant.com	Sun 10:30am - 2pm
Prices:	$$	

It's difficult to say which is the greater draw of this Zen oasis, the spectacular view or the inventive vegetarian cuisine. Occupying a former military warehouse at Fort Mason Center, Greens peers out over the marina and the Golden Gate Bridge beyond. Grab a table by the windows to take in the sunset, while you sip a wine from the award-winning list.

Established in 1979 by disciples of the San Francisco Zen Center, Greens gets its organic produce from the center's Green Gulch Farm in Marin County. Chef Annie Somerville's healthy meals don't require any badgering to get you to eat your veggies. If you're impressed by artichoke and grilled onion pizzetta, fresh pea ravioli, and Vietnamese yellow curry, purchase one of her cookbooks, *Fields of Greens* or *Everyday Greens*, before you leave.

ISA

Contemporary ✗

012

3324 Steiner St. (bet. Chestnut & Lombard Sts.)

Phone:	415-567-9588	Mon – Sat 5:30pm - 10pm
Fax:	415-409-1879	Closed Sun & July 4 - 11
Web:	www.isarestaurant.com	
Prices:	$$	

Owners Luke and Kitty Sung pay homage to their daughter, Isabelle, by naming their restaurant for her. In the sleek, narrow space you'll have a view of the little open kitchen. If you're after a more intimate atmosphere, keep walking back to the tented and heated patio.

Chef Luke cooked in the likes of La Folie, Masa, and the Ritz Carlton San Francisco before opening his own place. His concept here borrows from "small plates," though the portions are generous and intended for sharing. Spicy tuna tartare, lobster broth with tiger prawns (for two), potato-wrapped sea bass, and roasted rack of lamb with zucchini are just a few of the menu choices.

The service could use some work to reach the level of "warm and friendly."

Lettüs Café Organic

Vegetarian ✗

013

3352 Steiner St. (bet. Chestnut & Lombard Sts.)

Phone: 415-931-2777   Open daily 7:30am - 10:30pm
Fax: 415-931-2719
Web: www.lettusorganic.com
Prices: ᝡ

This organic cafe in the heart of the Marina fits San Francisco's health-conscious lifestyle like a glove. Opened in 2005, Lettüs serves breakfast, lunch and dinner, so there's no excuse not to eat food that's as good for you as it is for the earth. Order and pay at the counter, and the plates will be brought to your table.

It's food that's yummy, too. Start your day with lemon ricotta pancakes or scrambled tofu; for lunch, try a portobello panini or create your own salad from a list of more than 40 ingredients. Dinner entrées include an oven-roasted chicken breast with fingerling potatoes for those who want to cheat on their vegetarian diet. Fresh-squeezed juices, smoothies, and organic free-trade coffees and teas share the beverage list with beer, wine and sake cocktails.

Maki

Japanese ✗

014

1825 Post St. (bet. Fillmore & Webster Sts.)

Phone: 415-921-5215   Tue – Sun 11:30am - 1:45pm & 5:30pm - 8:45pm
Fax: N/A   Closed Mon & major holidays
Web: N/A
Prices: ᝡ

Hidden away on the second floor of the Kinokuniya Building in Japantown, Maki is a sliver of a place, with spare décor and only 17 seats, plus a smattering of tables in the adjoining Japan Center mall. A largely Japanese clientele favors this little place, where chef/owner Hidehiko Makiguchi creates a menu of sushi and maki rolls, teriyaki and tempura, and even vegan sushi rolls. The real attraction, however, is a dish rarely found in the United States: the house specialty, *wappa meshi*, rice cooked in a bamboo steamer and topped with vegetables, seafood or meat.

There's a good selection of sake to go with your meal. If you don't have a reservation, you may have to wait for one of the few seats.

Mamacita

015

2317 Chestnut St. (bet. Divisadero & Scott Sts.)

Phone: 415-346-8494

Fax: 415-346-8495

Web: www.mamacitasf.com

Prices: $$

Mon – Fri 5:30pm - midnight
Sat – Sun 10:30am - 2pm
& 5:30pm - midnight

A Marina newcomer, Mamacita opened at the end of 2005. Since then, the place has been packed with a lively crowd of well-heeled locals looking for good food and a good time. They find both at this vibrant Mexican restaurant.

A taste of old Mexico presides from the adobe "house," which partially encloses the kitchen, to the sky-blue walls and the metal star-burst chandeliers. While Mexican tradition forms the basis for the cuisine at Mamacita, the chef adds a New World twist to dishes such as pan-seared scallops in red mole sauce, and fish Veracruzano accompanied by soft roasted-garlic chile polenta.

So order up a batch of margaritas—billed as some of the best around—and join the party. You'll be glad you did.

Mifune

016

1737 Post St. (bet. Buchanan & Webster Sts.)

Phone: 415-922-0337

Fax: N/A

Web: N/A

Prices: 🍜

Open daily 11am - 9:30pm

Oodles of noodles is what you'll get at Mifune. Located in the Kintetsu Mall at Japan Center, surrounded by Asian restaurants and gift shops, this popular place sports deep-red walls and specializes in noodle dishes—both hot and cold—at inexpensive prices.

At lunch, go for the fixed-price menu. For $10, it's a real bargain for a choice of sushi, rolls or don, topped off by a copious bowlful of house-made soba or udon noodles. If you crave cold noodles, the Mifune Special (a mix of udon and soba noodles with shrimp and vegetable tempura all served aboard a lacquered wooden boat) is sure to please.

Can't get into Mifune? Go next door to its little sister, Mifune Don, on the upper level of the Miyako Mall.

San Francisco City Marina District

PlumpJack Cafe

Californian

017

Californian

3127 Fillmore St. (bet. Filbert & Greenwich Sts.)

Phone:	415-563-4755	Mon – Fri 11:30am - 2pm & 5:30pm - 10pm
Fax:	415-776-5808	Sat – Sun 5:30pm - 10pm
Web:	www.plumpjack.com	
Prices:	$$$	

At this Cow Hollow cafe refined California cuisine, served in an intimate setting of taupe tones and custom-designed shield-back chairs, wins the popular vote with city sophisticates. The menu changes often to incorporate remarkably fresh ingredients, but local Dungeness crab cake with Meyer lemon-infused guacamole, and grilled Snake River Farms Kobe beef tri-tip with foie gras Madeira sauce hint at chef Jeff Smock's versatility.

On the award-winning wine list you'll discover hard-to-find French and California vintages, at a wide range of prices—all attractively close to retail.

Ask the knowledgeable sommelier for sage advice regarding which wines to pair with your courses.

Ruth's Chris Steak House

Steakhouse

018

1601 Van Ness Ave. (at California St.)

Phone:	415-673-0557	Mon – Thu 5pm - 10pm
Fax:	415-673-5309	Fri – Sat 5pm - 10:30pm
Web:	www.ruthschris.com	Sun 4:30pm - 9:30pm
Prices:	$$$$	

With locations across the United States, Ruth's Chris ranks as a true restaurant institution. Ruth Fertel started her empire of eateries in 1965, with Chris Steak House in New Orleans. Now her influence stretches as far away as Taiwan and Hong Kong, and encompasses more than 90 restaurants.

Steak, of course, stars at Ruth's place: filet, T-bone, cowboy ribeye, New York strip, Porterhouse for two, all seared in an 1,800-degree custom-designed oven and served sizzling hot. Appetizers like shrimp remoulade and Louisiana gumbo recall the restaurant's place of origin, while a smattering of seafood entrées satisfy non-meat eaters.

It won't be easy to save room for dessert, but if you do, go for the warm bread pudding with whiskey sauce—and bring a friend to help you finish it.

San Francisco City Marina District

Shabu-Sen

Japanese ✗

019

1726 Buchanan St. (bet. Post & Sutter Sts.)

Phone:	415-440-0466	Sun – Thu 11:30am - 10pm
Fax:	415-440-6623	Fri – Sat 11:30am - 11pm
Web:	N/A	
Prices:	⮾	

You won't have to make many choices at Shabu-Sen. This inexpensive Japantown establishment only offers two types of dishes, shabu-shabu and sukiyaki—two preparations that derive from the Japanese practice of families gathering around a fire to warm themselves and make a meal together.

If you order shabu-shabu, you'll cook thin slices of beef, Chinese cabbage, shiitake mushrooms, tofu noodles and more in a hot pot of boiling broth at your table. You'll get two sauces on the side (*gomadare*, with a sesame-and-peanut base; and *ponzu-shoyu*, with a base of soy sauce and vinegar) for dipping. Sukiyaki (vegetarian, beef or pork) is cooked for you in soy sauce enriched with sweetened sake and seaweed broth. It's served with fresh vegetables, udon, tofu and steamed rice.

Sociale

Italian ✗✗

020

3665 Sacramento St. (bet. Locust & Spruce Sts.)

Phone:	415-921-3200	Mon 5:30pm - 10pm
Fax:	415-921-3186	Tue – Sat 11:30am - 2:30pm & 5:30pm - 10pm
Web:	www.caffesociale.com	Closed Sun
Prices:	$$	

"Eat well, drink well, live well" are the three rules to follow at this Italian charmer tucked away down an alley in Presidio Heights. It's worth seeking out, though, because once you're installed on the dreamy little patio out back, you'll feel miles away from the big-city buzz.

Sitting inside, where pastel hues set off black-and-white photographs of the Old Country, isn't so bad, either. Wherever you end up, though, you'll be treated to the same tasty Italian menu, which changes about every two weeks. The chef's discreet California twist stands out in *concentrare* (main dishes) like parsnip gnocchi with Oregon truffles and Parmigiano Reggiano, and seared Kobe bavette with cardoon gratin.

Just don't forget to make reservations, or you'll end up eating at home.

Vivande

021

2125 Fillmore St. (bet. California & Sacramento Sts.)

Phone:	415-346-4430	Open daily 11:30am - 10pm
Fax:	415-346-2877	Closed major holidays
Web:	www.vivande.com	
Prices:	$$	

Honest Italian cooking is the hallmark of this unpretentious Pacific Heights trattoria, where chef/owner Carlo Middione plumbs his Sicilian heritage for additions to the menu. Middione opened Vivande in 1981 with a commitment to producing authentic Italian dishes. Ingredients such as pasta made in-house from egg, durum and semolina flours, and Sicilian-style pork and fennel sausage, handmade according to an old family recipe leave little wonder as to why the Italian government recognized this restaurant for staying true to its Italian roots.

You can even take a taste of Italy home with you. The take-out counter here offers a veritable cornucopia of products to go, from imported olives and prosciutto to Tuscan bean salad and house-made pasta sauces. Now, that's Italian!

Zushi Puzzle

022

1910 Lombard St. (at Buchanan St.)

Phone:	415-931-9319	Open daily 5pm - 10:30pm
Fax:	415-931-9321	
Web:	www.zushipuzzle.com	
Prices:	☜	

Lines spilling onto this busy block of Lombard Street at peak hours will lead you to Zushi Puzzle. The Marina district sushi joint welcomes the crowds to its simply decorated dining space, furnished with wooden tables, red banquettes, and a tiny sushi bar in the back of the room.

Once known only to a handful of sushi aficionados, Zushi Puzzle now welcomes hosts of raw-fish lovers who come for the impressive selection of nigiri sushi, sashimi, makimono, noodles, and two boards announcing a list of specials—including rolls designed by the restaurant's regulars. Chef Roger Chong uses expensive soy paper instead of seaweed to wrap some of the more delicate fish and high-end rolls. Although maki names like "I Hate Salmon" and "Killer Josh" may be humorous, their ingredients are seriously fresh.

San Francisco City Marina District

Mission District
Bernal Heights, Mission Bay, Potrero Hill

This sunny southern neighborhood *(bounded by Duboce, Cesar Chavez and Church Sts., and Potrero Ave.)* is San Francisco at its most bohemian, with artists, dot-commers and activists coexisting with a vibrant Latino community. It's a fun place to hang out for a day. Aside from the historic **Mission Dolores**—the oldest building in San Francisco—there are dozens of good, cheap (and not-so-cheap) restaurants, plentiful bars and cafes, several first-rate bookshops, and block after block of pastel-painted Italianate row houses, some dating as far back as the 1870s.

Mission Dolores anchored a small village here in the early 1800s, but the area wasn't developed in earnest until after the Gold Rush. Some wealthy San Franciscans had weekend homes here, but by the turn of the 20th century, the neighborhood was mainly populated by European immigrants who worked in the warehouses, breweries and factories South of Market. Forced out of their homeland by the revolution, Mexicans began arriving in the 1920s. Central and South Americans have followed in the decades since.

Though gentrification has pushed many Latinos out of the area, the stretch of 24th Street between Mission and Potrero streets still dances to a salsa beat. Known as *El Corazón de la Misione*, or "the heart of the Mission," it's where the annual Carnaval festival takes place. To get a feel for the Latino art scene, check out the **Mission Cultural Center for Latino Arts** *(2868 Mission St.),* and don't forget to sample a big, juicy, "Mission-style" burrito.

Potrero Hill – Hemmed in by freeways, **Potrero Hill** lies east of the Mission. Defined by Alameda, 3rd, and Cesar Chavez streets and Potrero Avenue, this quiet residential district was originally part of a land grant deeded to Don Francisco de Haro, who grazed Mission Dolores' cattle on the *potrero*

Mission District Mural

Brigitta L. House/MICHELIN

nuevo ("new pasture" in Spanish). The neighborhood offers clear views of the Bay Area and downtown, as well as trendy cafes and family-owned restaurants that dish up comfort food.

Bernal Heights – Crowning a steep, grassy hill at the southern end of the Mission Valley, this bohemian suburb caters to families as well as price-conscious hipsters. The area once formed part of the *Rancho de las Salinas y Potrero Neuvo*. Bernal Heights takes its name from Jose Cornelio de Bernal, to whom the Mexican government granted the land in 1839. It's worth making the uphill trek for the nationally famous restaurants, local coffee shops and neighborhood bars.

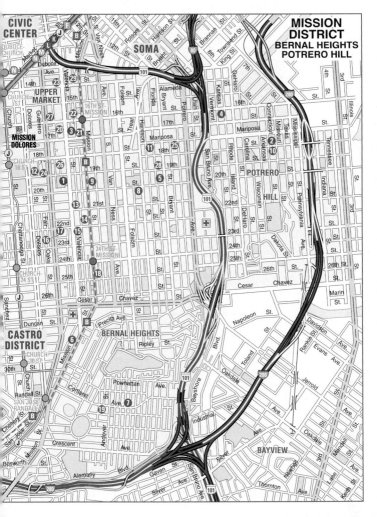

Range ✿

001

842 Valencia St. (bet. 19th & 20th Sts.)

Phone:	415-282-8283
Fax:	415-282-8828
Web:	www.rangesf.com
Prices:	$$

Sun – Thu 5:30pm - 10pm
Fri – Sat 5:30pm - 11pm

Range/Rose Gray

Food lovers gallop in from all over the city to eat at Range, which opened in summer 2005. Here, owners Phil West (he cooked at Bacar) and his wife, Cameron (she managed the waitstaff at Delfina), have fashioned a cool 70-seat dining environment marked by zinc-topped tables and a glassed-in kitchen.

In keeping with the restaurant's name, which conjures up visions of the Old West, specialty cocktails sport names like Blazing Saddle and Smoking Gun. You won't find huge sizzling steaks on Range's menu, though. What you will find is a concise list of well-realized contemporary dishes that changes daily, and combine French, Italian, Asian and Californian influences. For starters, silky chicken liver mousse may be accompanied by peppercress and toasts; fresh sautéed Maine monkfish might follow, paired with roasted endive, trumpet mushrooms and crispy pancetta. The wine list is on the short side, too, but offers an interesting range of bottles from California, France, Spain and Italy.

Cameron instructs the waitstaff in mannerly practices, such as announcing each course and folding diners' napkins if they leave the table during their meal.

Appetizers

Goat Cheese and Sorrel-Stuffed Pasta with Lime Butter and Chives

Raw Hawaiian Ono with Shaved Fennel and Preserved Lemon

Chicken-Liver Mousse with a Frisée Salad and Toast

Entrées

Coffee-rubbed Pork Shoulder with Creamy Hominy and Braised Greens

California Bass with Braised Artichokes, Spring Onions, Almonds and Mint

Pan-roasted Bavette Steak with Trumpet Mushrooms, Fresh-dug Potatoes and Horseradish Sauce

Desserts

Bittersweet Chocolate Soufflé with Espresso Crème Anglaise

Coconut Bavarian with Passion Fruit Tapioca and Lime Sherbet

Black-Walnut Crêpes with Caramelized Bananas and Crème-Fraîche Ice Cream

Aperto

Italian ✗

002

1434 18th St. (at Connecticut St.)

Phone:	415-252-1625	Mon – Fri 11:30am - 2:30pm & 5:30pm - 10pm
Fax:	415-252-1036	Sat 11am - 2:30pm & 5:30pm - 10pm
Web:	www.apertosf.com	Sun 10am - 2:30pm & 5:30pm - 9pm
Prices:	$$	

Potrero Hill is home to this unpretentious little Italian restaurant, where windows offer neighborhood views and you can watch the chefs in the open kitchen. There the team prepares a tasty and reasonably priced bill of fare, complemented by daily specials noted on the blackboard. Fulton Valley poultry, organic Australian lamb, Niman Ranch meats and wild caught seafood forms the base for seasonal dishes, from rustic orecchiette with housemade sausage, fava beans, dried tomato and oregano to a slow-braised lamb shank served with fava beans, sweet peas, cipollini onions and natural jus.

Kids are welcome here with a special pasta plate: their choice of pasta shapes and sauces. If you're coming with a small group, keep in mind that Aperto only accepts reservations for parties of six or more.

Bar Tartine ☺

Californian ✗

003

561 Valencia St. (bet. 16th & 17th Sts.)

Phone:	415-487-1600	Sun – Wed 6pm - 10pm
Fax:	415-487-1605	Thu – Sat 6pm - 11pm
Web:	N/A	Closed Mon
Prices:	$$	

When Bar Tartine opened in fall 2005, it gave fans of Elisabeth Prueitt and Chad Robertson's wildly popular Tartine Bakery (a few blocks away on Guerrero Street) another place to savor their superb baked goods. There's no sign out front, so look for the menu posted in the front window.

The narrow candlelit space at Bar Tartine, with its white walls, dark woods and elk-antler chandelier, nurtures a contemporary-bistro-meets-hunting-lodge vibe. On the plate, Mediterranean accents perk up such dishes as steamed Manila clams Basquaise, creamy potage St. Germain, and herb-crusted sturgeon with orange-saffron sauce.

You'll kick yourself later if you don't save room for one of Prueitt's luscious desserts, like rustic Shaker lemon pie, or Scharffen Berger chocolate soufflé cake.

Bistro 350

004

Contemporary ✗✗

350 Rhode Island St. (at 16th St.)

Phone:	415-216-4329	Tue – Fri 11:30am - 1pm & 6pm - 8pm
Fax:	N/A	Closed Sat – Mon
Web:	www.baychef.com	Closed April 2 - 10, August 27 - September 5
Prices:	⊖⊜	& December 24 - January 9

Practice makes perfect, and this new restaurant staffed by students of the California Culinary Academy will prove that point. Located in a contemporary building in Potrero Hill, this member of Le Cordon Bleu program welcomes the public (the Academy's original location is at 624 Polk St.). Your food will be cooked by future chefs, and students also act as waiters, so be indulgent if there is a slip-up now and then. The seasonal menu presents contemporary cuisine based on French technique and executed with a California accent.

For foodies, the best seat in the house is at the counter, where you can watch the kitchen team at work and perhaps pick up a tip or two. No matter where you sit, the prices are definitely right.

Blowfish Sushi

005

Japanese ✗

2170 Bryant St. (bet. 19th & 20th Sts.)

Phone:	415-285-3848	Mon – Thu 11:30am - 2:30pm & 5:30pm - 11pm
Fax:	415-285-0286	Fri 11:30am - 2:30pm & 5:30pm - midnight
Web:	www.blowfishsushi.com	Sat 5:30pm - midnight
Prices:	⊖⊜	Sun 5:30pm - 10pm

From the techno tunes to the Japanese animé clips that play on wall-mounted video screens, Blowfish Sushi rocks with a pulsing beat. Warehouses may dominate the blocks around this little sushi place, but inside, an urbane Tokyo vibe holds sway.

Tokyo native Ritsuo Tsuchida, who opened Blowfish in 1996 and now owns outposts in San Jose (335 Santana Row) and West Hollywood, combines traditional nigiri and sashimi with contemporary creations (like the tofu Napoleon, or the UFD—Unique Fusion Dish—dumplings filled with beef and vegetables served with avocado and mango salsa). At lunch the Bento Box, a choice of two items served with rice, miso soup, gyoza and salad, is the best bargain.

Check out the fascinating list of specialty cocktails, most of them made with sake.

Blue Plate

American American 🍴

006

3218 Mission St. (bet. 29th & Valencia Sts.)

Phone: 415-282-6777
Fax: 415-282-8053
Web: www.blueplatesf.com
Prices: $$

Mon – Thu 6pm - 10pm
Fri – Sat 6pm - 10:30pm
Closed Sun

This modest bistro near the border of Bernal Heights is as American as mom's apple pie, starting with the diner-style neon sign inviting passersby to "EAT." The concept of the blue-plate special is updated here to mean dining that is not only affordable but responsible in terms of the source of the ingredients. Nightly changing dishes kick mom's homey fare up a notch with the likes of roasted chicken livers with pancetta and charred dates, and Bloomsdale spinach ravioli with fava beans, asparagus and truffle butter.

Fashioned from local materials and found items, and decorated with works by area artists, the three little dining rooms have a funky feel that matches the restaurant's independent spirit. On a warm day, the best seat in the house is in the leafy back garden.

Café Chez Maman

French 🍴

007

803 Cortland Ave. (at Ellsworth St.)

Phone: 415-593-0944
Fax: N/A
Web: www.chezmamansf.com
Prices: $$

Open daily 11am - 10pm
Closed major holidays

Simple comforts are what you'll find at Chez Maman, set on a pleasant street in Bernal Heights. So what if the French-inspired menu lists paninis and quesadillas alongside crêpes and mussels marinière? The locals who've been filling the place since it opened in fall 2005 don't seem to care. They come for the warm, cozy ambience, the turn-of-the-20th-century vintage décor, and, most of all, for the fresh, uncomplicated and tasty food.

This is the second location of Chez Maman; the first is on 18th Street in Potrero Hill, and there's now a third location on Union Street in the Marina District. All three share the same menu and casual cafe feel.

Café Gratitude

008

2400 Harrison St. (at 20th St.)

Phone:	415-824-4652	Open daily 9am - 10pm
Fax:	415-824-4125	
Web:	www.cafegratitude.com	
Prices:	💳💳	

No matter your mood, the positive vibe here is designed to be uplifting, starting with the words "a world of plenty," on the façade. The concept of abundance is evident in every part of this place, including the cafe's own Abounding River board game, painted on the top of each table.

Then there are the organic vegan dishes with names like "I Am Magical" (mushrooms stuffed with sunflower and walnut pâté), "I Am Divine" (spicy carrot and avocado soup), and "I Am Happy" (sprouted almond-sesame hummus). Add to that a fine selection of salads, live pizzas (no, they don't bite back), just-squeezed juices and nut milks, and you've got something to be happy about.

None of the three locations—the other two are in Sunset *(1336 9th Ave.)* and Berkeley *(1730 Shattuck Ave.)*—take reservations for less than six people.

Charanga

009

2351 Mission St. (bet. 19th & 20th Sts.)

Phone:	415-282-1813	Tue – Wed 5:30pm - 10pm
Fax:	N/A	Thu – Sat 5:30pm - 11pm
Web:	www.charangasf.com	Closed Sun & Mon
Prices:	$$	

With a name that refers to both a Cuban dance party and a Latin flute-and-strings band, Charanga pulses with a lively atmosphere where neighbors enjoy good times and good food. Hemingway would have liked this Caribbean hideaway, with its weathered wood-plank floors, slowly turning ceiling fan, island music and mounted cigar boxes.

Billing itself as pan-Latin, the menu encompasses the cuisines of the Caribbean, Spain and Latin America. Think of Cuban-style roast pork leg (marinated in citrus, garlic and oregano) and *tostones a la tica* (fried green plantains layered with roasted-garlic goat cheese, pea shoots and black beans) as large tapas, and order several plates to share. Island-style libations like passionfruit mojitos, guava-ritas and caipirinha guajiros keep the party alive.

San Francisco City Mission District

Chez Papa

French ✗

010

1401 18th St. (at Missouri St.)

Phone:	415-255-0387	Mon – Thu 11:30am - 3pm & 5:30pm - 10pm
Fax:	N/A	Fri – Sat 11:30am - 3pm & 5:30pm - 11pm
Web:	www.chezpapasf.com	Sun 5:30pm - 10pm
Prices:	$$	

South of France comes to Potrero Hill via this casual bistro. Brought to you by the same folks who own nearby Baraka and Café Chez Maman, Chez Papa features the subtle, rustic recipes of Provence.

Fennel, tomatoes, artichokes, olives, and rosemary flavor authentic dishes such as lamb daube in red wine, salade Niçoise, and apple tarte Tatin. *Petites assiettes* (appetizers) and *grandes assiettes* (entrées), as the menu bills them, appeal to equally small and large appetites.

The dining room is tiny, colored by claret walls and chocolate-brown banquettes, and crowded with little zinc-topped tables. A scattering of tables on the sidewalk out front adds extra seating on a nice day.

Circolo

Contemporary ✗✗

011

500 Florida St. (at Mariposa St.)

Phone:	415-553-8560	Sun – Thu 5pm - 10pm
Fax:	415-553-8561	Fri – Sat 5pm - 11pm
Web:	www.circolosf.com	
Prices:	$$$	

Touting itself as a restaurant/ultra lounge, Circolo seduces its hip patrons with a sexy atmosphere complete with cascading water, bamboo walls, and a metallic mesh curtain forming the boundary between the dining room and the bar. The latter is where you'll want to start (with exotic house concoctions like the Watini) and end your evening (dancing to trendy tunes). The sleek dining room is extended by a mezzanine where the high leather booths are much requested by diners seeking privacy.

Chef Patrick Kehler fuses Nuevo Latino and Asian cuisines in such signatures as tres frijoles soup, miso-glazed tofu salad with noodles, halibut and shrimp duet with yucca chips, and adobo-crusted rack of lamb. At Circolo dessert means warm lychee bread pudding, and coconut flan with lychee and ginger granita.

Delfina

012

3621 18th St. (bet. Dolores & Guerrero Sts.)

Phone:	415-552-4055
Fax:	415-552-4095
Web:	www.delfinasf.com
Prices:	$$

Sun – Thu 5:30pm - 10pm
Fri – Sat 5:30pm - 11pm

This neighborhood gem near Mission Dolores Park was one of the city's hottest tables when it opened in 1998 and it's still a challenge to get in. There's a good reason for this. Innovative food and friendly service rule in the narrow, contemporary-style dining room, which is filled with wooden banquettes and zinc-topped tables. Two small bars—one for liquor and one for food—create a friendly vibe.

Craig Stoll and his wife, Anne, run the place, he as chef and she as general manager. Stoll cleverly personalizes the Italian recipes (such as house-made mint tagliatelle with chanterelles and mascarpone, or grilled swordfish with warm lentil salad and anchovy aioli) on the daily changing menu.

The waitstaff bubbles with energy, catering as much to new customers as they do to regulars.

Dosa

013

995 Valencia St. (at 21st St.)

Phone:	415-642-3672
Fax:	415-643-8823
Web:	www.dosasf.com
Prices:	⊜⊜

Tue – Thu 5:30pm - 10pm
Fri 5:30pm - 11pm
Sat 11am - 3pm & 5:30pm - 11pm
Sun 11am - 3pm & 5:30pm - 10pm
Closed Mon

Since Dosa opened in December 2005, this hot spot in the hub of the Mission always seems to be abuzz. That's because fans of South Indian cuisine make a beeline for the boisterous dining room, where dangling pendant lamps cast a warm glow on tangerine-colored walls.

The restaurant's name is synonymous with the thin crêpe that is its signature. Savory dosas are served filled, plain, or as open-faced versions called *uttapams*. All come with chutneys (coconut and/or tomato) and *sambar*, a dip made from spiced lentils. South Indian curries, rice dishes and traditional breads round out the offerings.

For the uninitiated, the menu does a good job of explaining the regional Indian dishes and how best to enjoy them. No reservations are accepted for parties less than five people.

San Francisco City Mission District

Foreign Cinema

014

2534 Mission St. (bet. 21st & 22nd Sts.)

Phone:	415-648-7600	Mon – Thu 6pm - 10pm
Fax:	415-648-7669	Fri 6pm - 11pm
Web:	www.foreigncinema.com	Sat 11am - 3:30pm & 6pm - 11pm
Prices:	$$	Sun 11am - 3:30pm & 6pm - 10pm

"Outside or inside?" will be the first question put to you upon entering Foreign Cinema. Choose the former and you'll be seated in a covered and heated courtyard, where, beginning at dusk, you can view foreign and independent films while you eat (reminiscent of drive-in movies of old). Pick the latter and you'll find yourself in a soaring, industrial space with concrete walls.

Chefs Gayle Pirie and John Clark produce a nightly menu that shows a list of oysters as a prelude, then moves on to "premieres" of house-cured sardines and natural beef carpaccio to spark your appetite. Feature attractions of Catalonian-style toasted noodles, and fried harissa-spiced chicken echo the films' foreign accents.

The adjoining Modernism West gallery does a double take as a private dining room.

Garçon

015

1101 Valencia St. (at 22nd St.)

Phone:	415-401-8959	Mon – Sat 5:30pm - 11pm
Fax:	415-401-8960	Sun 10:30am - 2:30pm & 5:30pm - 11pm
Web:	www.garconsf.com	
Prices:	$$	

"Garçon!" is more than just a way to summon your waiter in a French cafe. In the ethnic melting pot of eateries that is San Francisco's Mission District, Garçon ranks as one of the new crowd-pleasers.

As Gallic as duck confit, this spot decks out its dining room with blue banquettes, bistro chairs, mirrors and a curving bar. But instead of the Left Bank, windows here afford a view of the animated street scene on Valencia. Still, you won't need *beaucoup de* euros to afford tasty standards like the charcuterie plate, onion soup gratinée, goat cheese terrine, and mussels marinières.

As it happens, the owner, chef and most of the waitstaff are French, so if you call for the *garçon*, it's a pretty sure bet that someone will respond.

San Francisco City **Mission District**

Kiji

Japanese 🍴

016

1009 Guerrero St. (at 22nd St.)

Phone:	415-282-0400	Tue – Thu 5:30pm - 10:30pm
Fax:	415-282-0444	Fri – Sat 5:30pm - 11pm
Web:	www.kijirestaurant.com	Sun 5:30pm - 10pm
Prices:	🍴🍴	Closed Mon

Look for the red paper lantern that marks the entrance to Kiji, located between the Mission District and Noe Valley. Opened in October 2005, this little Japanese newcomer carries on the same theme inside with tea-green walls, red beaded lampshades, leafy plants and Asian artifacts—all designed by chef/owner Eddie Hong.

For an authentic experience, take a seat at the sushi bar, where you can watch the chefs carve rich toro, seared beef, sea eel, salmon belly and house-cured mackerel into silky slices of nigiri. Otherwise, you can choose among makimono, sashimi, or mains such as broiled black cod, pan-seared scallops and beef teriyaki.

Premium sakes come by the glass, carafe or bottle. Can't decide? Try a sake sampler.

La Provence

French 🍴

017

1001 Guerrero St. (at 22nd St.)

Phone:	415-643-4333	Tue – Sat 5:30pm - 11pm
Fax:	N/A	Sun 11am - 3:30pm & 5:30pm - 11pm
Web:	www.laprovencerestaurant.net	Closed Mon
Prices:	$$	

No time for that trip to Provence? Don't despair; the fragrant cuisine of the sun shines at this Mission District bistro, surrounded by the cheery yellows and warming reds of the dining room.

Here, the kitchen crew crafts authentic pissaladière, soup au pistou perfumed with basil, house-made duck rillettes, and tender roasted rabbit basted with lavender honey. While the dishes respect their origins in the South of France, the chef is known to add little twists such as substituting orange zest for black olives in the daube Provençale.

On Sunday, brunch puts a Gallic spin on an American tradition with the likes of croque monsieur, *pain perdu* (French toast), and scrambled eggs served with ratatouille.

La Taqueria

Mexican ✕

018

2889 Mission St. (bet. 24th & 25th Sts.)

Phone:	415-285-7117
Fax:	N/A
Web:	N/A
Prices:	🫘

Open daily 11am - 9pm
Closed December 17 – January 5

A Mission mainstay, La Taqueria offers authentic, good-quality Mexican food. It may not be the cheapest in town, but you can still get your fill here for well under $15. Although the eatery's basic counter design doesn't encourage lingering, the place is always packed.

While you wait in line to place your order, you'll have time to contemplate your choices: burritos and tacos can be stuffed with beef (including beef head and tongue), pork, sausage, chicken or just veggies. They all come with beans, fresh salsa, tomatoes, onions and cilantro; avocado, sour cream and cheese will set you back another 40 cents (bring cash, since that's all they accept). Wash down your meal with a sweet fresh-fruit drink, or a Mexican beer.

Look for the satellite location in San Jose *(15 S. First St.)*.

Liberty Cafe & Bakery

American ✕

019

410 Cortland Ave. (bet. Bennington & Wool Sts.)

Phone:	415-695-8777
Fax:	N/A
Web:	www.thelibertycafe.com
Prices:	$$

Tue – Fri 11:30am - 3pm & 5:30pm - 10pm
Sat – Sun 10:30am - 2pm & 5:30pm - 10pm
Closed Mon
Closed December 23 - January 2

If you lived in Bernal Heights, you'd likely be a regular at this diminutive bistro. It's the kind of convivial place that locals love, even more so because it's open for breakfast (at the bakery), lunch and dinner.

Tucked inside an old house, the cafe features a short monthly changing menu that takes fresh ingredients and turns them into dishes—chicken pot pie; culotte steak with shallot and sage marmalade; pizza with green garlic, Meyer lemon, pine nuts and house-made sausage—that satisfy sophisticates as well as lovers of comfort food.

Breads and desserts are prepared in the cottage out back, which does double duty as a wine bar serving light fare (beginning at 5:30pm) from Thursday through Saturday. The no-reservations policy means that you may have to wait for a table.

San Francisco City **Mission District**

Limón

020

524 Valencia St. (bet. 16th & 17th Sts.)

Phone: 415-252-0918
Fax: 415-252-1262
Web: www.limon-sf.com
Prices: $$

Mon – Thu 11:30am - 3pm & 5pm - 10:30pm
Fri 11:30am - 3pm & 5pm - 11pm
Sat noon - 11pm
Sun noon - 10pm
Closed July 4

Limón is a family affair. Executive chef Martin Castillo works with his brothers Antonio and Eduardo, as well as sister Ana, brother-in-law Aldo, and mother, Luz, who helps out in the kitchen. "Nuevo latino fusion food" is served here in the smartly decorated dining room, whose green walls echo the restaurant's name.

A fascinating combination of traditional Peruvian recipes and more contemporary dishes, all of which have roots in South America, satisfy diners at Limón. *Perihuela*, Peru's version of bouillabaisse, *lomo saltado* (slices of top sirloin sautéed with onions, tomatoes and fries), *camarones* Limón (braised whole calamari stuffed with aji amarillo, shrimp and breadcrumbs), and a separate menu section just for ceviche are just a few of the carefully prepared specialties.

Maverick

021

3316 17th St. (at Mission St.)

Phone: 415-863-3061
Fax: 415-863-3131
Web: www.sfmaverick.com
Prices: $$

Mon 5:30pm - 11pm
Thu – Fri 11:30am - 2:30pm & 5:30pm - 11pm
Sat – Sun 11am - 3pm & 5:30pm - 11pm

You won't find many cowboys eating in this shoebox-sized Mission restaurant. What you will find is a mix of neighbors and business people who come for well-prepared regional American cuisine (check out the abstracted map of the United States that hangs over the tiny bar in front).

For lunch, sandwich plates include Cincy BBQ, fried oyster po' boy, East Coast hoagie, and, of course, the all-American burger. In the evening, the menu morphs to feature selections like Iowa salad, Creekstone Farms grilled ribeye, Cornish game hen, and East Providence-style pan-roasted monkfish.

If you're lunching here and have to go back to the office, you'll appreciate the fact that the menu offers half-glasses of wine. On Monday night you can get a whole bottle of wine for half-price.

San Francisco City Mission District

Pancho Villa Taqueria

Mexican ✗

3071 16th St. (bet. Mission & Valencia Sts.)

Phone:	415-864-8840	Open daily 10am - midnight
Fax:	415-864-3484	
Web:	www.panchovillasf.com	
Prices:	💰💰	

 ♿

Named for the Mexican revolutionary whose portrait and statue adorn the back wall of this tiny taqueria, Pancho Villa packs in Mexican food aficionados all day long. Behind the long counter where the food is prepared, hands fly like bullets as an army of employees takes and plates orders at a frenetic pace.

Choose among the fresh array of burritos, tacos, quesadillas, or create your own combo meal. Once you've paid the cashier, pull up a stool to one of the basic tables and dig in. A meal here is inexpensive enough that you'll have a few coins left in your pocket to give to the musicians who often entertain diners with lively Mexican tunes.

Check out Pancho Villa's other location south of the city in San Mateo *(365 B St.)*.

Pauline's Pizza 😊

Pizza ✗

260 Valencia St. (bet. Duboce Ave. & 14th St.)

Phone:	415-552-2050	Tue – Sat 5pm - 10pm
Fax:	415-431-4535	Closed Sun & Mon
Web:	N/A	Closed December 23 - January 1
Prices:	$$	

 ♿

Some of the best pizza in San Francisco can be found in the Mission at Pauline's. It's not the least expensive pizza around, but you pay a price for quality.

Perfectly thin and crispy handmade crusts can be strewn with "regular" (mushrooms, black olives, sausage, pepperoni) toppings or with seasonal "eccentric" ingredients (pancetta, artichoke hearts, goat cheese, house-made chicken sausage). The signature pie is slathered with pesto, and the chef offers a special "eccentric combination" each night in both meat and vegetarian versions. For a sweet ending, try the homemade ice cream, dark-chocolate mousse or butterscotch pudding.

Pauline's doesn't take reservations (for parties of less than eight people), so it's no wonder that the line streams out the door most nights.

San Francisco City **Mission District**

Pizzeria Delfina

024

Pizza

3611 18th St. (bet. Dolores & Guerrero Sts.)

Phone:	415-437-6800	Mon 5:30pm - 10pm
Fax:	415-437-6828	Tue – Thu 11:30am - 10pm
Web:	www.pizzeriadelfina.com	Fri 11:30am - 11pm
Prices:	⊜⊜	Sat noon - 11pm
		Sun noon - 10pm

Next door to big sister, Delfina, this petit pizzeria is new on the city's restaurant scene. Opened in July 2005 by the successful team of Craig and Anne Stoll, the 20-seat (including eight seats on the sidewalk out front) eatery was designed with an urban attitude.

Artful thin-crust Neapolitan pizzas are made to order, or to go. A blackboard announces the short menu, which includes several antipasti (delicious eggplant caponata, fresh mozzarella stretched in-house), and six variations on pizza, with toppings running the gamut from house-made fennel sausage to cherrystone clams.

Unlike its sister, Pizzeria Delfina doesn't accept reservations. You can avoid a line by going later in the afternoon; the pizzeria offers continuous service every day but Monday, when they're closed for lunch.

Slow Club ⊜

025

Californian

2501 Mariposa St. (at Hampshire St.)

Phone:	415-241-9390	Mon – Thu 11:30am - 2:30pm & 6:30pm - 10pm
Fax:	415-241-8371	Fri 11:30am - 2:30pm & 6:30pm - 11pm
Web:	www.slowclub.com	Sat 10am - 2:30pm & 6pm - 11pm
Prices:	$$	Sun 10am - 2:30pm

Located on the border of the Mission District and Potrero Hill in a neighborhood composed mainly of warehouses, Slow Club sports a techno-chic décor realized by a varnished concrete floor, charcoal-gray walls, and exposed metal beams. The hip, young clientele seems to blend in perfectly with the surroundings.

The menu changes daily to propose a short selection of California cuisine based, as much as possible, on products that come from farms and ranches that adhere to ecologically sound practices. The result? Impeccably seasoned grilled pork loin with cremini mushrooms and port wine reduction, carrot soup scented with curry, and a dark chocolate cake that will satisfy the most confirmed chocoholic.

This laid-back place doesn't take reservations.

San Francisco City Mission District

Tartine Bakery

026

600 Guerrero St. (at 18th St.)

Phone:	415-487-2600	Mon 8am - 7pm
Fax:	415-487-2605	Tue – Wed 7:30am - 7pm
Web:	www.tartinebakery.com	Thu – Fri 7:30am - 8pm
Prices:		Sat 8am - 8pm
		Sun 9am - 8pm

On weekends, let the line on the sidewalk and the wonderful smells wafting out the door lead you to Tartine Bakery. Otherwise, you might not notice the simple façade of this tiny place. That would be a shame, because then you'd miss Chad Robertson's crusty loaves, fresh from his wood-fired oven. This bread forms the cover for sandwiches (*tartines* in French) stuffed with Niman Ranch pastrami, tapenade, and Humboldt Fog goat cheese. They also offer quiche, croque monsieur and salads.

Delectable pastries, fashioned daily by Robertson's wife, Elisabeth Prueitt, will tempt you from the refrigerator case. Prepare to agonize over frangipane croissants, lemon cream tarts and morning buns with cinnamon and orange. The best solution? Keep coming back so you can try them all.

Tokyo Go Go

027

3174 16th St. (bet. Guerrero & Valencia Sts.)

Phone:	415-864-2288	Mon – Thu 5:30pm - 10:30pm
Fax:	415-864-2331	Fri – Sat 5:30pm - 11pm
Web:	www.tokyogogo.com	Sun 5:30pm - 10pm
Prices:	$$	

Modeled on a Japanese *izakaya*, a place to dine, drink and socialize, this mod sushi bar with its blaring hip-hop and acid jazz is where the Mission's hip twentysomethings gather before a night of partying.

Specialty rolls like Off the Wall (tempura shrimp and cucumber topped with spicy tuna, avocado, and wasabi tobiko), and original presentations (croquettes of American Kobe beef and Yukon gold potatoes) reflect a Japanese cuisine that cuts above the rest. A glass of premium sake makes the perfect complement to your meal.

Prices are especially low during Handroll Happy Hour (Monday to Saturday 5:30pm to 7pm, Sunday 5pm to 6:30pm), when you can order a handroll and a Kirin, a sake or a well cocktail for $6. Note that Tokyo Go Go doesn't take reservations for parties of less than four.

San Francisco City **Mission District**

Universal Cafe

028

2814 19th St. (bet. Bryant & Florida Sts.)

Phone:	415-821-4608
Fax:	415-285-6760
Web:	www.universalcafe.net
Prices:	$$

Tue – Thu 5:30pm - 9:30pm
Fri 11:30am - 2:30pm & 5:30pm - 10:30pm
Sat 9am - 2:30pm & 5:30pm - 10:30pm
Sun 9am - 2:30pm & 5:30pm - 9:30pm
Closed Mon

A find for foodies, Universal Cafe sits off the beaten track on the eastern edge of the Mission district, near Potrero Hill. Smart post-industrial décor has transformed the building into a chic den, outfitted with gray marble tables, a long wooden banquette lining one wall, and, across from it, a curving bar opening onto the kitchen.

Chef/owner Leslie Carr Avalos favors organic products procured from ranches and farms that practice sustainable agriculture. Her short well-balanced menu of nightly changing fare focuses on what's fresh: ravioli may be stuffed with Bellwether Farm ricotta and wild nettles; rare-grilled yellowfin tuna could be paired with avocado-kumquat salsa.

Warm, friendly service and a casual cosmopolitan atmosphere make Universal Cafe a place to go out of your way for.

Woodward's Garden

029

1700 Mission St. (at Duboce St.)

Phone:	415-621-7122
Fax:	N/A
Web:	www.woodwardsgarden.com
Prices:	$$

Tue – Sat 6pm - 10pm
Closed Sun & Mon

A diamond in the not-so-rough Mission district, Woodward's Garden hides under the Highway 101 overpass between the Mission and the Castro. In the mid-19th century, this was the site of an amusement park and gardens—the subject of Robert Frost's poem *At Woodward's Garden*, and namesake of the quaint restaurant that chef Dana Tommasino and Margie Conard opened here in 1992.

At this Woodward's Garden, no walls or windows buffer diners from the sights, sounds and smells of the integrated kitchen. Dishes spell satisfying down-home comfort with the likes of a meaty fennel-crusted Niman Ranch pork chop accompanied by caramelized fennel and apples, blue lake beans and white cornbread stuffing. Irresistible desserts such as the Scharffen Berger bittersweet chocolate-almond tart are good as gold.

San Francisco City Mission District

Nob Hill
Russian Hill, Chinatown

In the northeast corner of the city, three adjoining areas, Nob Hill, Russian Hill and Chinatown, may share boundaries, but each retains its own distinct personality.

Nob Hill – Though it pokes into the sky like a knobby knee, Nob Hill actually got its name from the titans of industry who once lived here—"nob" is a contraction of "nabob," a term for European adventurers who made huge fortunes in India and the East.

These nabobs came in two waves. The first were the "Big Four" railroad magnates—Leland Stanford, Charles Crocker, Mark Hopkins and Collis **Huntington**—who built sprawling mansions atop Nob Hill in the 1870s. They were joined in the 1880s by two of the four "Bonanza Kings," James Fair and James Flood, who profited off Nevada's Comstock silver lode. Engineer Andrew Hallidie's "folly"—the cable car—brought more development to the 376-foot summit after the establishment of the California (1878) and Powell Street (1888) lines.

Today residential Nob Hill *(edged by Van Ness, Geary, Mason and Washington Sts.)* is peppered with upscale restaurants and several of the city's poshest hotels.

Russian Hill – Along with its neighbor, Russian Hill offers some of the best vistas in the city. It wasn't until the 1880s, when the cable car provided easy access to its summit, that people started moving here *en masse*. The Powell-Hyde and Powell-Mason lines are still the best way to get to the top.

Over the years, the neighborhood defined by Francisco, Taylor, Pacific and Polk streets has provided inspiration for many literary figures, from Mark Twain to Beat writer Jack Kerouac. Today

Huntington Park

Brigitta L. House/MICHELIN

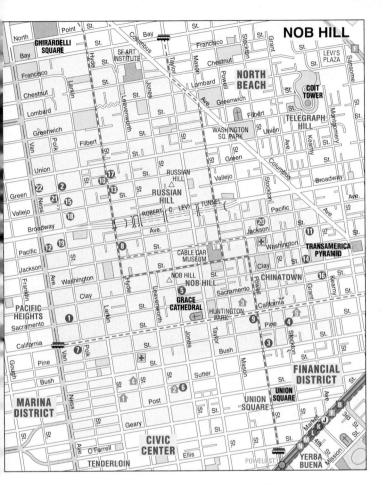

it attracts thrill seekers to navigate the 100 block of **Lombard Street**, where eight dramatic switchbacks mark the steep (16 percent) grade between Hyde and Leavenworth.

Chinatown – Chinatown, which got its start around 1849 when thousands of Cantonese treasure seekers ventured up toward Sutter's Mill in search of gold, spills down the eastern slope of Nob Hill, bridging the Financial District and North Beach. Pass through the **Chinatown Gate** (Grant Ave. at Bush St.) and you'll find dim sum "palaces," tea shops, vegetable markets, souvenir emporiums and temples. **Grant Avenue**, Chinatown's main street, abounds in architectural chinoiserie, while on **Stockton Street** shoppers throng the produce, fresh fish and poultry markets flanking the blocks between Clay Street and Broadway. The densely populated neighborhood—with some 30,000 residents—remains a tight-knit community that fiercely protects its Asian heritage.

Acquerello ❀

001

1722 Sacramento St. (bet. Polk St. & Van Ness Ave.)

Phone: 415-567-5432
Fax: 415-567-6432
Web: www.acquerello.com
Prices: $$$$

Tue – Sat 5:30pm - 10:30pm
Closed Sun & Mon

©Marty Kelly

Soft as a watercolor (which is how the restaurant's name translates in Italian), Acquerello elevates this former chapel into a cathedral of fine cuisine. Maitre d' and co-owner Giancarlo Paterlini graciously leads the services in the 50-seat dining room, where walls are awash in butter yellow under a vaulted ceiling lined with dark wood rafters.

At comfortably spaced white-clothed tables illuminated by the glow of Murano glass lamps, diners converse *sotto voce*, so as not to disturb the other worshipers of chef Suzette Gresham's delicate Italian cooking. Gresham exhibits a reverence for outstanding ingredients in preparations such as Parmesan budino with pea tendrils and Meyer lemon, and asparagus tortellini with black truffles. You can order à la carte, or feast on her nightly tasting menu, which combines four courses with select wines. Whichever you choose, count on Giancarlo for seamless service and expert advice regarding Italian wine pairings (he personally selected the 700 labels on the list).

For dessert, bourbon-caramel semifreddo sprinkled with amaretti crumbs and house-made vanilla gelato drizzled with aged balsamic vinegar will incite hallelujahs from your taste buds.

Appetizers

Ridged Pasta with Foie Gras, Scented with Black Truffles

Delicate Parmesan Budino with Pea Tendrils and Meyer Lemon

Lobster Panzerotti in a Spicy Lobster Brodo with "Diavolicchio"

Entrées

Boneless Saddle of Lamb with Olive Oil and Braised Potatoes in a Soft-roasted Garlic Sauce

Crisply Grilled Whole Dorade over Romano Beans, Tender Potatoes and House-Cured Pancetta

Lemon-infused Breast of Guinea Hen over Sautéed Salsify in an Umbrian Truffle Sauce

Desserts

Bourbon Caramel Semifreddo with Amaretti Crumbs and Drizzle of Chocolate Sauce

Saffron Panna Cotta with Pine-Nut and Fig Crostata and Balsamic Sauce

House-made Vanilla Gelato with Aged Balsamico Tradizionale di Modena

La Folie ❀

French 🍴🍴🍴

2316 Polk St. (bet. Green & Union Sts.)

Phone:	415-776-5577	Mon – Sat 5:30pm - 10:30pm
Fax:	415-776-3431	Closed Sun & major holidays
Web:	www.lafolie.com	
Prices:	$$$$	

San Francisco City Nob Hill

La Folie

Despite the restaurant's name, there's nothing foolish about La Folie. Jamie Passot, the chef's wife, greets guests at the entrance, then ushers them into one of two recently remodeled dining spaces: the first is the main wood-paneled room dressed with mirrors and coppery drapes; the second is an intimate private space embellished with green-upholstered walls and French country-style paintings.

No matter where you sit at this family-run restaurant on Russian Hill, a host of stylish and efficient servers will be at your beck and call. From the changing menu, you can choose between three, four, and five courses (ranging from $65 to $85), depending on the size of your appetite—and your wallet. Chef/owner Roland Passot, who hails from Lyon, shows off his versatility in whimsical creations such as quail and foie gras lollipops, sautéed branzini with truffle gnocchi, and coconut tapioca with passion fruit sorbet. In addition, a thematic menu expresses the season by designing dishes around ingredients such as asparagus in April or truffles in January.

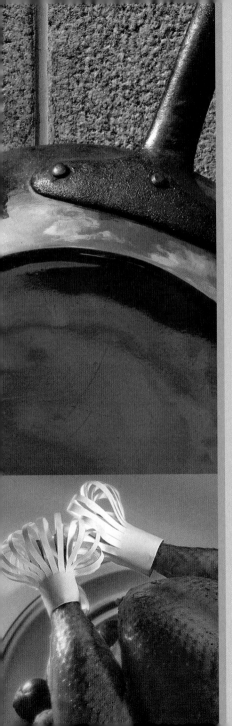

Appetizers

*Parsley and Garlic Soup
with a Ragoût of Snails
and Shiitake Mushrooms*

*Quail and Foie Gras
Lollipops with Leek
and Wild Mushroom
Cannelloni*

*Dungeness Crab Napoleon
layered with Crispy
Pineapple Chips on Apple
Gelée*

Entrées

*Rôti of Quail and Squab
Stuffed with Mushrooms,
Crispy Potato Strings and
Natural Jus with Truffles*

*Pan-roasted Sturgeon on
Braised Leeks with Crispy
Polenta Gâteau and
Oxtail, Red-Wine Thyme
Reduction*

*Seared Liberty Farm Duck
Breast on Crispy Rice, with
Spring Onions and Spiced
Kumquat Sauce*

Desserts

*Le Coco et La Passion:
Coconut Tapioca with
Passion Fruit Sorbet, Basil
Infusion and Coconut Tuile*

Masa's ✿

003

648 Bush St. (bet. Powell & Stockton Sts.)

Phone:	415-989-7154	Tue – Sat 5:30pm - 9:30pm
Fax:	415-989-3141	Closed Sun & Mon
Web:	www.masasrestaurant.com	
Prices:	$$$$	

Masa's/Scott Moules

A redo in 2001 transformed Masa's dining room into a sleek space bathed in warm brown tones with chocolate-colored mohair banquettes, toile-covered chairs, and shirred red-silk lampshades overhead. On one side of the room stands a hammered bronze sculpture by local artist Albert Guibara, entitled *Les Muses de La Cuisine*.

The kitchen muses do indeed seem to spark chef Gregory Short's creative juices. Short, who worked with Thomas Keller at The French Laundry, crafts refined contemporary cuisine using solid French technique and seasonal products. His considerable culinary skill dazzles nightly in four-, six-, and nine-course tasting menus. Dishes such as rouelle of wild striped bass with short-rib ravioli, succulent lamb chops with a fricassée of chanterelles, and a chocolate millefeuille accompanied by Irish coffee and creamsicle sherberts will no doubt inspire you to come back for more.

Located two blocks north of Union Square adjacent to the Hotel Vintage Court, Masa's regales diners at the table with Frette linens, frosted-glass vases of fresh roses, fine china and Riedel stemware—the better to show off selections from the award-winning wine list.

Appetizers

Maine Crab Salad with English Peas, Himalayan Truffles and Pea Shoots

Hamachi and Hawaiian Hearts of Palm with Aji Panca, Red Shiso and Trout Caviar

Confit of Liberty Valley Duck Leg with Minted Couscous, Grey Shallot Chutney, Mâche and Aged-Sherry Vinaigrette

Entrées

Whole Roasted Tolenas Farms Quail, *farcie aux Truffles Noires et Foie Gras, servie avec Purée de Chou-fleur et Épinards*

Roasted Ribeye of Colorado Lamb with Fresh Chickpeas, Roasted Peppers, Japanese Eggplant, Panisse Cake and Curry Oil

Loin of Four Story Hills Farms Veal with Spring Vegetable "Matignon," Himalayan Truffles and Natural Sauce

Desserts

Thai Coconut-Pineapple and Lime Thai Coconut Sherbet and Hand-cut "Noodles," Textures of Pineapple, Lemongrass and Lime

Dessert "Tacos": Honey and Cornmeal Shells with Fillings of Chocolate Mole, Banana and Cajeta Foam

Basmati Rice Clouds with Cinnamon Meringues, Textures of Rum-Raisin and Tangerine

Ritz-Carlton Dining Room ✿

Contemporary ✗✗✗✗

004

600 Stockton St. (at California St.)

Phone:	415-773-6198	Tue – Thu 6pm - 9pm
Fax:	415-951-8730	Fri – Sat 5:30pm - 9:30pm
Web:	www.ritzcarlton.com	Closed Sun & Mon
Prices:	$$$$	

Ron Starr/The Ritz-Carlton

As one of the most luxurious hotels in the city, it's only fitting that the Ritz-Carlton atop Nob Hill should house an equally lavish dining room. Formality enfolds well-heeled guests in this bastion of elegance, where picture-frame moldings set off contemporary artwork, lustrous draperies frame large windows, and sparkling white Limoges china, fresh tulips and delicate glassware dress the tables.

Amid all this grand tradition, you'd expect the food to follow suit. But chef Ron Siegel (formerly at Masa's) injects his cuisine with Asian-inspired notes as in grilled hirame with dashi gelée and crispy yuba, and sashimi of live spot prawns with wasabi and Japanese sea salt.

Whether you choose one of the multicourse tasting menus or fashion your own three-course meal, expect to spend several hours over dinner here. You'll be tended to by a brigade of well-trained and discreet waiters who are always present when needed, as well as a sommelier who can decipher the encyclopedic wine list, which cites some of the best varietals from Europe and the U.S.

Appetizers

Hot Foie Gras with Spicy Pickled Cherries, Crouton, and Apple Juice Infused with Black Pepper

Tahitian Vanilla Sea Salt and Muntock with White Pepper Seared Toro, Beech Mushrooms, Mirin Reduction (from the Salt & Pepper Tasting menu)

☺ Sashimi of Live Spot Prawns with Wasabi, Japanese Sea Salt, Lemon Juice, Sautéed Heads and Yuzu Gelée

Entrées

Slow-cooked King Salmon with Fennel and Leek Purée, Melted Squid, Meyer Lemon Shellfish Reduction

Duck Breast with Swiss Chard, Asparagus, and Bamboo Rice with Licorice Root and Pickled Cherries

Smoked Sea Salt and Espelette Pepper Maine Lobster, with Pork Belly, Baby Fennel and Clam Broth (from the Salt & Pepper Tasting menu)

Desserts

Strawberry Composition: Strawberry Honey Chèvre Tartlet, Strawberry Lemon-Cream Napoleon and Strawberry Sorbet

Chocolate Manjari Caramel Cake with Teccino Amaretto Ice Cream, Hazelnut Foam, Hazelnut Dentelle and Maldon Salt

Citrus Fleur de Sel and Tasmanian Pepper, with Strawberry Consommé, Honey Ice Cream, Tapioca Pearls and Lime Chiboust (from the Salt & Pepper Tasting menu)

C & L Steakhouse

005

American 🍴🍴🍴

1250 Jones St. (at Clay St.)

Phone: 415-771-5400
Fax: 415-771-3542
Web: www.cl-steak.com
Prices: $$$$

Open daily 11am - 3pm & 5:30pm - 10pm

Buoyed by their success with Aqua, restaurateur Charles Condy (the "C" of C & L) and Aqua chef Laurent Manrique (the "L") opened this joint venture in late 2004. Valet parking is one perk of the restaurant's location in the bottom floor of the Clay-Jones apartment building in residential Nob Hill.

Wood-paneled and clubby, the stylish dining room says "steakhouse" with its mirrored walls, massive columns and plush red banquettes. The menu, however, takes a more regional American approach. Sure, there are steaks (petit filet, New York strip, ribeye) and the requisite chilled wedge of iceberg, but you'll also find braised pork belly and roasted Cornish game hen. The chef kicks up Caesar salad with spicy crawfish and offers yucca fries and Yukon gold potato mousseline as sides.

Canteen

006

Californian 🍴

817 Sutter St. (bet. Leavenworth & Jones Sts.)

Phone: 415-928-8870
Fax: 415-923-6804
Web: N/A
Prices: $$

Wed – Fri 7am - 2pm & 6pm - 10pm
Sat 8am - 2pm & 6pm - 10pm
Sun 8am - 2pm
Closed Mon & Tue

Straddling the border of Nob Hill and the Tenderloin, the 20-seat diner next door to the Commodore Hotel seems an unlikely place to find the guy who took over Rubicon's kitchen from Traci Des Jardins. Yet at Canteen, chef/owner Dennis Leary and his team dish up breakfast, lunch and dinner for hotel guests and savvy foodies alike. The chef changes his menu weekly, offering perhaps a dozen dishes total. The likes of warm asparagus served atop a pool of pea purée, coriander-spiced roast chicken glazed with apricot, and fragrant vanilla soufflé are far from diner fare.

Bare bulbs hanging from the ceiling light soft gray walls inset with bookshelves, giving this eatery a coffee-shop ambience. Behind the bright-green counter, though, some big flavors come out of the galley kitchen.

Crustacean

007

Asian 𝄫𝄫𝄫

1475 Polk St. (at California St.)

Phone: 415-776-2722
Fax: 415-776-1069
Web: www.anfamily.com
Prices: $$$

Mon – Thu 5pm - 10pm
Fri – Sun 11:30am - 3:30pm & 5pm - 10pm

Behind Crustacean there's a fairy tale come true about the Ans, a well-to-do Vietnamese family who were forced to leave their country in the wake of the Communist invasion in 1975. Mother Helene started the family's culinary empire at Thanh Long in San Francisco. Crustacean, the second in their string of restaurants, opened its doors in 1991.

Take the elevator to the third floor, where Crustacean creates an exotic world filled with bamboo, potted palms, whimsical lanterns, and large picture windows. In the locked kitchen within the kitchen, An family members prepare their "secret specialties," such as royal tiger prawns, garlic noodles, and the much-ordered whole roasted Dungeness crab in garlic sauce.

1550 Hyde Cafe & Wine Bar

008

Californian 𝄫

1550 Hyde St. (at Pacific Ave.)

Phone: 415-775-1550
Fax: 415-775-1514
Web: www.1550hyde.com
Prices: $$

Tue – Thu 6pm - 10pm
Fri – Sat 6pm - 10:30pm
Sun 5:30pm - 9:30pm
Closed Mon

At this diminutive candlelit restaurant, Russian Hill residents have an intimate space for a quiet dinner with a view of passing cable cars through the windows. The kitchen staff favors growers who practice environmentally sustainable agriculture. Hoffman Game Birds chicken, James Ranch leg of lamb, and Point Reyes blue cheese represent a sampling of the local ingredients that figure in the California fare on the daily changing menu. As for wine, you'll find a reasonably priced selection of labels from California, France, Italy and Spain. Each night, a featured wine flight highlights three different wines from the same region.

Parking's not easy in Russian Hill, so if you don't live in the neighborhood, try taking the Hyde/Beach Street cable car, which goes right by the restaurant.

San Francisco City Nob Hill

Fournou's Ovens

Californian XXX

009

905 California St. (at Powell St.)

Phone: 415-989-1910
Fax: 415-986-8195
Web: www.fournousovens.com
Prices: $$

Open daily 6:30am - 2:30pm & 5pm - 10pm

Couched in the Stanford Court Hotel, Fournou's Ovens promotes a European aesthetic with wooden beams decorating the ceiling, tapestries hanging on the walls, and the rustic brick ovens for which the restaurant is named forming the centerpiece of the kitchen. Menu offerings span the globe from a grilled shrimp and crab cake with ancho chile sauce to Moroccan spiced scallops. The massive ovens turn out succulent rack of lamb, duck breast, and alderwood-planked Pacific salmon. For health-conscious diners, low-carb, low-fat and low-cholesterol dishes are singled out on the menu.

You'll find an award-winning selection of California labels on the wine list; the cellar's inventory counts more than 8,000 bottles.

Frascati

Mediterranean XX

010

1901 Hyde St. (at Green St.)

Phone: 415-928-1406
Fax: 415-928-1983
Web: www.frascatisf.com
Prices: $$

Open daily 5:30pm - 9:45pm

Set on a tree-shaded block of Russian Hill with a European village vibe, Frascati attracts a casually elegant cadre of neighbors and other city dwellers. The welcoming staff treats everyone like a friend here, whether you're part of the large group of regulars or a first-timer. If it's privacy you seek, ask for a table on the romantic upstairs balcony.

Refined and flavorful Mediterranean cuisine here ranges from mahi mahi with creamy polenta to Maple Leaf duck breast, and includes signatures like grilled pork Porterhouse with Italian sausage and cannellini ragout, and dark-chocolate bread pudding.

Don't even try finding a parking space in this crowded Russian Hill neighborhood; hop on the Powell-Hyde cable car, which stops right in front of the restaurant.

Great Eastern

011

649 Jackson St. (bet. Grant Ave. & Kearny St.)

Phone:	415-986-2500	Open daily 10am - 1am
Fax:	415-986-5603	
Web:	N/A	
Prices:	🅑🅑	

You won't find a gaggle of tourists at this bright, attractive, chandelier-lit dining room in Chinatown; the authentic fare at Great Eastern appeals to a largely Asian audience. The lengthy menu hones in on seafood, and large tanks swimming with crustaceans and fish in the back of the dining room attest to the freshness of dishes such as steamed abalone, lobster with XO sauce, Geoduck clam sashimi, and Dungeness crab. There's a wide variety of meat, vegetarian and noodle and rice dishes, as well as several choices of family-style meals. Clay-pot creations include squab with dried lily flowers and cloud bar mushrooms, sizzling fresh frog, and taro and preserved duck with coconut sauce.

Expect polite and well-organized service.

Harris'

012

2100 Van Ness Ave. (at Pacific Ave.)

Phone:	415-673-1888	Mon – Thu 5:30pm - 9:30pm
Fax:	415-673-8817	Fri 5:30pm - 10pm
Web:	www.harrisrestaurant.com	Sat 5pm - 10pm
Prices:	$$$$	Sun 5pm - 9:30pm

Any doubts that this is a steakhouse will be dispelled once you spy the butcher counter just inside. From the entrance, the clubby Pacific Lounge beckons with its mahogany bar, classic martinis (shaken, not stirred) and live jazz music Thursday through Saturday nights. It's a fine place to sip a cocktail before adjourning to the skylit dining room decorated with Victorian-style brass chandeliers, curved leather banquettes, and a mural of the Kings River in California covering one wall.

This makes a fitting setting to carve into a wide selection of dry-aged midwestern Angus beef, ranging from the Harris steak (a thick, bone-in New York cut) to filet mignon Rossini (served with Sonoma foie gras, black truffle and Cabernet sauce).

San Francisco City Nob Hill

Luella

Mediterranean ✕✕

1896 Hyde St. (at Green St.)

Phone: 415-674-4343   Open daily 5:30pm - 9:45pm
Fax: 415-674-4344
Web: www.luellasf.com
Prices: $$

Opened in late 2004 by Ben de Vries (formerly chef at Andalu) and his wife, Luella fills an L-shaped space with subtle earthy tones and an urbane décor. At the entrance a tiny lounge and a casual wine bar ensure a comfortable, albeit bustling, place to wait for a table. Despite the trendy ambience, the charming staff stays rooted in attentive service. Signatures like tender Coca-Cola-braised pork shoulder served over white-bean purée, and other seasonal Cal-Med cuisine keep the crowds coming back for more. Short but well selected, the wine list leans toward southern Europe, with a good choice by the glass.

Bring the kids on Sunday night, when the Little Luella menu (served from 5pm to 8pm) caters to young diners with chicken pot pie, mac and cheese, and ice-cream sundaes for dessert.

Oriental Pearl

Chinese ✕

760 Clay St. (bet. Grant & Kearny Sts.)

Phone: 415-433-1817   Open daily 11am - 3pm & 5pm - 9:30pm
Fax: 415-433-4541
Web: www.orientalpearlsf.com
Prices: ⤸

A good pick for an authentic and tasty meal in Chinatown, Oriental Pearl occupies the second floor of this Clay Street building. Here you'll dine in comfort at well-separated tables, with classical music playing softly in the background—all conditions that are conducive to conversation.

The restaurant's excellent and freshly prepared dishes emphasize Hong Kong-style cuisine, such as *yee mein* (noodles that are fried and then braised with Chinese vegetables), chicken meatballs wrapped in an egg-white pancake, and barbecue pork buns. A remarkable number of set dim sum menus (priced from $9.75 to $38 per person) can be prepared for two people or more—sorry, but you're out of luck if you're dining alone.

San Francisco City **Nob Hill**

Pesce

015

2227 Polk St. (bet. Green & Vallejo Sts.)

Phone:	415-928-8025	Mon – Thu 5pm - 10pm
Fax:	N/A	Fri 5pm - 11pm
Web:	N/A	Sat – Sun noon - 4pm & 5pm - 11pm
Prices:	$$	

Most everything about Pesce is small, beginning with the dining room and ending with the *cichetti*, or small plates like those served at bars in Venice. Even the prices are relatively small, especially given the swanky Russian Hill neighborhood.

Tastes here, however, are big. Ruggero Gadaldi, chef/owner of sibling Antica Trattoria down the street, presides over this cozy self-styled "seafood bar" where cichetti are classified as either cold or hot. Among the former, you'll find house-smoked salmon, trout and sturgeon; a Dungeness crab tower; and an oyster shot. The latter might include braised octopus salad, Sicilian swordfish rolls, and Merlot-braised lamb shank (they focus on fish, but not exclusively). For dessert, try the excellent tiramisu, creamy and redolent of liquor.

R & G Lounge

016

631 Kearny St. (bet. Clay & Sacramento Sts.)

Phone:	415-982-7877	Sun – Thu 11:30am - 9:30pm
Fax:	415-982-1496	Fri – Sat 11:30am - 10pm
Web:	www.rnglounge.com	
Prices:	$$	

This well-run, classically Chinese place on the edge of Chinatown (within two blocks of the Transamerica Pyramid) is popular with business types at lunch. At dinner, groups and families add to the mix in the boisterous, low-ceilinged downstairs dining room with its wall of aquarium tanks. If you prefer a quieter atmosphere, the airy and refined space upstairs better accommodates private conversations.

Signature dishes are illustrated on the menu to unravel any mystery concerning the Cantonese cuisine. Spend some time leafing through the wide selection before you narrow your choices. You won't go wrong with a house specialty like the fresh-from-the-tank salt-and-pepper crab, or chef's specials such as stir-fried minced seafood in lettuce cups, shark-fin soup, and Peking duck.

San Francisco City **Nob Hill**

Sushi Groove

Japanese ✗

017

1916 Hyde St. (bet. Green & Union Sts.)

Phone: 415-440-1905
Fax: N/A
Web: N/A
Prices: $$

Sun – Thu 5:30pm - 10pm
Fri – Sat 5:30pm - 10:30pm

You can take your pick of cuisines (Italian, French, Spanish, Californian) in this posh residential Russian Hill neighborhood, but you can't beat Sushi Groove for good Japanese food at reasonable prices. The freshest fish at the market makes up both traditional and more innovative nigiri, maki, sashimi and tempura offerings. Some of the special maki rolls (like Pete's Roll, spicy baked salmon wrapped around zesty white tuna and scallions) are named for the sushi chefs who invented them.

If you're looking for a quiet atmosphere, skip this place. Loud modern music and a twenty-something crowd rules the roost here. Even more boisterous, Sushi Groove South *(1516 Folsom St.)* near hip SoMa nightclubs entertains diners with DJ music.

Tablespoon ☺

Contemporary ✗✗

018

2209 Polk St. (at Vallejo St.)

Phone: 415-268-0140
Fax: 415-268-0143
Web: www.tablespoonsf.com
Prices: $$

Mon – Thu 5:30pm - 10:30pm
Fri – Sat 5:30pm - midnight
Sun 5pm - 10pm

Chef Robert Riescher gave up his gig at Erna's Elderberry House near Yosemite National Park to partner with John Jasso (who worked the front of the house at Gary Danko and Fifth Floor) at Tablespoon. A line of tables parallels the long bar in this narrow bistro warmed by cherry wood paneling.

Riescher's cuisine meets the measure with fresh organic ingredients in inventive New American preparations such as an excellent poached Atlantic haddock filet served atop a mix of fava beans, spring onions and asparagus, or a tasty salad of Dungeness crabmeat with shiso, Asian pear and endive. Order signature dishes (pan-roasted calamari, lobster and black-truffle ravioli, pasilla-pepper-spiced Ahi tuna loin) as either a starter or a main course. The three-course Sunday Dinner is a steal at under $25.

Tai Chi

Chinese

019

2031 Polk St. (bet. Broadway & Pacific Sts.)

Phone:	415-441-6758	Mon – Sat noon - 10pm
Fax:	415-441-4258	Sun 4pm - 10pm
Web:	N/A	
Prices:	☜☜	

You'll get more for your money at Tai Chi. Specifically, copious portions of authentic, freshly prepared Chinese food. In an area where most of the restaurants have limited offerings like sandwiches and salads, this canteen-style establishment provides an attractive alternative. And unlike the majority of restaurants in this section of Nob Hill, Tai Chi is open for lunch and dinner.

Once you're seated at your table, you'll receive a complimentary bowl of hot chicken soup and a pot of green tea. Leaf through the long menu to find chef's specials including garlic shrimp, orange beef, and spicy Szechuan minced chicken, along with a wide selection of meat, seafood and vegetarian dishes. When you leave Tai Chi, both your stomach and your wallet will be happy.

Y. Ben House

Chinese

020

835 Pacific Ave. (bet. Powell & Stockton Sts.)

Phone:	415-397-3168	Open daily 7am - 9pm
Fax:	N/A	
Web:	N/A	
Prices:	☜☜	

This Chinatown dim sum restaurant is the real thing. The large room is always packed with Chinese families, and you may wind up at a table with strangers if you want to find a seat. Think of it as making new friends, ignore the clatter and noise, and do as the regulars do. At lunchtime, flag down the carts as they pass by to sample authentic dim sum. The likes of fried wontons, pork meat balls, dumplings stuffed with shrimp and chives, all exhibit excellent quality for a reasonable price.

For dinner there's a full list of entrées, from clay-pot specials to a long list of seafood dishes. If you're dining with a crowd, the restaurant offers several different banquet menus designed to feed 10 people.

Yabbies Coastal Kitchen

021

2237 Polk St. (bet. Green & Vallejo Sts.)

Phone:	415-474-4088	Mon – Fri 5:30pm - 10:30pm
Fax:	415-474-4962	Sat – Sun 11am - 3:30pm
Web:	www.yabbiesrestaurant.com	& 5:30pm - 11:30pm
Prices:	$$	

Weeknights are the best times to dine at Yabbies if you want a quiet meal. During the weekends, a crush of Russian Hill urbanites hovers around the seafood bar and the separate wine bar (the full menu is served at both).

Start by selecting some oysters on the half shell among the half-dozen kinds listed. If you have a party in tow, go for one of the chilled seafood platters, piled high with Dungeness crab, oysters, prawns, mussels and littlenecks (the larger, more expensive platters add Maine lobster to the mix). Besides the roster of predominantly seafood entrées, nightly specials—from fish and chips to clambake for two—are offered Monday through Thursday.

Simple paper dresses the tabletops and a bustling ambience prevails.

Yaya

022

2424 Van Ness Ave. (bet. Green & Union Sts.)

Phone:	415-440-0455	Tue – Sun 5:30pm - 9:30pm
Fax:	415-440-4547	Closed Mon
Web:	www.yayacuisine.com	
Prices:	⊜	

With more than 15 years of restaurant experience in the city, chef Yahya Salih now holds sway on Russian Hill at Yaya. Here, well-spaced brown-paper-covered tables and wall murals of ancient Babylon provide the backdrop for what Salih bills as "Mesopotamian-California-style" food. This translates to an exotic and original cuisine scented with cinnamon, coriander, ginger, allspice, cardamom and curry powder.

Middle Eastern specialties like *perdaplow* (phyllo dough filled with shredded chicken, saffron rice, almonds, golden raisins and cardamom), and *makhlama* (mashed potatoes mixed with curry and vegetables) can be ordered as "nomads"; these combinations come with a crunchy diced-vegetable salad. For dessert, you won't go wrong with honeyed baklava, served atop a rice and saffron pudding.

Live in Italian

At finer restaurants in Los Angeles, Melbourne, Cape Town and of course, Positano.

North Beach Area
Fisherman's Wharf, Telegraph Hill

Nestled between bustling Fisherman's Wharf and the steep slopes of Russian and Telegraph hills, North Beach is one of the liveliest neighborhoods in the city. You can thank the Italians who came to dominate the area in the late 1800s. Though they're no longer in the majority, dozens of Italian cafes, restaurants, and bars attest to their interpretation of the good life.

Hanging out in North Beach can be a full-time job, which is what attracted a ragtag array of beret-wearing poets here in the 1950s. These so-called beatniks—among them Allen Ginsberg and Jack Kerouac—were eventually driven out by the busloads of tourists who came to see what all the fuss was about. Beatnik spirits linger at landmarks like City Lights bookstore *(261 Columbus Ave.)*, founded by poet Lawrence Ferlinghetti in 1953.

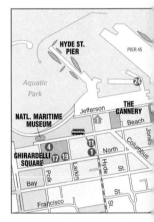

Today the majority of North Beach's eating and drinking establishments lie on busy **Columbus Avenue**, which cuts diagonally from the Transamerica Pyramid to Fisherman's Wharf. Check out the avenue's Italian delis, where imported meats and cheeses make the perfect ingredients for a picnic in Washington Square Park.

Telegraph Hill – Punctuating the eastern edge of North Beach, the abrupt 274-foot rise of Telegraph Hill is named for a long-vanished semaphore that used varicolored flags to signal the arrival of ships through the Golden Gate. Most of the early structures built on the hill were destroyed in the 1906 fire, save some on the eastern slope that were saved by Italian Americans, who, reportedly, beat back the flames with blankets soaked with red wine. The svelte 180-foot-high column of **Coit Tower tops** Telegraph Hill, and a climb to the top of the tower affords the best views in a city that, as Alfred Hitchcock said, doesn't have a bad angle.

Fisherman's Wharf – For family entertainment, you can't beat this teeming bazaar of shops, eateries and attractions set on a mile-long stretch of waterfront *(along Jefferson St. and the Embarcadero between Van Ness and Kearny Sts.)*. Once an industrial zone, Fisherman's Wharf is San Francisco's most popular tourist destination. Six piers offer everything from carousel rides and shopping on **Pier 39** to maritime history on **Hyde Street Pier**. Take a ferry to Alcatraz or to Sausalito, or just hang out and enjoy a sourdough bread "bowl" of fresh clam chowder.

Telegraph Hill

Brigitta L. House/MICHELIN

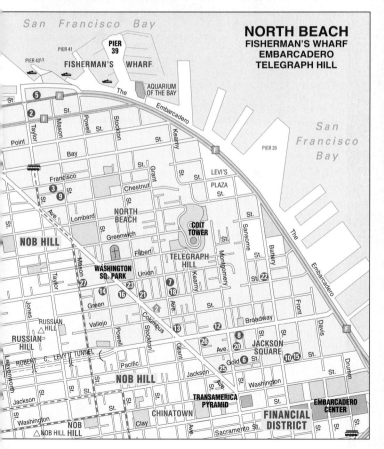

San Francisco Bay

PIER 41

PIER 43½

PIER 39

FISHERMAN'S WHARF

NORTH BEACH
FISHERMAN'S WHARF
EMBARCADERO
TELEGRAPH HILL

❺

❷

Point

Taylor

Mason

Powell St.

Stockton St.

The Embarcadero

AQUARIUM OF THE BAY

Kearny

PIER 29

LEVI'S PLAZA St.

San Francisco Bay

Bay

❸

❾

St.

Francisco

Lombard Ave.

Grant

Chestnut

NORTH BEACH

Greenwich

COIT TOWER

Sansome St.

Battery

St.

Filbert

NOB HILL

WASHINGTON SQ. PARK

TELEGRAPH HILL

㉗

⑭

⑯

㉓

㉑

Union

Kearny

❼

⑱

㉒

Taylor

Jones

Green

Montgomery St.

❷

Broadway

Front

Vallejo

Powell

Stockton

Columbus

⑬

⑫

Davis

RUSSIAN HILL

RUSSIAN HILL

ROBERT C. LEVY TUNNEL

Leavenworth

Pacific

Grant Ave.

㉖

⑳

❽

JACKSON SQUARE

⑩⑮

Gold ❻ St.

㉕

St.

NOB HILL

Jackson

Washington

EMBARCADERO CENTER

Jackson

TRANSAMERICA PYRAMID

Drumm

Washington

NOB HILL HILL

CHINATOWN

Clay

FINANCIAL DISTRICT

Sacramento St.

Gary Danko ✿

001

800 North Point St. (at Hyde St.)

Phone:	415-749-2060	Open daily 5pm - 10pm
Fax:	415-775-1805	
Web:	www.garydanko.com	
Prices:	$$$$	

Kingmond Young/S.F.

Behind this black marble façade, set on a quiet corner a block from Fisherman's Wharf, lurks an oasis of elegance. Plantation shutters, soft lighting, Asian accents, and honey tones provide the backdrop for modern artwork, while red roses and candlelight add color to tables dressed with white linen and porcelain.

The producer behind this show is chef/owner Gary Danko, whose experience encompasses the kitchens at Chateau Souverain and the Dining Room at The Ritz-Carlton San Francisco. It was at the latter that Danko met his partner Nick Peyton, who is responsible for the large brigade of skilled and knowledgeable waiters who always seem to be there when needed, pampering diners with polished service.

Lobster, foie gras and lamb are some of the chef's favorite ingredients and he interprets them differently, depending on the season. Whether you make your choice among three-, four- and five-course prix-fixe menus, or go for the chef's tasting, you'll experience Danko's beautifully presented takes on classic recipes.

The 1,500-label wine list, which includes an impressive selection of half-bottles, celebrates the best of California and French varietals.

San Francisco City **North Beach Area**

Appetizers

Roast Maine Lobster with Chanterelles, White Corn and Tarragon

Glazed Oysters with Osetra Caviar, Zucchini Pearls and Lettuce Cream

Pan-seared Branzini with Fennel Purée, Niçoise Olives, Cara Cara Oranges and Saffron

Entrées

Quail Stuffed with Wild Mushrooms and Foie Gras, Cabbage Compote and Pomegranate Gastrique

Sautéed Breast of Guinea Hen with Braised Leg and Cardamom Poached Pears

Lemon-Herb Duck Breast with Duck Hash and Warm Bing Cherries

Desserts

Meyer Lemon Soufflé Cake with Raspberry Crème-Fraîche Ice Cream

Roasted Pears with Gingerbread and Nutmeg Ice Cream

French Macaroon Ice-Cream Sandwiches

CONTEMPORARY

A. Sabella's

Seafood

002

2766 Taylor St. (at Jefferson St.)

Phone:	415-771-6775	Open daily 5pm - 11pm
Fax:	415-771-6776	
Web:	www.asabellas.com	
Prices:	$$$	

What a relief it is to find an elegant and sophisticated restaurant amid the teeming bazaar of bad eateries that marks this tourist area. Run by the Sabella family for four generations now, A. Sabella's provides an oasis of calm inside its long third-floor dining room, where arched floor-to-ceiling windows look out over the bay to Alcatraz and the Golden Gate Bridge. The view is good from any table, but the best vantage point is right by the windows.

The restaurant maintains saltwater tanks for Dungeness crab and Monterey Bay red abalone, two of their signature dishes. Classic clam chowder will warm you on a chilly day, and the selection of fresh Pacific fish (Alaskan halibut, blue nose sea bass, King salmon) varies with the season. There's even a children's menu, if you've got the kids in tow.

Albona

Italian

003

545 Francisco St. (bet. Mason & Taylor Sts.)

Phone:	415-441-1040	Tue – Sat 5pm - 10pm
Fax:	415-441-5107	Closed January 1 - 8 & June 26 - July 10
Web:	www.albonarestaurant.com	
Prices:	$$$	

It's the warm spirit of owner Bruno Viscovi that makes Albona so special. Since 1998, Viscovi has personally welcomed guests to his distinctive restaurant, located a few blocks from Fisherman's Wharf. Here, he freely chats with diners, offering advice about specials and sharing the history of his native city, Albona, which commands a view of the Adriatic Sea.

This area near the intersection of Italy, Slovenia and Croatia shares its foodways and its geography with Eastern Europe. Along with northern Italian dishes such as the excellent *calamari al forno* roasted in marinara, you'll find pork loin stuffed with sauerkraut, veal shank à la Triestina, and Adriatic fish stew. For dessert, the signature *crema di gelato* (creamy gelato mousse topped with Maraska cherries soaked in brandy) is a must.

Ana Mandara

004

Vietnamese 🍴🍴🍴

891 Beach St. (at Polk St.)

Phone:	415-771-6800	Mon – Thu 11:30am - 2pm & 5:30pm - 9:30pm
Fax:	415-771-5275	Fri 11:30am - 2pm & 5:30pm - 10:30pm
Web:	www.anamandara.com	Sat 5:30pm - 10:30pm
Prices:	$$$	Sun 5:30pm - 9:30pm

Although its entrance lies on the bay side of Ghirardelli Square, Ana Mandara doesn't need a view to entertain. Its exotic ambience provides ample eye candy with a stunning Vietnamese temple décor, punctuated by potted palms and populated by a chic cadre of diners who dress to impress.

This is more than a "beautiful refuge," as the restaurant's name translates. It's a stylish venue in which to relish the refined Vietnamese cuisine of chef Khai Duong, whose Parisian training provides him with the classical technique on which he bases piquant ceviche of striped bass and cucumber, and grilled lamb rack rubbed with cinnamon and star anise.

Two more reasons to go: the restaurant will validate parking for the Ghirardelli garage, and a live jazz band sets up on the mezzanine lounge on weekends.

Bistro Boudin

005

American 🍴

160 Jefferson St. (at Mason St.)

Phone:	415-928-1849	Mon – Fri 11:30am - 10pm
Fax:	415-351-5579	Sat – Sun 10am - 10:30pm
Web:	www.boudinbakery.com	
Prices:	$$	

No visit to San Francisco is complete without a stop at Boudin Bakery on Fisherman's Wharf. Started in 1849 by a family of French immigrants, the bakery is now renowned for its crusty sourdough bread, which is still made from the "mother dough" starter that traces its roots back to the original starter brought to California by French immigrant Isidore Boudin during the Gold Rush.

You'll want to go by and watch the bakers in action, visit the museum, and, of course, take away some of their sourdough French bread—a real San Francisco treat. If you come by around lunchtime, head for the second floor, where you'll find Bistro Boudin with its bay views. Their distinctive bread covers sandwiches, accompanies soups and salads, and forms the crust for brick-oven-fired pizzas.

San Francisco City North Beach Area

Bix

006

XX

56 Gold St. (bet. Montgomery & Sansome Sts.)

Phone:	415-433-6300	Sun – Wed 5:30pm - 10pm
Fax:	415-433-4574	Thu 5:30pm - 11pm
Web:	www.bixrestaurant.com	Fri – Sat 5:30pm - midnight
Prices:	$$$	

Duck into the little alley off Jackson Square to find this slinky 1930s-style supper club, recognizable by the neon sign boasting "Bix Here." Opened in 1988 by Doug "Bix" Biederbeck, the restaurant caters to a stylish crowd that dresses to impress and harmonizes well with the fluted columns, grand staircase, plush banquettes and mahogany paneling that grace this glamorous two-story space.

To match the mood, a jazz group entertains diners nightly—that is, when patrons can turn their attention away from Bruce Hill's updated American cuisine. A basket of warm *gougères* is the way to start, followed by a Kobe *bavette* with *pommes purée*, or the Bix truffled cheeseburger.

Locals like to stop by the bar for a classic cocktail (perhaps a Sazerac or a huckleberry gin fizz).

Café Jacqueline

007

X

1454 Grant Ave. (bet. Green & Union Sts.)

Phone:	415-981-5565	Wed – Sun 5:30pm - 11pm
Fax:	N/A	Closed Mon & Tue
Web:	N/A	
Prices:	$$$	

You'll find Jacqueline Margulis in the kitchen here. Born in Bordeaux, the grandmotherly chef has been running this place in North Beach for 27 years. She's passionate about her food and she loves compliments from her clients, so be sure to pass one on.

This won't be difficult to do, since the soufflés here—the house specialty—come out seductively puffed and airy, flavored with the likes of asparagus and cauliflower, shiitakes and chanterelles, lobster and crab, Gruyère and Roquefort, and, of course, intense chocolate for dessert.

With its lace curtains, long-stemmed wine glasses and fresh roses on each table, the cafe makes a romantic setting to linger over a meal. Soufflés require 30 minutes to cook, so don't order one if you're in a hurry.

Coi

Contemporary ✗✗✗

373 Broadway St. (bet. Montgomery & Sansome Sts.)

Phone:	415-393-9000	Tue – Sat 6pm – 10pm
Fax:	415-358-8446	Closed Sun & Mon
Web:	www.coirestaurant.com	
Prices:	$$$$	

One of the most ambitious newcomers of 2006, Coi opened in April on the fringe on the Financial District. You'll enter into a sleek wood-paneled lounge area, where jazz music creates a hip vibe.

In the intimate 30-seat dining room, a minimalist but posh style colored by earthy tones and textures from nature sets the scene for avant-garde cuisine by former Frisson chef Daniel Patterson. Diners have a choice of two nightly prix-fixe menus: 4 or 10 courses. Not one to go with the flow, Patterson experiments with complicated combinations and bold flavors that result in dishes like a wonderful cracked-wheat "risotto" with a fragrant stew of morels, fava beans and baby leeks.

The service here is some of the best in the city, elegant, knowledgeable and full of thoughtful touches.

Fior d'Italia

009

Italian ✗✗

2237 Mason St. (bet. Chestnut & Francisco Sts.)

Phone:	415-986-1886	Open daily 11:30am - 10:30pm
Fax:	415-441-8774	
Web:	www.fior.com	
Prices:	$$	

Opened in 1886, the "Flower of Italy" bills itself as the city's oldest restaurant. This establishment has moved around over the years, from its original location on Broadway (where it catered to the resident bordello) to its current venue in the San Remo Hotel. Fior d'Italia took up this spot after a fire destroyed its former digs on the corner of Union and Stockton. Despite its new space, the eatery retains its old spirit in pastel tones, velvet curtains and its black-and-white photographs of "the Fior" in the 20th century.

A brigade of conscientious bow-tie-clad waiters take their time serving old-fashioned Italian-American fare from veal saltimbocca to tagliatelle alla Bolognese. But the mature, well-dressed crowd doesn't need to rush; many of them are neighborhood regulars.

San Francisco City North Beach Area

Frisson

010

244 Jackson St. (bet. Battery & Front Sts.)

Phone:	415-956-3004	Mon – Wed 11:30am - 2pm & 5:30pm - 11pm
Fax:	415-956-3661	Thu – Fri 11:30am - 2pm & 5:30pm - midnight
Web:	www.frissonsf.com	Sat 5:30pm - midnight
Prices:	$$$	Closed Sun

Think of Frisson as an updated Art Deco supper club. Located a block from Jackson Square, the restaurant boasts a stunning décor. Its round dining room is decked out in sensuous shades of red, gold and tangerine, with semicircular orange booths and a back-lit dome covering the two-tiered space (bathrooms are unisex). Private dining spaces include the Garden Room, the Cinema Room for private screenings, and the 10-seat chef's table, adjacent to the kitchen.

The contemporary menu lists a large selection of raw items (sea bream sashimi, tuna or steak tartare), along with a choice of carefully prepared entrées (as in fino sherry-braised short ribs with vanilla bean-parsnip purée) that use premium ingredients. You can order anything off the menu in the lively bar area.

Grandeho's Kamekyo

011

2721 Hyde St. (bet. Beach & North Point Sts.)

Phone:	415-673-6828	Sun – Wed 11am - 10:30pm
Fax:	415-673-6863	Thu – Fri 11am - 11pm
Web:	N/A	Sat noon - 11pm
Prices:	$$	

Located two blocks from Ghirardelli Square, this little spot stands out for its particularly fresh sushi, friendly service and entertaining sushi chefs.

Sushi rolls form the basis of the menu here, with unique selections such as the Alcatraz roll (rock shrimp, crabmeat, wakame and vegetables), the Dynamite (deep-fried roll with eel, spicy tuna and asparagus), and the Lombard Street (smoked salmon and vegetables with thinly sliced lemon wrapped in dry soy bean paper). If you're not up for sushi, you can choose from an entrée list that includes *karrage* (deep-fried shellfish) and Korean-style barbecue ribs.

Kame ("turtle" in Japanese) symbolizes a long and happy life. The restaurant shares this wish with its customers by displaying little turtles along the sushi bar.

San Francisco City **North Beach Area**

The Helmand

012

Afghan

430 Broadway St. (bet. Kearny & Montgomery Sts.)

Phone: 415-362-0641
Fax: 415-362-0862
Web: www.helmandrestaurantsanfrancisco.com
Prices: 😊😊

Tue – Fri 11:30am - 2:30pm & 5:30pm - 10:30pm
Sat – Mon 5:30pm - 10:30pm

You'll need to venture a bit off the beaten track to get to The Helmand. It's not in the most attractive neighborhood and the façade provides no view of the interior, but once inside, you'll be transported by the cuisine of a faraway land.

Fresh flowers, antique cabinets and Afghan artifacts brighten the narrow dining room, which brims with regulars who know good *aushak* (ravioli stuffed with leeks and scallions, and served on a bed of house-made yogurt, mint and garlic and topped with ground beef and mint) when they taste it.

A menu of excellent kebabs and other specialties, offered with either challow rice (spiced with cumin seeds) or pallow rice (with cardamom, cinnamon, nutmeg and black pepper) makes an unbeatable value for the money.

The House

Contemporary Asian

013

1230 Grant Ave. (bet. Columbus Ave. & Vallejo St.)

Phone: 415-986-8612
Fax: N/A
Web: www.thehse.com
Prices: $$

Sun – Thu 11:30am - 3pm & 5:30pm - 10pm
Fri – Sat 11:30am - 3pm & 5:30pm - 11pm

This slip of an Asian eatery shines amid the profusion of Italian restaurants in North Beach. Larry and Angela Tse run the place; he's the executive chef and she takes care of the front of the house. It's tiny but trendy, with a young crowd and a lively (it can get pretty noisy) vibe.

Your waiter will rattle off the day's specials, which could include deep-fried salmon roll with Chinese hot mustard, soy-glazed sea bass with wonderful garlic noodles, or Niman Ranch pork chop with pomegranate-currant sauce. A Hong Kong native, Tse is inspired by what he finds at the market. His creative cuisine brings down the house with its top-quality ingredients.

A word to late-night revelers: you'd best come here before going out, since the kitchen closes at 10pm.

San Francisco City North Beach Area

Iluna Basque

Basque ✗

014

701 Union St. (at Powell St.)

Phone:	415-402-0011	Sun – Thu 5:30pm - 10:30pm
Fax:	415-402-0099	Fri – Sat 5:30pm - 11:30pm
Web:	www.ilunabasque.com	
Prices:	$$	

One of San Francisco's youngest chefs, Mattin Noblia brings his Basque roots to the Italian enclave of North Beach. In 2003, at the tender age of 23, Noblia opened Iluna Basque, overlooking Washington Square. Since then, the restaurant has won acclaim as a place to go for late-night tapas and a glass of Spanish wine.

Small plates and *petite entrées* tempt diners with the distinguished specialties of southwestern France and northwestern Spain: piquillo peppers stuffed with bacalao (salt cod), piperade with sautéed Serrano ham and a poached egg, hearty chicken Basquaise, and gâteau Basque, a rich almond cream cake.

Bordeaux-red walls, velvet curtains and candlelight accent the modern décor. A young crowd pours in beginning at happy hour, making for a more rambunctious than romantic scene.

Kokkari Estiatorio 😊

Greek ✗✗

015

200 Jackson St. (at Front St.)

Phone:	415-981-0983	Mon – Thu 11:30am - 2:30pm & 5:30pm - 10pm
Fax:	415-982-0983	Fri 11:30am - 2:30pm & 5:30pm - 11pm
Web:	www.kokkari.com	Sat 5pm - 11pm
Prices:	$$	Closed Sun

If you missed your holiday in the Mediterranean this year, you can make up for it in part by dining at Kokkari. Named for a small fishing village on the island of Samos, Kokkari Estiatorio will transport you to Aegean climes in its taverna-style rooms—one with a huge stone fireplace, bar and booths, the other with its communal table and open kitchen.

Begin your journey by sharing several meze, especially the delicious grilled octopus dressed with lemon, oregano and olive oil, and served with house-made pita. Then move on to the superlative whole grilled fish with braised greens, the lemon-oregano roasted chicken or the aromatic braised lamb shank.

Although your sojourn must inevitably end, rest assured that this is one trip you won't soon forget.

L'Osteria del Forno

016

519 Columbus Ave. (bet. Green & Union Sts.)

Phone:	415-982-1124	Sun – Mon & Wed – Thu 11:30am - 10pm
Fax:	N/A	Fri – Sat 11:30am - 10:30pm
Web:	www.losteriadelforno.com	Closed Tue
Prices:	$$	

Columbus Avenue, the hub of North Beach, holds a plethora of Italian eateries, but this little gem, run by two Italian women since 1990, always seems to be packed. "Packed" is an adequate term for the shoebox of a dining room, where you may feel like a sardine, but you won't care once you taste the delicious Italian food.

L'Osteria del Forno prepares most of its dishes in the namesake oven, where pork braised in milk and fresh herbs is roasted, and thin-crust pizzas are baked. Before you dig in, spark your appetite with an antipasto such as speck (smoked prosciutto with white beans, arugula and Parmigiano Reggiano), or *bresaola della Valtellina* (paper-thin slices of air-cured beef drizzled with white truffle oil).

Two things to remember: Osteria doesn't take reservations or credit cards.

The Mandarin

017

900 North Point St. (bet. Larkin & Polk Sts.)

Phone:	415-673-8812	Open daily 11:30am - 10pm
Fax:	415-673-5480	
Web:	www.themandarin.com	
Prices:	$$	

Located on the top floor of the Woolen Mill Building in Ghirardelli Square, The Mandarin impresses at first glance with its imperial setting: striking multicolored tile floor, cane furniture and Chinese lanterns juxtaposed against the exposed brick and timber of this 150-year-old structure.

It's a treat to find such a serious restaurant in this touristy area, and this one is a stalwart; Cecelia Chang founded The Mandarin in 1968. The extensive—and pricy—menu covers the highlights of northern Chinese cuisine from mu-shu platters to Yang Chow fried rice, with many dishes tending toward the spicy side. Signatures like tea-smoked duck, shark-fin soup, and abalone with mushrooms will bring you back for more.

One last perk: the restaurant will validate parking in the Ghirardelli garage.

Maykadeh

018

470 Green St. (bet. Grant Ave. & Kearny St.)

Phone:	415-362-8286	Mon – Thu 11:45am - 10:30pm
Fax:	N/A	Fri – Sat 11:45am - 11pm
Web:	www.maykadehrestaurant.com	Sun 11:45am - 10pm
Prices:	$$	

North Beach isn't all about Italian food. Maykadeh, for example, presents a rare opportunity to have Persian food in San Francisco. Historically, a maykadeh was a tavern where intellectuals would meet to socialize. This contemporary incarnation recalls its roots with the colorful photographs of Iranian villages that line the walls of the dining room.

Succulent lamb is a signature dish here. Ground lamb is skewered in shish kebabs; lamb shanks are stewed with vegetables; and lamb chops are marinated in lime juice, basil, onion and garlic. For dessert, don't pass up the *bastani*, a fragrant Persian ice cream, studded with pistachios and scented with rosewater.

The restaurant also offers valet parking, a relief in a neighborhood where finding a place to leave your car is always a challenge.

McCormick & Kuleto's

019

900 North Point St. (at Larkin St.)

Phone:	415-929-1730	Sun – Thu 11:30am - 10pm
Fax:	415-567-2919	Fri – Sat 11:30am - 11pm
Web:	www.mccormickandschmicks.com	
Prices:	$$$	

The San Francisco outpost of a well-known national chain, McCormick and Kuleto's claims a prime piece of real estate in Ghirardelli Square. From any table in the classy, bi-level dining room, you'll have impressive views of several city icons—the bay, Alcatraz and the Golden Gate Bridge—through large picture windows. (Hint: reserve a window table at sunset.)

Fish is the focus of the changing menu here. Stick with shellfish (they offer a good choice of oysters) or grilled selections from the Fresh List, which includes denizens of oceans around the world. McCormick & Kuleto's really packs 'em in for weekend dinners and Sunday brunch. So, if you don't like crowds, come on weekdays, when Ghirardelli Square isn't quite so jammed with tourists.

San Francisco City **North Beach Area**

Myth

020

470 Pacific Ave. (bet. Montgomery & Sansome Sts.)

Phone: 415-677-8986
Fax: 415-677-8987
Web: www.mythsf.com
Prices: $$$

Tue – Thu 5:30pm - 9:30pm
Fri – Sat 5:30pm - 10pm
Closed Sun & Mon

Seek out this sexy Jackson Square hot spot when you're looking for a chic atmosphere and creative California cuisine. Chef Sean O'Brien, a Gary Danko protégé, presides over the open kitchen, hitting his mark with the likes of aromatic wild mushroom soup, pancetta-wrapped rabbit loin with beluga lentils, and garganelli with foie gras cream and marsala.

After it took the place of MC^2 in 2004, Myth quickly became the talk of the town for its lovely dining room, which occupies the first level of a historic building. A flock of moneyed young patrons packs the bar at the front, while diners feast amid warm woods and tones of chocolate-brown and olive-green.

A thoughtful touch: several dishes are available in half-portions for those who have less of an appetite.

North Beach Restaurant

021

1512 Stockton St. (bet. Green & Union Sts.)

Phone: 415-392-1700
Fax: 415-421-4489
Web: www.northbeachrestaurant.com
Prices: $$$

Open daily 11:30am - 11:45pm

Decked out with Carrera marble, Venetian granite and Florentine tile, this North Beach institution was founded in 1970 by Lorenzo Petroni and chef Bruno Orsi. Regulars keep coming back for authentic Tuscan cuisine and Old World service from a staff of waiters who know the menu backward and forward.

Go for pastas—they're made fresh daily—or sample signature dishes including sand dabs, cioppino, prochetta al Barolo, and veal saltimbocca all Nerone, a creation of the chef. The impressive wine list encompasses more than 600 different labels, both Italian and domestic. There are several rooms available for private functions, but if you happen to be dining with an actor wannabe, the Prosciutto Room, hung with haunches of cured meat, is an appropriate setting for the biggest ham in any group.

San Francisco City North Beach Area

Piperade

022

1015 Battery St. (at Green St.)

Phone:	415-391-2555	Mon – Fri 11:30am - 3pm
Fax:	415-391-1159	& 5:30pm - 10:30pm
Web:	www.piperade.com	Sat 5:30pm - 10:30pm
Prices:	$$	Closed Sun

Chef/owner Gerald Hirigoyen may have lived in California for some 25 years now, but he hasn't forgotten his Basque roots. That's why green-red-and-white-striped runners (colors of the Basque flag) grace every table, and the homey dining room exudes the ambience of an auberge in the Pyrenees.

Fragrant, flavorful Basque cuisine takes on a California attitude here, as the chef fuses his native region's recipes—like the stew of tomatoes and sweet bell peppers for which the restaurant is named—with local products and contemporary sensibilities. For dessert, Piperade's gâteau Basque vies with any you'll find in France or Spain.

You'll often see Hirigoyen in the dining room, as he comes out to greet his guests and chat with the regulars. You can pick up copies of his cookbooks on your way out.

Rose Pistola

023

532 Columbus Ave. (bet. Green & Union Sts.)

Phone:	415-399-0499	Sun – Thu 11:30am - 4pm
Fax:	415-399-8758	& 5:30pm - 11pm
Web:	www.rosepistolasf.com	Fri – Sat 11:30am - 4pm
Prices:	$$	& 5:30pm - midnight

This lively North Beach hot spot, with its heated outdoor terrace, open kitchen and large, bustling dining space, has long been a city favorite. Inspired by North Beach's original residents, who hailed from the Ligurian coast of Italy, Rose Pistola focuses its menu on seafood, from whole grilled Petrale sole to a mix of shellfish braised in white wine. The likes of Petaluma braised rabbit, osso buco, and rotisserie-roasted Hill Farms pork loin will satisfy meat lovers. Whatever you order, don't pass up the delicious olives and fresh foccacia that start off a meal here.

For that special-occasion dinner, ask for the reserve wine list; it contains the best selection of Italian and Napa varietals.

Scoma's

024

Seafood ✗

Pier 47 on A1 Scoma Way (bet. Jefferson & Jones Sts.)

Phone:	415-771-4383	Sun – Thu 11:30am - 10pm
Fax:	415-775-2601	Fri – Sat 11:30am - 10:30pm
Web:	www.scomas.com	
Prices:	$$	

Scoma's is the place for good seafood in the heart of Fisherman's Wharf. Started by brothers Al and Joe Scoma in 1965 as a six-stool coffee shop on Pier 47, Scoma's has mushroomed into this 360-seat restaurant, with a second location—boasting wonderful views—in Sausalito *(588 Bridgeway)*.

Inside, the place shows its age, but the service is genuinely friendly and it's fun to look out and see the fishing boats while you eat. Hosts of diners, including many tourists, flock here to enjoy Dungeness crab Louis, cioppino, California red abalone doré, and fresh wild-caught fish (Scoma's doesn't serve farm-raised seafood).

At lunchtime the three-course fixed-price menu is the way to go after you've worked up a big appetite sightseeing.

Scott Howard

025

Contemporary ✗✗

500 Jackson St. (at Columbus Ave.)

Phone:	415-956-7040	Mon – Sat 5:30pm - 10pm
Fax:	N/A	Closed Sun
Web:	www.scotthowardsf.com	
Prices:	$$$	

The young and the moneyed flock to this hot spot, opened in September 2005. Named for the chef who founded Fork in San Anselmo, Scott Howard is the perfect place to broker a business deal—especially if you're on an expense account.

Occupying the space most recently held by 500 Jackson, Howard's newest venture divides the ample room into two levels where nearly all the bare-wood tables have a view of the kitchen. The latter serves as an arena in which the chef and his crew compete for diners' taste buds. A protégé of Norman Van Aken, Howard recently revamped his menu from ambitious cross-cultural cuisine to more rustic fare. Entrées range from skate wing to Colorado lamb loin.

A seven-course chef's selection augments the thematic à la carte menu.

San Francisco City **North Beach Area**

Tommaso's

I t a l i a n

026

1042 Kearny St. (bet. Broadway St. & Pacific Ave.)

Phone:	415-398-9696	Tue – Sat 5pm - 10:30pm
Fax:	415-989-9415	Sun 4pm - 9:30pm
Web:	www.tommasosnorthbeach.com	Closed Mon
Prices:	$$	

Tommaso's has been a North Beach institution since 1935, when the restaurant (then called Lupo's) introduced San Francisco to the city's first wood-oven-fired pizzas. Owned and run today by the Crotti family, Tommaso's claim to fame is still its pizzas; 12 different pies feature toppings from simple cheese and tomato sauce to spinach and shaved parmesan. Three monthly specials are the only changes to the standing menu, but you won't go wrong with staples like house-made manicotti and ravioli, or oven-baked veal Marsala, picata, or parmigiana.

This is a fun place to bring friends or family, with informal service and Southern Italian dishes plenty big for sharing. It's a good value, too, which combined with its other attributes makes Tommaso's one busy restaurant.

Trattoria Contadina

I t a l i a n

027

1800 Mason St. (at Union St.)

Phone:	415-982-5728	Sun – Thu 5:30pm - 9pm
Fax:	415-982-5746	Fri – Sat 5:30pm - 10pm
Web:	www.trattoriacontadina.com	
Prices:	$$	

Locals love this little North Beach corner trattoria, with its cramped dining room, warm service and simple décor. Although judging from the signed photos of celebrities that paper the walls, this place is no neighborhood secret.

Established in 1983 by Dick and Sandra Correnti, Trattoria Contadina serves copious quantities of Italian comfort food; house-made ricotta gnocchi in a tomato cream sauce with asiago cheese, rigatoncelli alla Carlesimo (with pancetta and porcini in a spicy vodka-tomato sauce), and pollo or vitello Correnti (sautéed scallopini of chicken or veal in a cream sauce served over penne) will stick to your ribs while not putting a big dent in your wallet.

If you don't want to hassle with parking, the Powell-Mason cable-car line will drop you off right in front.

LOUIS ROEDERER

C H A M P A G N E

Richmond and Sunset

These two residential neighborhoods edging the Pacific Ocean share several things in common. With Golden Gate Park as their backyard, Richmond (to the north of the park) and Sunset (to the south) both have a middle-class small-town feel; both are fog-shrouded (owing to their proximity to the ocean); and their populations incorporate an ethnic mix that is apparent in the area's myriad restaurants.

Expansive **Ocean Beach** creates a broad, sandy seam between both areas and the Pacific Ocean. A paved promenade, landscaped with dune-stabilizing grasses and shrubs, extends north three miles from Sloat Boulevard to just south of Cliff House, making the beach extremely popular with bikers, walkers and runners (the Pacific's water is too cold for swimming).

Richmond – At the turn of the 20th century, Richmond's western reaches were condemned as "The Great Sand Waste." In 1912 the establishment of a municipal railway along Geary Boulevard opened the district to serious settlement. As single-family row houses sprang up, ethnically diverse residents clamored to fill them.

Today Richmond's main shopping and dining thoroughfare, **Clement Street**, teems with inexpensive Chinese, Thai, Burmese, Vietnamese and Korean eateries and markets. In fact, the 12-block stretch of Clement Street between Arguello and Park Presidio boulevards rivals Chinatown for its concentration of Chinese restaurants. A culturally heterogeneous community adds French and Italian cafes and Irish pubs.

Sunset – South of Golden Gate Park sits the Sunset District, which was also a windswept region of sand dunes until developer Aurelius Buckingham built the first row houses on present-day Lincoln Way in 1887. Bounded on the east by Stanyan Street, on the west by the Pacific Ocean and on the north by Golden Gate Park, the Sunset District encompasses a broad, flat grid of regularly spaced residential streets with row after orderly row of modest bungalows.

Clement Street

Often veiled in fog, the Sunset district harbors mom-and-pop diners alongside coffee shops and hip new restaurants. When planning your visit to this neighborhood, keep in mind that the fog rolls in early, and some days, the sun never shows through.

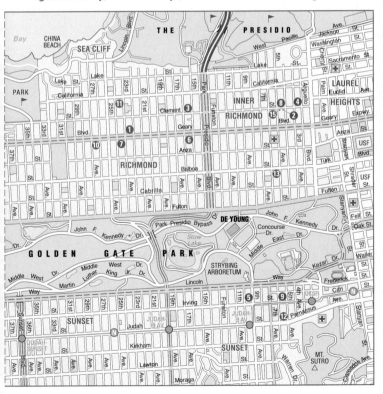

Aziza

001

5800 Geary Blvd. (at 22nd Ave.)

Phone:	415-752-2222	Wed – Mon 5:30pm - 10:30pm
Fax:	415-752-3056	Closed Tue
Web:	www.aziza-sf.com	
Prices:	$$	

Aziza beckons like a desert oasis on this lively stretch of Geary Boulevard. You'll feel a sultry, spice-market vibe in the dimly lit space, where sharply dressed servers and cool jazz substitute for trinket vendors and the music of snake charmers. Red-glass lanterns cast a rosy glow over azure suede chairs, and on weekend evenings, belly dancers shimmy between the hand-carved tables.

Chef/owner Mourad Lahlou, who hails from Marrakech, honors his roots as he translates Berber tagines and Moroccan vegetable stews into modern Moroccan cuisine using California products. Cocktails are the beverage of choice at the tile-clad bar. Will it be a Fez Fizz (champagne infused with pomegranate purée), or a heady Marrakech Express (cardamom espresso spiked with Kahlua, Bailey's and vodka)?

Burma Superstar

002

309 Clement St. (bet. 4th & 5th Sts.)

Phone:	415-387-2147	Sun – Thu 11am - 3:30pm & 5pm - 9:30pm
Fax:	N/A	Fri – Sat 11am - 3:30pm & 5pm - 10pm
Web:	www.burmasuperstar.com	
Prices:	🍴🍴	

This Burmese restaurant seems right at home among the multitude of other ethnic establishments in Richmond. Burma Superstar doesn't take reservations, so be prepared to wait to pack yourself into the cramped dining room, adorned with Burmese masks and other exotic artifacts.

New to Burmese cuisine? The helpful staff will gladly aid you in deciphering the menu. Since Burma shares borders with India, China and Thailand, you'll see—and taste—the influences of those countries in the food here. If you're interested in authentic Burmese cuisine, look for the stars that mark dishes like *Moh Hinga* (catfish chowder), tea-leaf salad, pumpkin shrimp stew, and yellow bean curry.

You won't have to worry when the bill comes; prices are low and most of the budget-friendly dishes are big enough for two.

Chapeau!

003

French ✗✗

1408 Clement St. (at 15th Ave.)

Phone: 415-750-9787
Fax: 415-750-9677
Web: N/A
Prices: $$$

Tue – Thu & Sun 5pm - 10pm
Fri – Sat 5pm - 10:30pm
Closed Mon

♿

Boisterous and convivial, this well-established French bistro has been a Richmond fixture for years. Owner Philippe Gardelle, a native of Toulouse, spends much of his time chatting with customers and offering wine suggestions in the butter-yellow dining room. Meanwhile, his wife, Ellen, manages the waitstaff and helps take orders.

White-clothed tables crowd together at this casual place, where, to lay down your hat (*chapeau* in French), is to call the restaurant home. Leg of rabbit stuffed with spinach and garlic in a Dijon mustard sauce, coq au vin, and cassoulet à la Toulousaine constitute a sampling of the comforting French country fare.

Choose your courses à la carte, or select one of several prix-fixe menus. The "early bird" (before 6pm) special is a real deal.

Clementine ☺

004

French ✗✗

126 Clement St. (bet. 2nd & 3rd Aves.)

Phone: 415-387-0408
Fax: 415-387-0782
Web: N/A
Prices: $$

Mon – Sat 5:30pm - 10pm
Closed Sun

♿

A little piece of Paris hides on Clement Street behind this bottle-green façade. From the gracious French waiters, who greet customers with a cheery "bonjour," to chef/owner Didier Labbé, who hails from Brittany, Clementine respects Gallic traditions in both its ambience and food—much to the delight of diners.

Labbé worked at Spago before opening his own place in 1998; since then he's established Clementine as one of the best French restaurants in the Bay area. All the standards (escargots, duck confit, crème brûlée) are here, and while Clementine's fish may come from American waters, they're prepared à la Française, as in grouper in red-wine sauce, or sautéed salmon with tapenade.

For dessert, French toast, or *pain perdu*, topped with hazelnut ice cream, will titillate any sweet tooth.

San Francisco City Richmond and Sunset

Ebisu

005

Japanese ✗

1283 Ninth Ave. (at Irving St.)

Phone:	415-566-1770	Mon – Wed 11:30am - 2pm & 5pm - 10pm
Fax:	N/A	Thu – Fri 11:30am - 2pm & 5pm - 11pm
Web:	www.ebisusushi.com	Sat 11:30am - 11pm
Prices:	⊜⊜	Sun 11:30am - 10pm

Located in a lively section of Sunset, near Golden Gate Park, this little sushi bar appeals with its sweet Japanese waitresses, its quiet ambience (the place is always crowded, but diners seem to honor the serene mood by speaking in low voices), and its fresh assortment of original sushi rolls. Ebisu is named for one of the seven Japanese deities of good fortune, the one who is honored as the god of the kitchen.

Regulars know to order from the board of daily specials, created according to the freshest ingredients available and the inspiration of the sushi chefs. Of course, there's also a long list of tempura, teriyaki and sashimi, and more on the menu.

If you're headed out of town, you can get one last Ebisu fix at the food court in San Francisco International Airport (Terminal G).

Kabuto

006

Japanese ✗

5121 Geary Blvd. (at 15th Ave.)

Phone:	415-752-5652	Tue – Sun 5pm - 10:30pm
Fax:	N/A	Closed Mon
Web:	www.kabutosushi.com	
Prices:	$$	

Chef Sachio Kojima built his renowned reputation at the sushi counter of this Richmond establishment, which he founded more than 20 years ago. Kojima retired in spring 2006 for personal reasons, leaving the reins in the hands of Jinsoo Kim and Eric Cho. Fortunately for Kabuto fans, who form a line outside at dinnertime, the new chef adheres to Kojima's principles of using wonderfully fresh fish and combining it with other ingredients in innovative and artful presentations.

The cheerful Japanese staff maintains a warm ambience in the tiny dining space, and knowledgeable waitresses can help you pare down the large list of sushi. Choose from the ambitious selection of makimono rolls, vegetable sushi, spicy fish, tempura or teriyaki. Green-tea tempura ice cream makes a fitting finale.

Khan Toke Thai House

007

5937 Geary Blvd. (bet. 23rd & 24th Aves.)

Phone: 415-668-6654   Open daily 5pm - 10pm
Fax: N/A
Web: N/A
Prices: 🥜

Save your good socks to wear to Khan Toke Thai House, since you'll be required to remove your shoes before entering. This slice of old Siam in the Richmond district envelopes diners in a lavish environment of carved teak, woven tapestries, and a lush Asian garden out back. To add to the Bangkok feel, you'll sit cross-legged on cushions on the floor, or dangle your legs in wells set beneath the carved-wood tables.

The exhaustive menu roams from lemongrass soup and standard curries to *Meing Com*, a dish that allows diners to wrap any combination of seven favorite Thai ingredients (shrimp, coconut, peanuts, peppers) in butter lettuce. Try the fixed-price Thai dinner if you're having trouble deciding.

Reasonable prices will leave you with enough money to tip the "shoeman" when you leave.

King of Thai

008

346 Clement St. (at 5th Ave.)

Phone: 415-831-9953   Open daily 11am - 2am
Fax: N/A
Web: N/A
Prices: 🥜

$

The price is definitely right at this spotless neighborhood haunt in Inner Richmond. For less than $20 you can dine well in the mauve-walled room on such Thai dishes as *Poh Pier Tod* (deep-fried vegetarian rolls stuffed with noodles, black mushrooms, carrots and cabbage), and *Kao Nar Pad* (boneless roast duck and yho choy, topped with Thai-style duck sauce).

One in a chain of seven San Francisco area noodle houses, King of Thai dishes up steaming bowls of aromatic noodle soup as well as stir-fried flat rice noodles, both with your choice of meat or vegetarian add-ins. The cuisine is well-balanced, fragrant with herbs, and accented by spicy sauces.

San Francisco City Richmond and Sunset

Koo 😊

009

408 Irving St. (bet. 5th & 6th Aves.)

Phone:	415-731-7077	Tue – Thu 5:30pm - 10pm
Fax:	N/A	Fri – Sat 5:30pm - 10:30pm
Web:	www.sushikoo.com	Sun 5pm - 10pm
Prices:	$$	Closed Mon

This Richmond sushi restaurant balances the concepts of yin and yang, starting with its name. Koo derives from the masculine form (more commonly spelled *ku*) of "to eat" in Japanese. That covers the yang, while delicate lithographs and polite Japanese waitresses take care of the yin.

Innovative Japanese cuisine, masterminded by Tokyo-trained chef/owner Kiyoshi Hayakawa, appeals across the board to a coterie of connoisseurs. For a tête-à-tête with the sushi master, take one of the seven seats at the sushi bar. There you'll appreciate the harmony of flavors in rolls like Tokyo Crunch (spicy tenkasu, yellowtail and cucumber with wasabi tobiko).

Your best bet is to select from the Catch of the Day, where you'll find the freshest fish and the chef's latest creations.

Mayflower

010

6255 Geary Blvd. (at 27th Ave.)

Phone:	415-387-8338	Mon – Fri 11am - 2:30pm & 5pm - 10pm
Fax:	N/A	Sat – Sun 10am - 2:30pm & 5pm - 10pm
Web:	N/A	
Prices:	🍜	

The fact that the Chinese sign on the façade outsizes the English one should give you an indication of the authenticity of Mayflower's cuisine. Your next clue will be the dearth of Westerners among the clientele. The freshness of the seafood won't be in doubt either, after you glimpse the large aquarium tank swimming with shellfish just inside the entrance.

Set on the corner of Geary Boulevard and 27th Avenue, this Hong Kong-style restaurant is renowned in the multiethnic Richmond area for its dim sum. Perhaps the best way to eat here is to make your selection from the trays of attractive offerings that waiters carry slowly between the crowded tables. If you prefer to order off the copious menu, shark is one of Mayflower's signature ingredients.

Pizzetta 211

011

211 23rd Ave. (at California St.)

Phone:	415-379-9880	Mon 5pm - 9pm
Fax:	415-379-9881	Wed – Fri noon - 2:30pm & 5pm - 9pm
Web:	N/A	Sat – Sun noon - 9pm
Prices:	&#x1F36A;	Closed Tue

Cached in a quiet neighborhood of Victorian houses tucked between the Presidio and Geary Boulevard, Pizzetta 211 is so small it hardly even ranks as a sit-down restaurant. The no-frills pizzeria only has four tables inside and four outside, so locals looking for a cheap and tasty meal know to order take-out to eat at home.

The choices change weekly, but the short menu always includes a handful of pizzas, an artisanal cheese plate, and a few mouth-watering homemade sweets, like saffron biscotti. This is mystic pizza with a small "m." Tasty pies here come out thin-crusted and light, like those you'd find in southern Italy. Unique premium toppings follow the seasons from Fiori Sardo sheep cheese, toasted pine nuts and rosemary to eggs, artichokes and ricotta.

Pomelo

012

92 Judah St. (at 6th Ave.)

Phone:	415-731-6175	Mon – Fri 11:30am - 2pm & 5:30pm - 10pm
Fax:	N/A	Fri – Sun 5:30pm - 10pm
Web:	www.pomelosf.com	
Prices:	&#x1F36A;	

In an Inner Sunset area that's far from restaurant-rich, Pomelo provides UCSF students and residents a much-needed respite from the ordinary. The menu, divided into Side Trips (appetizers and small plates) and Destinations and Upgrades (main courses), will transport you from Italy (black pepper tagliatelle with pulled duck braised in red wine) to Thailand (spicy coconut curry) to Cuba (Cuban-style fried rice with black beans, plantains and chipotles, served with grilled skirt steak) and back. Dishes change, one by one, every couple of months.

One caution: you can't make reservations for this trip. Eighteen seats make for a casual, elbow-to-elbow ambience, where your neighbor may just end up a friend. The Noe Valley location *(1793 Church Street)* is known for its weekend brunch.

San Francisco City Richmond and Sunset

Sushi Bistro

Japanese 🍴

013

445 Balboa St. (at 6th Ave.)

Phone:	415-933-7100	Open daily 5pm - 11pm
Fax:	415-387-4666	
Web:	www.sushibistrosf.com	
Prices:	$$	

Set on a quiet block in Inner Richmond, this discreet sushi bar offers one of the best bargains in the city. At Sushi Bistro you can feast on a variety of fresh Japanese fare and still have money left over.

For something different try the Hot Love (baby lobster, avocado and crabmeat rolled in white fish and baked in a sweet and spicy sauce), or the 7-flavor Albacore Appetizer, a lightly seared albacore filet peppered with seven types of spices. Then again, the wide range of chef's special rolls—from shrimp tempura to freshwater eel—will appeal to most everyone's palate.

Sunny colors, friendly service and a convivial vibe are but more reasons to visit. The only downside? It's nearly impossible to find parking nearby.

Sutro's

Californian 🍴🍴🍴

014

1090 Point Lobos Ave. (at Ocean Beach)

Phone:	415-386-3330	Open daily 11:30am - 3pm & 5pm - 9:30pm
Fax:	415-387-7837	
Web:	www.cliffhouse.com	
Prices:	$$$	

Spectacular vistas of the Pacific surf have long attracted visitors to Cliff House, which perches atop a bluff above the ocean. A San Francisco landmark since 1909, the present version of Cliff House (the first two were destroyed by fire) reopened in September 2004 after a $14 million makeover. The remodel includes a spiffy new restaurant, Sutro's, decked out in maritime décor with multistory window walls to drink in the views.

Today locals join visitors at Sutro's to savor the scenery as well as the serious cuisine. Pacific fish and Dungeness crab enjoy starring roles on the menu, alongside American Waygu beef, Fulton Valley organic chicken and Kurobuta pork. Call ahead if you wish to reserve a window table.

Upstairs, a casual bistro serves less ambitious fare at modest prices.

Troya

015

349 Clement St. (at 5th Ave.)

Phone: 415-379-6000
Fax: N/A
Web: www.troyasf.com
Prices: ☕☕

Mon – Thu 11:30am - 10pm
Fri – Sat 11:30am - 10:30pm
Sun 11:30am - 9:30pm

Troya adds a new face to Richmond's restaurant scene. Opened in early 2006, this corner Turkish spot pays homage to the ancient city of Troy, the ruins of which were discovered in western Turkey in the mid-19th century.

Start with the meze platter; the waiter will tempt you with a colorful sampling of the day's choices. Good bets are the *esme* (a garlicky red-pepper and tomato paste), and the *cacik* (diced cucumbers and garlic tossed with yogurt, olive oil, mint and dill). If you're waffling about your entrée, go for the *beyti*, the signature dish of ground lamb and beef doused with the house special sauce and wrapped in flatbread; it's served with yogurt-garlic sauce for dipping.

End your meal with thick, strong Turkish coffee poured into tiny cups from a traditional copper vessel.

San Francisco City Richmond and Sunset

South of Market

San Francisco's hardscrabble history meets its high-tech future in the large, heterogeneous region known as **SoMa** (for South of Market). In the Gold Rush days, this industrial area bounded by 12th, Market and King streets and the Embarcadero was known as "South of the Slot," a reference to its location on the "wrong side" of the Market Street cable-car track.

Mainly industrial until the mid-1990s, South of Market now attracts hordes of visitors to the **San Francisco Museum of Modern Art** *(151 3rd St.)* and **Yerba Buena Gardens** *(Mission St., between 3rd and 4th Sts.)* and its **Center for the Arts**, cultural powerhouses on SoMa's northern border with the Financial District. Plans to add the Contemporary Jewish Museum and the Mexican Museum in 2007 will bolster this burgeoning museum district. In between, you'll find scores of old warehouses, many converted into swank nightclubs and some of the city's hottest new restaurants.

A Bit of History – In 1847 city planner Jasper O'Farrell gave SoMa its distinctive look, making its streets twice as wide and its blocks four times as large as those north of Market Street, and setting the whole area at a 45-degree angle. The idea was to make room for industry, and it worked. Foundries, gasworks, shipyards, refineries and breweries took hold here. As manufacturing declined in the mid-20th century, architects, graphic designers, software companies and publishers divvied up former industrial buildings and warehouses into loftlike offices. When the Internet bubble burst in 2001, nearly half of the offices were left vacant.

Along Market Street, historically the city's major commercial thoroughfare, you'll find the new **Westfield San Francisco Centre** *(between 4th and 5th Sts., with entrances on Market and Mission Sts.)*, which adds Bloomingdale's and a nine-screen movie theater to the existing five levels of the San Francisco Shopping Centre anchored by Nordstrom. Nearby, the **Moscone Convention Center** draws hundreds of thousands of conventioneers and trade-show exhibitors each year.

Defining SoMa's southern border, breathtaking **AT&T Park** *(3rd and King Sts., at the Embarcadero)* is home to the San Francisco Giants baseball franchise. Just north of the stadium, South Park centers on a grassy oval surrounded by townhouses, shops, cafes and restaurants. This pleasant neighborhood was built in the 1850s to resemble London's Berkeley Square.

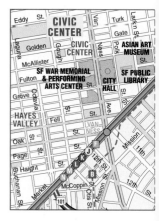

San Francisco Museum of Modern Art and Yerba Buena Gardens

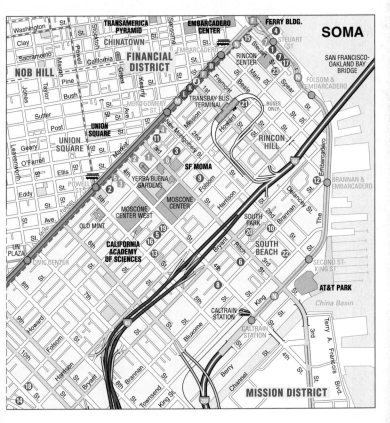

Boulevard ❀

001

1 Mission St. (at Steuart St.)

Phone: 415-543-6084
Fax: 415-495-2936
Web: www.boulevardrestaurant.com
Prices: $$$

Mon – Fri 11:30am - 2pm & 5:30pm - 10pm
Sat – Sun 5:30pm - 10pm

Boulevard

Opened in 1993, Nancy Oakes' SoMa restaurant constantly wins raves as one of San Franciscans' favorite places to eat. Why do Bay Area diners love this place so much? Start with the location on the first floor of the lovingly preserved 1889 Audiffred Building. Here Pat Kuleto beautifully spells Belle Époque brasserie with art-glass light fixtures, a vaulted brick-lined ceiling in the front, and multicolored mosaics framing the windows on the wall opposite the exhibition kitchen.

Then there's the buzz of a restaurant that stays busy day and night (be sure to reserve ahead), and the friendly, black-bow-tied brigade who choreographs service to the mixed clientele with the all grace of a corps de ballet. Last, but far from least, is Oakes' storied cuisine. Oakes changes the menu constantly, several dishes at a time. Any palate would be pleased by sublime grilled Florida butterfish with a mousseline of roasted baby artichokes and picholine olives, or dry-aged California lamb chops and lamb osso buco with Barolo risotto and spring asparagus.

As if you needed another reason to come, the 500-label wine list spotlights California, France and Italy.

Appetizers

Pan-roasted Squab and Hudson Valley Foie Gras, Cipollini Onion Stuffed with Braised Kobe Short Ribs, Dried Bing Cherry Gastrique

Ahi Tuna Tartare and Hamachi Sashimi with Avocado, Jalapeno, Ginger and Key Lime, Crispy Taro and Shiso Salad

Monterey Red Abalone with Sautéed Abalone Mushrooms, Vine-Ripe Cherokee Tomatoes, Razor Clam, Lime Vinaigrette and Green-tomato Sauce Vierge

Entrées

Wood-oven-roasted Berkshire Pork Prime Rib Chop Stuffed with Artichoke Hearts, Melted Garlic and Herbs, Tarbais Beans, Spanish Chorizo and Spinach, Crunchy Manchego and Arugula, Roast-pork Jus

Dry-aged California Lamb Chops and Lamb Osso Buco with Barolo Risotto, California Spring Asparagus, Salsa Verde and Braising Jus

Desserts

White Chocolate Banana Cream Pie and Huckleberry Gelée, with Candied Walnuts, Huckleberry Sauce, White-Chocolate and Banana Caramel

Warm Blackberry Galette with Mango Carpaccio and Vanilla Ice Cream

Chocolate, Chocolate, Chocolate: House-made Glazed Chocolate Doughnuts, Mocha Milkshake, Dark-Chocolate Fondue with Assorted Sweets for Dipping

Fifth Floor ✿

Contemporary XXXX

002

12 4th St. (at Market St.)

Phone: 415-348-1555
Fax: 415-348-1551
Web: www.fifthfloorrestaurant.com
Prices: $$$$

Mon – Thu 5:30pm - 9:30pm
Fri – Sat 5:30pm - 10:30pm
Closed Sun

Fifth Floor

The name of this acclaimed restaurant will lead you to its location inside the Hotel Palomar *(see SoMa hotel listings)* on the corner of Fourth and Market streets. At Fifth Floor, subtle lighting plays across red leather banquettes, setting off the dark polished woods against the chic zebra-striped carpet.

In this sleekly elegant setting, you'll be treated to chef Melissa Perello's ever-changing tasting menu (there's a "garden," or vegetarian, version, too), which smartly contrasts textures and flavors in seasonal combinations such as Kaffir lime-scented Maine lobster, supple skate wing crowned with truffles and baby artichokes, squab breast au poivre in a concentrated red wine jus, and a comfortingly warm Valrhona chocolate cake drizzled with Guinness crème anglaise. A short à la carte menu rounds out the nightly offerings.

Adding to the experience, a professional and attentive waitstaff renders flawless formal service. Ask sommelier Emily Wines (her real name!) to help you choose among the 1,400 bottles on the award-winning wine list, which hones in on French, German and California labels.

Appetizers

Alder-smoked Foie Gras with Caramelized Shallot and English Pea Ragoût

Chilled Maine Lobster "en gelée" with Lemongrass, Lime Oil and Tapioca Pearls

Salad of Fiddlehead Ferns and Morel Mushrooms with Walnut Vinaigrette and Pecorino

Entrées

Roasted Guinea Hen with Blenheim Apricot, Chanterelle Mushrooms and Riesling Jus

Butter-poached Alaskan Halibut with Crème Fraîche and Spring Onion Soubise

Fennel Pollen-crusted Venison with Black Cherry Confiture and Caramelized Fennel Marmalade

Desserts

Manila Mango Tarte Tatin with Dulce de Leche Ice Cream and Lime Caramel

Thai Chile-scented Chocolate Custard with Dark Fudge Cake and Crisp Phyllo

Rosemary Gâteau with Poached d'Anjou Pear, Beurre de Chèvre and Poire Williams Sorbet

Ame

Contemporary XXX

003

689 Mission St. (at 3rd St.)

Phone:	415-284-4040	Open daily 11:30am - 2pm & 6pm - 10pm
Fax:	415-284-4043	
Web:	www.amerestaurant.com	
Prices:	$$$	

Opened in November 2005 in the St. Regis Hotel *(see SoMa hotel listings)*, Ame is the newest venture by chef Hiro Sone and his wife and pastry chef, Lissa Doumani (long known for their Napa Valley restaurant, Terra). Diners are greeted at the entrance by a custom-designed sashimi bar, which flows past a wooden screen into the large L-shaped dining room.

A selection from the sashimi bar proves a fitting introduction to a meal here—perhaps Japanese sea bream, or "Lissa's Staff Meal," cuttlefish noodles tossed with sea urchin, quail eggs, wasabi and umami soy sauce. Sone's signature fusion of Japanese, Italian and French cuisines shines in dishes like sake-marinated Alaskan black cod. Whatever you order, you'll revel in premium ingredients rendered with Asian sensibilities by chef Greg Dunmore.

Americano

Californian XX

004

8 Mission St. (at The Embarcadero)

Phone:	415-278-3777	Mon – Thu 11:30am - 2:30pm & 5:30pm - 10pm
Fax:	415-278-3770	Fri 11:30am - 2:30pm & 5:30pm - 11pm
Web:	www.americanorestaurant.com	Sat 10:30am - 3pm & 5:30pm - 11pm
Prices:	$$$	Sun 10:30am - 3pm & 5:30pm - 10pm

Overlooking the waterfront, Americano is part of the slick Hotel Vitale *(see SoMa hotel listings)*, which opened in March 2005. Look up to see the most distinctive feature of the restaurant's contemporary design; life-size portraits on the ceiling depict four "Americano Dreamers" who anticipated a better life in America after World War II. From the spacious heated terrace (with its new wine bar menu) or the dining room with its picture windows, you'll have great views of the Bay Bridge.

Italian at heart, the cuisine here adds a California kick to dishes such as artichoke hearts stuffed with baccalà, lobster ravioli with gorgonzola sauce, and skate wing parmesan. Brick-oven-baked pizzas include Margarita, topped with fontina cheese, prickly-pear cactus leaves, jalapeno, lime and sea salt.

Azie

005

826 Folsom St. (bet. 4th & 5th Sts.)

Phone:	415-538-0918	Mon – Sat 5pm - 10pm
Fax:	415-538-0916	Closed Sun
Web:	www.azierestaurant.com	
Prices:	$$	

Little sister to LuLu next door, Azie transfigured a former warehouse in the heart of trendy SoMa during the dot-com frenzy of the 1990s. Here it aims to re-create the buzz of an Asian street in the soaring bi-level space.

You can grab a quick bite at the casual bar, claim a stool in front of the exhibition kitchen, or take a seat in the wood-paneled dining room (ask for one of the curtained booths for an intimate dinner). On the table, innovative Asian fare fuses with classic French technique in crab spring rolls scented with mint, or steamed fish in black bean sauce served with baby bok choy and Thai chiles.

With more than 600 labels, the wine list takes a straightforward approach to California, France and Italy. A nice selection of green, black and herbal teas rounds out the menu.

bacar

Californian ✗✗

006

448 Brannan St. (bet. 3rd & 4th Sts.)

Phone:	415-904-4100	Sun – Thu 5:30pm - 11pm
Fax:	415-904-4113	Fri 11:30am - midnight
Web:	www.bacarsf.com	Sat 5:30pm - midnight
Prices:	$$$	

This SoMa hot spot bills itself as a "restaurant and wine salon" (*bacar* is Latin for "wine goblet"). A three-story wine wall on one side of the loftlike brick-walled space holds the stock described in the 1,400-label hardcover volume that passes for a wine list (a less intimidating softcover version is available). If you're not interested in a bottle, an extensive selection of wines (more than 60) can be had by the glass, by the 2-ounce pour, or by a 250- or 500-milliliter decanter.

Luckily, the menu is not as daunting, although it does present a good range of wine-worthy California-style dishes. Start, perhaps, with some Kumomoto oysters, then move on to a harissa-roasted chicken or a mesquite-grilled Painted Hills ribeye. Prices are reasonable considering the top-notch ingredients used.

San Francisco City SoMa

Chaya Brasserie

007

132 The Embarcadero (bet. Howard & Mission Sts.)

Phone: 415-777-8688
Fax: 415-247-9952
Web: www.thechaya.com
Prices: $$

Mon – Wed 11:30am - 2:30pm & 6:30pm - 10pm
Thu – Fri 11:30am - 2:30pm & 5:30pm - 10:30pm
Sat 5:30pm - 10:30pm
Sun 6:30pm - 10pm

Take traditional Japanese cuisine, mix it with California products, add a pinch of French savoir faire, and you've got Chaya Brasserie (the name blends the Japanese term for "teahouse" with the French *brasserie*). Set on the Embarcadero with stellar views of the Ferry Building and the Bay Bridge, Chaya opened in 2000 as the San Francisco outpost of a small chain whose first cousins live in Los Angeles and Venice Beach.

Chef Shigefumi Tachibe learned French technique in Japan, and he interprets it California-style in the likes of cumin-crusted mahi mahi with crab and celery remoulade, and Chaya's burger, topped with grilled onions, Jack cheese and an exotic touch of mango chutney. Even drinks marry east and west, as in the Chaya Vitamin V (V for vodka, in this case infused with pineapple).

Fringale

008

570 4th St. (bet. Brannan & Bryant Sts.)

Phone: 415-543-0573
Fax: 415-905-0317
Web: www.fringalerestaurant.com
Prices: $$

Mon – Thu 11:30am - 3pm & 5:30pm - 10pm
Fri 11:30am - 3pm & 5:30pm - 11pm
Sat 5:30pm - 11pm
Sun 5:30pm - 10pm

The next time you find yourself ravenous (or *fringale* in French), make tracks for this little piece of France in the SoMa district. Fringale has been going strong since 1991, when it was launched by chef Gerald Hirigoyen and partner J.B. Lorda. They have both since moved on, leaving the restaurant in the capable hands of Jean-Marie Legendre (who's been at Fringale since it opened) and chef Thierry Clement. Your hunger will be sated here by refined Mediterranean and Basque fare (think prawns sautéed in pastis with sun-dried tomatoes; crispy polenta with spinach; piperade and frisée) and desserts like Mme. Angèle's gâteau Basque, a velvety almond torte filled with a layer of custard cream.

A sophisticated epicurean crowd soaks up the bistro atmosphere in a room done in soft earth tones.

Hawthorne Lane

Californian 🍴🍴

22 Hawthorne St. (bet. Folsom & Howard Sts.)

Phone: 415-777-9779
Fax: 415-777-9782
Web: www.hawthornelane.com
Prices: $$$

Mon – Thu 11:30am - 1:30pm & 5:30pm - 9pm
Fri 11:30am - 1:30pm & 5:30pm - 10pm
Sat 5:30pm - 10pm
Sun 5:30pm - 9pm

Steps from SF MOMA, the two-story 1922 brick building that once held the San Francisco Newspaper Company now houses Hawthorne Lane. Two large dining rooms on the first floor (the second floor caters to private dining) recall the building's history with a changing array of fine art prints from Crown Point Press.

Dive into the bread basket for a tasty house-made assortment of rolls, brioches and chive biscuits. Then delight in chef Bridget Batson's hand-picked products that grace signatures like Chinese-style roasted duck with steamed green-onion buns, and grilled loin of Berkshire pork with sweet corn and fava beans.

Want to do it yourself? Sign up for one of Hawthorne Lane's Saturday cooking classes. These hands-on tutorials begin with mimosas in the bar and end with a luscious lunch.

Jack Falstaff

Contemporary 🍴🍴🍴

598 2nd St. (at Brannan St.)

Phone: 415-836-9239
Fax: 415-836-9243
Web: www.jackfalstaff.com
Prices: $$$

Mon – Fri 11:30am - 11pm
Sat – Sun 3pm - 11pm

Newest star in the PlumpJack Group's constellation of restaurants, Jack Falstaff rockets up the glamour factor in industrial-chic SoMa. The young and the fashionable flock here to see and be seen in the posh grey-green-suede-lined dining room, with its dark wood-paneled ceiling, and sexy lighting to offset the booming music.

Slow is a key word in the cuisine here. The chef slow-cooks Niman Ranch ancho chile pork belly, and salt-bakes red snapper whole. Located just two blocks from SBC Park, Jack Falstaff takes tailgating to new heights with its game-day menu, served rain or shine on the enclosed and heated patio. Stop by before the game for a Jack's burger served with Kennebec fries and arugula salad.

San Francisco City **SoMa**

Kyo-ya

011

2 New Montgomery St. (at Market St.)

Phone: 415-546-5090
Fax: 415-537-6299
Web: www.kyo-ya-restaurant.com
Prices: $$$

Mon – Fri 11:30am - 2pm & 6pm - 10pm
Closed weekends & major holidays

Between the serene atmosphere, the kimono-clad waitresses and the fabulously fresh fish, you'll feel more like you're in Asia here than on one of San Francisco's main avenues. Kyo-ya, with its separate entrance, is part of the 1909 Palace Hotel *(see SoMa hotel listings)*, which graces a busy corner of Market Street.

This little sushi bar makes a great stop for lunch or dinner if you're sightseeing at the nearby San Francisco Museum of Modern Art or Yerba Buena Gardens. But it's worth going out of your way for tempting tempura, maki, special rolls and sushi ranging from buttery toro (fatty tuna) to miru gai (giant clam). The chef also proposes a six-course kaiseki menu that showcases different preparation techniques and changes monthly to focus on seasonal offerings.

La Suite

012

100 Brannan St. (at The Embarcadero)

Phone: 415-593-9000
Fax: 415-593-9002
Web: www.lasuitesf.com
Prices: $$

Sun – Thu 5:30pm - 10pm
Fri – Sat 5:30pm - midnight

Boasting an expansive view of Bay Bridge from the Embarcadero, La Suite is brought to you by the same team that founded Chez Papa on Potrero Hill. Its Belle Epoque look is enhanced with a mosaic-tile floor, a pressed-metal ceiling, and a long zinc-topped bar where you can sample a good selection of French and domestic wines by the glass. Classic bistro dishes like mussels marinière and terrine of foie gras share menu space with California-inspired offerings (think Dungeness crab salad with fennel tuile; Liberty Farms duck breast with sunchokes; Ahi tuna tartare).

With all this going for it, it's no surprise that getting a table at La Suite is no easy feat. Even with a reservation, you may have to linger at the lively bar before your table is ready.

Le Charm

013

315 5th St. (bet. Folsom & Shipley Sts.)

Phone:	415-546-6128	Mon 11:30am - 2pm
Fax:	415-546-6712	Tue – Fri 11:30am - 2pm & 5:30pm - 9:30pm
Web:	www.lecharm.com	Sat – Sun 5:30pm - 9:30pm
Prices:	$$	

Whether you're looking for a place for a brief business lunch or a venue for a romantic dinner, Le Charm can oblige. The lofty dining room with its cinnamon-colored walls has an intimate feel and a European flair, and the food is sure to satisfy any cravings for Gallic cuisine.

A fricassée of tender escargots comes with wild mushrooms; cassoulet is filled with lamb, duck confit and garlic sausage; juicy pan-seared bavette steak is napped with red-wine sauce and served with crispy frites; boudin blanc is made in-house. Can't decide? Go for the three-course prix-fixe dinner; it's a great value for under $30.

The lush candlelit patio (heated in winter) is de rigueur for an intimate tête-à-tête. That's "Le Charm" of it.

Manora's Thai Cuisine

014

1600 Folsom St. (at 12th St.)

Phone:	415-861-6224	Mon – Fri 11:30am - 2:30pm & 5:30pm - 10:30pm
Fax:	415-861-1731	Sat 5:30pm - 10:30pm
Web:	www.manorathai.com	Sun 5pm - 10pm
Prices:	⊜⊜	Closed major holidays

You can't ask for more powerful flavors for the money than at this little family-run Thai restaurant, making it a natural for any Bay Area "cheap eats" list. For lunch you can get a plate of Thai-style fried rice with prawns, calamari and crabmeat for under $7. At dinner there's a wide choice of modestly priced meat and vegetable dishes, many seasoned with fragrant lemongrass, zesty garlic and red-hot chiles (be sure to tell your server how spicy you want your food). Check out the Chef's Favorites to quickly narrow down your selection.

Although it was here long before SoMa became a cool destination, Manora's location near the district's trendy nearby nightclubs means it's a good bet for dinner before an evening of club-hopping—as the cool young crowd attests.

San Francisco City SoMa

One Market

Contemporary ✗✗

015

1 Market St. (at Steuart St.)

Phone: 415-777-5577
Fax: 415-777-3366
Web: www.onemarket.com
Prices: $$$

Mon – Fri 11:30am - 2pm & 5:30pm - 9pm
Sat 5:30pm - 9pm
Closed Sun

Celebrity chef Bradley Ogden's downtown restaurant couldn't be better located. Boasting a laid-back bar and an urbane main dining room filled with natural light from large picture windows, One Market sits on a prime corner bordering the city's busiest commercial thoroughfare and facing the Ferry Building across the street.

Chef/partner Mark Dommen makes regular stops at the Ferry Plaza Farmers' Market to find the best produce to flesh out his seasonal menu. Dommen sources his meat (Berkshire pork, Liberty duck, Prime top sirloin) and seafood (Eastern striped bass, Alaskan halibut, Petrale sole) directly from ranchers and fishermen to assure that what's on your plate is exceedingly fresh. The attractively priced two-course Business Lunch appeals to Financial District wheeler-dealers.

Oola

Californian ✗

016

860 Folsom St. (bet. 4th & 5th Sts.)

Phone: 415-995-2061
Fax: 415-995-2065
Web: www.oola-sf.com
Prices: $$

Open daily 6pm - 1am

Named for its chef/owner Ola Fendert (formerly of Plouf, Chez Papa and Baraka), this hip bi-level bar and restaurant is a sultry candlelit lair of exposed brick walls, gauzy fabric panels and cushy upholstered booths. While it may be sexy, it's far from quiet, so if you want a place for intimate conversation, keep walking. However, if it's a party beat you're after, you've come to the right place.

Oola serves drinks until 2am nightly (and dinner until 1am), so you can always drop in for a late-night libation; try a watermelon cosmopolitan, or a ginger snap (Gentleman Jack whiskey with fresh ginger syrup). From the kitchen come the likes of grilled Creek Stone Farms hamburger, house-made pork sausage, baby back ribs, and potato-wrapped day boat scallops.

Ozumo

017

161 Steuart St. (bet. Howard & Mission Sts.)

Phone:	415-882-1333	Mon – Fri 11:30am - 2pm & 5:30pm - 10pm
Fax:	415-882-1794	Sat – Sun 5:30pm - 10pm
Web:	www.ozumo.com	
Prices:	$$$	

♿
☞🔑

Ozumo caters to many moods and palates with three different dining spaces and a wide range of Japanese dishes. Located a block from the Embarcadero, the capacious spot accommodates diners first in a dark, moody sake lounge (Steuart Street entrance) with a communal table, pulsing music, and an extensive sake menu.

The restaurant's procession of dark to light continues in the main room, done in stone and wood with cube-like wood-backed chairs. This is where you'll find the robata grill, where meat, fish or vegetables are grilled over imported *sumi* charcoal. Keep walking and you'll end up in the naturally lit sushi bar (Embarcadero entrance), accented by blond woods and bay views. Sushi fans favor this room, where they can watch the chefs assemble delicate pieces of sashimi and nigiri.

The Public

018

1489 Folsom St. (at 11th St.)

Phone:	415-552-3065	Tue – Sat 6pm - 9:30pm
Fax:	N/A	Closed Sun & Mon
Web:	www.thepublicsf.com	
Prices:	$$	

In August 2005, The Public got a new chef, in the form of Anna Bautista, who formerly worked at Jardinière. Bautista seems to be the right woman for the job; since she took over the kitchen, this place has reawakened with a seriously executed (and moderately priced) contemporary cuisine.

The ground level is devoted to the casual lounge, enlivened by modern music and set about with comfortable couches and a changing collection of work by local artists. Upstairs, the dining room with its caramel-colored walls and I-beamed ceiling is populated by enthusiastic diners and a young, friendly staff. This is the place to dig into Ahi tuna poke with watermelon radish salad, braised short ribs with Port-Cabernet sauce, or butternut squash and asparagus risotto.

Restaurant LuLu

019

Mediterranean

816 Folsom St. (bet 4th & 5th Sts.)

Phone:	415-495-5775
Fax:	415-495-7810
Web:	www.restaurantlulu.com
Prices:	$$

Sun – Thu 11:30am - 9:45pm
Fri – Sat 11:30am - 10:30pm

Bigger isn't necessarily better, but in LuLu's case it's pretty darn good. Installed in a refurbished 1910 warehouse, the cavernous vaulted space with its sunny colors and serpentine wall of banquettes rings nightly with the sounds of happy diners.

Acclaimed chef Reed Hearon (now at Rose Pistola) opened LuLu in early 1993; although he's no longer here, his concept of food cooked over an open fire remains the centerpiece, literally and figuratively, of this restaurant. Most of the dishes—duck breast, suckling pig, leg of lamb—are roasted in the oak-fired oven or rotisserie in the open kitchen, sending heady aromas wafting across the room. Food is served family style, perfect for sharing.

Be sure to check out the lengthy wine list, which features French, Italian and California labels.

South Park Cafe

020

French

108 South Park Ave. (bet. 2nd & 3rd Sts.)

Phone:	415-495-7275
Fax:	415-495-7295
Web:	www.southparkcafesf.com
Prices:	$$

Mon 11:30am - 2:30pm
Tue – Fri 11:30am - 2:30pm & 5:30pm - 10pm
Sat 5:30pm - 10pm
Closed Sun & major holidays

Exuding a village vibe with lovely little town houses flanking a central green, the South Park neighborhood is an oasis of serenity in the sprawling district of SoMa. Inside one of these houses you'll find South Park Cafe, recognizable by its green façade.

You're just as likely to see a guest strumming a folk guitar as dot-commers discussing business in this French-style charmer, where the short à la carte menu adds blackboard specials and a set bargain-priced three-course meal nightly. The bohemian feel at lunch dresses up at dinnertime with white linens, fresh roses and entrées like slow-roasted lamb shoulder with thyme, braised veal sweetbreads, and grilled hanger steak.

On a sunny day, grab a French newspaper on-site, stake out a sidewalk table and imagine you're on the Rive Gauche.

Town Hall

Contemporary 🍴

021

342 Howard St. (at Fremont St.)

Phone:	415-908-3900
Fax:	415-908-3700
Web:	www.townhallsf.com
Prices:	$$

Mon – Fri 11:30am - 2:30pm & 5:30pm - 10pm
Sat – Sun 5:30pm - 10pm

In America, the town hall forms the heart of a community, and so Town Hall, the restaurant, provides a lively gathering place for families, friends and colleagues in swanky SoMa. Occupying the beautifully renovated 1907 Marine Electric Building, the restaurant suggests an Adirondack eating hall with its exposed brick walls, early-American light fixtures and bright white wainscoting.

In the kitchen, brothers Mitchell and Steven Rosenthal (partners with Doug Washington, who works the front) dish up regional American fare like warm Bakewell cream biscuits with Smithfield ham and pepper jam, Niman Ranch ribeye with spicy creamed corn, and cedar-planked wild King salmon. Don't even think of leaving without trying the irresistible chocolate and butterscotch pot de crème.

Tres Agaves

Mexican 🍴

022

130 Townsend St. (at 2nd St.)

Phone:	415-227-0500
Fax:	415-227-0535
Web:	www.tresagaves.com
Prices:	$$

Mon – Thu 11:30am - 11pm
Fri 11:30am - 1am
Sat 11am - 1am
Sun 11am - 11pm

Opened in late 2005, this SoMa hot spot is well situated near the Embarcadero and SBC Park. Everything about the place pulses, from the music to the soaring industrial space. Regional Mexican fare focuses on the Central Highlands with dishes like Jaliscan-style slow-cooked beef, and spit-roasted chicken rubbed with epazote and sour orange. Tacos come with zesty marinated meat fired in the wood-burning oven.

Named for the three types of pure agave tequila, Tres Agaves is run by a partnership that includes chef Joseph Manzare (of Globe and Zuppa). It's not *all* about tequila here, although Mexico's infamous alcoholic beverage does star in the lounge, where some of city's best Margaritas are mixed. Remember, the signature spirit, 100-percent blue agave tequila, is for sipping, not shooting.

Yank Sing

Chinese ✗✗

101 Spear St. (bet. Howard & Mission Sts.)

Phone:	415-957-9300	Mon – Fri 11am - 3pm
Fax:	415-957-9322	Sat – Sun & holidays 10am - 4pm
Web:	www.yanksing.com	
Prices:	$$	

Dim sum spells mystery, with all those circulating carts of bamboo steamers hiding an exotic mix of bite-size gems. At Yank Sing, mystery is a beautiful thing, in the form of more than 60 different kinds of dumplings, spring rolls, lettuce cups filled with minced chicken, skewers of barbecue pork, and stuffed lotus leaves. Don't pass on the Peking duck, served by the slice with slivered scallions and a dab of Hoisin sauce on a steamed bun.

Housed in the Rincon Center (there's another SoMa location at 49 Stevenson Street) with a roomy indoor terrace in the lobby atrium, Yank Sing lives up to its reputation as one of the best places for dim sum on the West Coast. On weekends, you can park free at the Rincon Center (with validation from the restaurant).

San Francisco City SoMa

L'ERMITAGE
BRUT 1998
ESTATE BOTTLED · ANDERSON VALLEY
SPARKLING WINE

ROEDERER ESTATE

East
of San Francisco

Bay Bridge

East of San Francisco
Berkeley and Oakland

A short hop across the Bay Bridge—or on the BART—from San Francisco, the neighboring cities of Berkeley and Oakland have their own individual charms. Each is worth a visit in its own right, Berkeley for its lovely university campus and its liberal attitude, and Oakland for its revitalized downtown.

Berkeley – Synonymous with the renowned University of California at Berkeley, this college town is Oakland's erudite little sister—a small city with a big reputation for political activism. Though things have calmed down here since the Free Speech Movement was launched on Berkeley's campus in the 1960s, a bohemian air persists today.

Berkeley has long enjoyed a reputation for attracting intellectuals, idealists and eccentrics whose diverse tastes have left their mark on the city's history, architecture and ambience. One such resident, Alice Waters, changed America's food scene forever in 1971 when she opened Chez Panisse and gave rise to California cuisine. Today Waters' restaurant occupies the same Arts and Crafts-style bungalow on a bustling restaurant row on upper Shattuck Avenue *(between Rose and Virginia Sts.)* known as the "Gourmet Ghetto." Here, many Chez Panisse alumni have opened their own places, serving everything from pizza to tapas.

Oakland – Named for its expansive growth of oak trees, Oakland was incorporated in 1852 as a quiet bedroom community for the woollier city across the bay. Today this workaday city is experiencing a renaissance. New businesses have replaced vacant warehouses on downtown blocks, Port of Oakland has been expanded and modernized. Thanks go in part to Mayor Jerry Brown, whose 10K Initiative has catalyzed new retail

College Avenue, Oakland

Brigitta L. House/MICHELIN

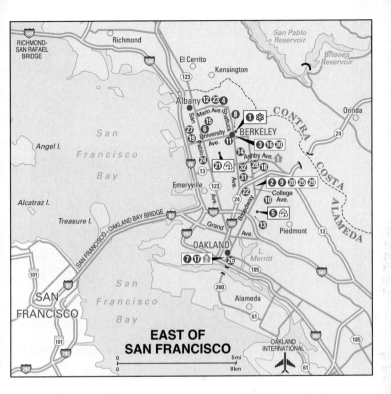

interest downtown. Some 36 new cafes and restaurants, 18 new nightclubs and bars, and 14 new galleries lure residents and visitors alike to the city's core. New farmers' markets eliminate the need for locals to cross the bay to buy fresh organic produce.

Another downtown draw is Jack London Square, a sparkling, pedestrian-friendly complex of shops, restaurants, entertainment and cultural attractions that nestles along Oakland Estuary at the site of the once-gritty dock area. The square is named for author Jack London, who lived in Oakland as a boy and a young man. One of London's favorite watering holes, Heinold's First and Last Chance Saloon *(45 Webster St., in Jack London Square)*, still operates as a bar, though it now ranks on the National Register of Historic Places.

Check out the upscale Rockridge area, a tony residential neighborhood on the border of Berkeley, which boasts a strip of trendy shops, markets and restaurants that makes a perfect place to while away an afternoon.

Chez Panisse ✿

1517 Shattuck Ave., Berkeley (bet. Cedar & Vine Sts.)

Phone:	510-548-5525	Mon – Sat 6pm - 9:45pm
Fax:	510-548-0140	Closed Sun
Web:	www.chezpanisse.com	
Prices:	$$$$	

Chez Panisse/Aya Brackett

One of the country's most influential culinary figures, Alice Waters is justly lauded for her revolutionary contributions to America's food scene. It was Waters who defined California cuisine in the 1970s as the pure expression of premium market-fresh products. Her storied restaurant started in 1971 in an Arts and Crafts-style bungalow on a quiet Berkeley street, now a busy restaurant row. Although the operation has expanded to include a casual cafe upstairs, the original wood-paneled dining room, hung with prints from the Marcel Pagnol film trilogy that inspired the restaurant's name, still has a bohemian air.

The concept, too, remains intact, with organic produce, meats and fish providing sublime raw materials for the changing bill of fare. Warm frisée and pancetta with fava bean soufflé, grilled Paine Farm squab with foraged morels, and chocolate crêpes topped with Cognac-spiked hazelnut ice cream are just a sampling of the delectable dishes on the set four-course menu.

Whereas the cafe welcomes walk-ins, the downstairs dining room requires reservations (call a month ahead, then check online the week of your reservation to see what's on the menu the night you plan to be there).

East of San Francisco

Appetizers

Dungeness Crab Salad with Meyer Lemon and Garden Lettuces

Spring Vegetable Ragoût with Morels, Fava Beans, and Sweet Peas

Chino Ranch Fritto Misto with Green-Garlic Aioli

Entrées

Bouillabaisse cooked in the fireplace

Spit-roasted Marin Sun Grass-fed Ribeye with Marrow and Garlic

Grilled Rack, Leg, and Loin of Dal Porto Spring Lamb

Desserts

Gravenstein Apple and Candied Meyer Lemon Galette

Baked Suncrest Peaches with Mulberry Ice Cream

Blenheim Apricot Soufflé

À Côté

002

French 🍴

5478 College Ave., Oakland (at Taft St.)

Phone:	510-655-6469
Fax:	510-655-6716
Web:	www.acoterestaurant.com
Prices:	$$

Sun – Tue 5:30pm - 10pm
Wed – Thu 5:30pm - 11pm
Fri – Sat 5:30pm - midnight

If you're looking for a festive neighborhood restaurant in the Oakland/Berkeley area, look no farther than this Rockridge hot spot. In keeping with À Côté's amicable theme, a communal table runs down the center of the dining room, inviting guests to share conversation as well as French-inspired small plates such as mussels in Pernod, warm lamb tongue salad, and rabbit boudin blanc.

One look at the wine list will tell you that the owner has a talent for buying wines that are rarely found in California. In fact, he regularly sniffs out artisanal wineries in Europe, and the list reflects his good nose. In addition, the beverage list includes an impressive selection of Belgian ales and aperitifs, as well as a first-class roster of liquors.

The downside: À Côté doesn't accept reservations.

Adagia

003

Californian 🍴🍴

2700 Bancroft Way, Berkeley (bet. College & Piedmont Aves.)

Phone:	510-647-2300
Fax:	510-647-2301
Web:	www.adagiarestaurant.com
Prices:	$$

Open daily 11am - 3pm & 5pm - 10pm

Across the street from the university campus, Adagia installed itself in 2005 inside the Tudor-style Westminster House, designed in 1926 by architect Walter Ratcliff. The interior retains its historic integrity, with wood paneling, a wrought-iron chandelier, stained-glass windows, rustic wood tables, and a huge fireplace.

While the décor may be Old World, the food is contemporary. Sophisticated cuisine leans toward Cal-Ital in dishes like braised lamb shanks with soft polenta, and asparagus risotto scented with parmesan cheese and Meyer lemon. Vegetables are especially well selected and flavorful (the kitchen uses organic and sustainable ingredients whenever possible). End with a sampling of wine-infused sorbets, perfumed pairings of Zinfandel and raspberry, and Merlot and strawberry.

Ajanta

Indian ✗

004

1888 Solano Ave., Berkeley (bet. The Alameda & Colusa Ave.)

Phone: 510-526-4373   Open daily 11:30am - 2:30pm & 5:30pm - 9:30pm
Fax: 510-526-3885
Web: www.ajantarestaurant.com
Prices: 🥜

Berkeley is known for its melting pot of ethnic cuisines, and Ajanta adds authentic Indian food to the mix. Push open Ajanta's carved wood door and you'll enter a world where sitar music plays softly in the background, waiters wear traditional embroidered waistcoats, and dishes range across the regions of Kashmir, Goa, Rajasthan and Punjab.

Lamb chops, game hen and swordfish are served sizzling from the tandoor oven, while flavorful standards include chicken tikka masala and lamb korma. New dishes (*machi tikki*, fish cakes made from mahi mahi; lamb biriyani) are introduced each month. The restaurant is "green certified," meaning they serve only free-range meats that contain no hormones or antibiotics, and sustainable seafood.

Bay Wolf 🥜

Californian ✗✗

005

3853 Piedmont Ave., Oakland (at Rio Vista Ave.)

Phone: 510-655-6004   Mon – Fri 11:30am - 2pm & 5:30pm - 9:30pm
Fax: 510-652-0429   Sat – Sun 5:30pm - 9:30pm
Web: www.baywolf.com
Prices: $$

A charming Victorian house encloses this Oakland favorite. Opened in 1975 by chef/owner Michael Wild, Bay Wolf divides its dining space into two rustic rooms and the pleasant heated veranda, which is open all year.

Wild's monthly changing take on Cal-Med cuisine results in updated versions of recipes from Italy, France and Spain. The freshest local ingredients are interpreted simply in such entrées as duck liver flan, tender slow-cooked pork loin with creamy potato-fennel gratin, and Bellwether Farms ricotta ravioli with broccoli rabe.

The serious young waitstaff knows the menu well and is happy to offer advice if you're wavering in your dinner decision. Elegantly presented dishes arrive at the table at a relaxed (not slow) pace.

East of San Francisco

Café Fanny

006

1603 San Pablo Ave., Berkeley (at Cedar St.)

Phone:	510-524-5447	Mon – Fri 7am - 3pm
Fax:	510-526-7486	Sat 8am - 4pm
Web:	www.cafefanny.com	Sun 8am - 3pm
Prices:	☜	

If you want to grab a quick but delicious bite for breakfast or lunch, this friendly little food bar is a must-stop. It's run by Alice Waters and named for her daughter; breakfast and lunch are the only meals available from the cafe's stand-up counter.

In the morning, scones and other mouth-watering baked goods share the menu with farm eggs, levain toast, and buckwheat crêpes filled with ham and Gruyère. At lunchtime, you'll likely have to stand in line, but it's worth waiting for some of the best sandwiches in the Bay area—made with products from local farms and sourdough and other loaves fresh from ovens of the Acme Bakery right next door. Lunch wouldn't be complete without a taste of the cafe's yummy homemade organic ice cream.

Caffè Verbena

007

1111 Broadway, Oakland (bet. 11th & 12th Sts.)

Phone:	510-465-9300	Mon – Fri 11:30am - 9pm
Fax:	510-465-9302	Closed Sat, Sun & major holidays
Web:	www.caffeverbena.com	
Prices:	$$	

Verbena gives business types a good reason to stay in downtown Oakland. It's located in the Walter Shorenstein building, close to the port. With tables in both the light-filled atrium and the brasserie-style dining room, the cafe caters to a boisterous lunch bunch, and brings in guests from around the area in the evening. Cherry wood paneling warms the main room, where banquettes bear plaques engraved with the names of well-known local regulars (Oakland's mayor, for example).

Lunch highlights the four Ps: pizza, pasta, panini and piatti principale. Dinner adds antipasti and a selection of steaks and chops (minus the pizza and panini). Combine all this with friendly service and a wine list of domestic and Italian varietals, and you have the ideal place to entertain business colleagues.

César

008

Spanish ✗

1515 Shattuck Ave., Berkeley (bet. Cedar & Vine Sts.)

Phone: 510-883-0222

Open daily noon - midnight

Fax: 510-883-0227

Web: www.barcesar.com

Prices: 💳💳

Next door to Chez Panisse, César appeals with its mixture of old and new: a mosaic bar, rustic wood tables, trendy tunes and contemporary tapas. The restaurant was founded by a group of Chez Panisse alumni who conceived it as an inviting neighborhood bar. Welcoming guests from noon until midnight, César dishes up a spirited selection of Catalan and Basque small plates such as the morcilla and wild mushrooms, salt cod and potato cazuela, and jamón Serrano and grilled d'Anjou pears, as well as the spicy marinated olives offered as a start to the meal.

What to drink? Check out the impressive array of American and Spanish wines and the intriguing beverage list, which includes French artisan cider, Belgian draft beer, and Austrian fruit-syrup sodas.

Citron

009

Contemporary ✗

5484 College Ave., Oakland (bet. Lawton & Taft Aves.)

Phone: 510-653-5484

Mon 5:30pm - 9:30pm

Fax: 510-653-9915

Thu – Fri 11:30am - 4:30pm & 5:30pm - 9:30pm

Web: www.citronrestaurant.biz

Sat – Sun 10am - 3pm & 5:30pm - 9:30pm

Prices: $$

Set on the main drag in tony Rockridge, sunny Citron showcases fresh products that are well selected and perfectly prepared. French, Mediterranean and California inflexions spark dishes such as herbed potato gnocchi with roasted chanterelles, and grilled beef tenderloin with Lyonnaise potatoes, that change every week. In addition to the à la carte fare at dinner, chef/owner Chris Rossi offers three-, four-, and five-course tastings (if you're really hungry, you can even add extra courses). Desserts like rich chocolate pot de crème and warm pecan rhubarb crumble will surely send you off to sweet dreams.

Start your weekend right with ricotta buttermilk pancakes, a croque monsieur, or eggs Benedict with poached salmon and Meyer lemon hollandaise at Citron's popular brunch.

East of San Francisco

Dopo

010

4293 Piedmont Ave., Oakland (at Echo St.)

Phone:	510-652-3676	Mon – Thu 11:30am - 2:30pm & 5:30pm - 10pm
Fax:	510-597-0265	Fri – Sat 5:30pm - 11pm
Web:	N/A	Closed Sun
Prices:	$$	

Although the kitchen occupies more than half of the dining space at this shoe-box size Italian place on busy Piedmont Avenue, the mix of Berkeley students, business people, and couples doesn't seem to give the cramped space a second thought. They're too busy concentrating on thin-crust pizza with gorgonzola and red onion, antipasti misti (a trio of tastes), and rigatoni with braised broccoli.

The menu is small (three pastas, four pizzas, a few salads and soups) and ever-changing, to insure the freshness of ingredients like organic greens, house-cured meats and house-made pâté. Prices are not the lowest in town, but the quality of the food justifies paying a bit more.

With such a tiny place (less than 30 seats), it's no wonder that Dopo doesn't accept reservations.

downtown

011

2101 Shattuck Ave., Berkeley (at Addison St.)

Phone:	510-649-3810	Mon – Thu 11am - 2pm & 5:30pm - 11pm
Fax:	510-649-8971	Fri 11am - 2pm & 5pm - midnight
Web:	www.downtownrestaurant.com	Sat – Sun 5pm - midnight
Prices:	$$	

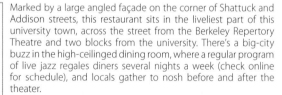

Marked by a large angled façade on the corner of Shattuck and Addison streets, this restaurant sits in the liveliest part of this university town, across the street from the Berkeley Repertory Theatre and two blocks from the university. There's a big-city buzz in the high-ceilinged dining room, where a regular program of live jazz regales diners several nights a week (check online for schedule), and locals gather to nosh before and after the theater.

Chef/partner David Stevenson works magic with fish, as grilled Monterey Bay sardines, whole roasted fish, and wild salmon with purple barley can attest. And his sleight of hand with braised oxtails, Niman Ranch pork loin and other meat entrées on the weekly changing menu wins applause, too.

Fonda Solana

012

Latin American ✗✗

1501 Solano Ave., Albany (at Curtis St.)

Phone: 510-559-9006
Fax: 510-559-9177
Web: www.fondasolana.com
Prices: $$

Mon – Fri 5:30pm - 12:30am
Sat – Sun 4pm - 12:30am

♿

The Albany hot spot for sophisticated cocktails and gourmet tapas, Fonda Solana is indeed a "cafe on a sunny corner" as its Spanish name suggests. It's set on Albany's main street, where a cool East Bay crowd comes to drink in the festive atmosphere, while sampling the likes of sautéed prawns with salsa negra, duck and pomegranate tacos, and grilled rack of lamb Churrasco style.

Portions may be small, but flavors are big (as are the prices—all those small plates can add up fast). The kitchen's not afraid of using a generous dose of Mexican chiles and spices to wake up your taste buds. Luckily, Fonda offers a long list of inventive cocktails from mojitos to flights of tequila served with a glass of Fonda's zesty house-made sangrita.

Jojo

013

Contemporary French ✗

3859 Piedmont Ave., Oakland (at Rio Vista Ave.)

Phone: 510-985-3003
Fax: 510-985-3033
Web: www.jojorestaurant.com
Prices: $$

Tue – Thu 5:30pm - 9:30pm
Fri – Sat 5:30pm - 10:30pm
Closed Sun & Mon

♿

With experience at Zuni Café, Olivetto and Chez Panisse to their collective credit, the husband-and-wife team of Curt Clingman and Mary Jo Thoresen founded Jojo in 1999. Located in a pleasant neighborhood, this cheery bistro with its butter-yellow walls emulates the South of France in both its ambience and cuisine.

Service is casual and welcoming; a faithful crowd of regulars packs the place at night, exchanging hugs with the chefs when they leave. It can be a challenge to snag a table, but have patience. Clingman's country-French cooking (think grilled wild sturgeon with sauce gribiche and house-made pâté de campagne) is worth waiting for. The à la carte menu is divided into three courses (starter, entrée and dessert), and always features a vegetarian selection.

East of San Francisco

Kirala

Japanese ✗

014

2100 Ward St., Berkeley (at Shattuck Ave.)

Phone:	510-549-3486	Mon 5:30pm - 9:30pm
Fax:	510-549-0165	Tue – Fri 11:30am - 2pm & 5:30pm - 9:30pm
Web:	www.kiralaberkeley.com	Sat 5:30pm - 9:30pm
Prices:	🍝	Sun 5pm - 9pm

This neighborhood favorite offers great value and they don't take reservations, so bring your patience. If you do have to wait for a table, the sake bar makes a good place to hang out and sample a glass—or a flight—of premium sake. Once you do get a seat, you'll have a choice of a long list of fabulously fresh nigiri (yellowtail, scallops, halibut, sea eel, to name a few) complemented by the day's market specials, announced on the whiteboard above the long sushi bar.

Kirala is also known for its robata grill, from which come such signatures as miso-marinated black cod, and delicious skewers threaded with the likes of ground chicken wrapped in shiso leaves, or sliced beef wrapped around asparagus. Service is efficient and friendly, no matter how many people are waiting for your table.

Lalime's

Contemporary ✗✗

015

1329 Gilman St., Berkeley (bet. Neilson & Peralta Aves.)

Phone:	510-527-9838	Sun – Thu 5:30pm - 9pm
Fax:	510-527-1350	Fri – Sat 5:30pm - 10pm
Web:	www.lalimes.com	
Prices:	$$	

Secreted away in Berkeley's Westbrae neighborhood, Lalime's (named for co-owner Cynthia Lalime Krikorian) is a little restaurant with a big heart. Outside, this Craftsman-style cottage blends in with the rest of the homes on the street. Inside, the small bi-level space gives diners the option of chatting with regulars at the bar, or going down a few stairs and enjoying a quiet meal in the main room, where lemon-colored walls and paintings of orchids set a warm tone for a changing bill of fare determined by the market.

Mediterranean-inspired dishes (crêpes filled with wild mushroom, asparagus and fromage blanc, and rack of lamb on pearl couscous with preserved lemon and charmoula) coupled with thoughtful service have made Lalime's a local favorite for more than 15 years.

La Rose Bistro

016

2037 Shattuck Ave., Berkeley (at Addison St.)

Phone:	510-644-1913	Tue – Fri 11:30am - 3pm & 5pm - 10pm
Fax:	N/A	Sat – Sun 5pm - 10pm
Web:	N/A	Closed Mon
Prices:	$$	

California-French fare at reasonable prices lures locals to this family-run neighborhood bistro. Painted with green walls and pastoral murals, the dining room welcomes a quiet crowd of Berkeley professors by day and a lively mix of theatergoers by night. Tables are well spaced in order to foster private conversations; ask for a seat at the front of the room, where windows survey Shattuck Avenue's bohemian street scene.

While you're munching on the warm bread that comes with cilantro dipping sauce, you can ponder the short unpretentious menu. Chef/owner Vanessa Dang offers a fine range of French-inspired selections from duck confit with cherry demi-glace to halibut with fig vincotto gastrique.

Le Cheval

017

1007 Clay St., Oakland (at 10th St.)

Phone:	510-763-8495	Mon – Sat 11am - 9:30pm
Fax:	N/A	Sun 5pm - 9:30pm
Web:	www.lecheval.com	
Prices:	⊜	

Housed in an old brick building near City Hall, Le Cheval was established in 1985 and enjoys a longstanding reputation for refreshing, family-style Vietnamese cuisine. Indeed, large parties are welcome in the spacious, high-ceilinged dining room, decorated with Vietnamese artifacts and paintings of—what else?—horses.

The voluminous bill of fare features something for just about everyone; its pages and pages list columns of firepot soups (the small version serves two), rice dishes, kebabs, stir-fried noodles, steamed whole fish, along with set-price multicourse tasting menus spotlighting beef or seafood.

If you're on the go in neighboring Berkeley, drop by little sister, Le Petit Cheval *(2600 Bancroft Way)*, set on the edge of the university campus.

East of San Francisco

Nan Yang

018

Burmese 🍴

6048 College Ave., Oakland (at Claremont Ave.)

Phone:	510-655-3298	Tue – Sun 11:30am - 3pm & 5pm - 10pm
Fax:	N/A	Closed Mon
Web:	N/A	
Prices:	🥜	

This is the kind of restaurant you wish you had around the corner from your house: the Burmese fare is simple and tasty; the small room is pleasant and clean; the service is fast and efficient; and the price is right. So much the better for Rockridge residents, who have easy access to Nan Yang.

For those not familiar with Burmese cuisine, the menu does a good job of describing the dishes; a "V" indicates vegetarian items. The food bears influences of the surrounding countries of China, India, Thailand and Vietnam. For starters, the ginger salad tosses cured shredded ginger, toasted yellow split peas, fava beans, peanuts and coconut chips in garlic oil and lemon juice. Main courses range from spicy curries to traditional vegetable dishes to garlic noodles with seafood, the house specialty.

O Chamé

Japanese 🍴

1830 4th St., Berkeley (bet. Hearst Ave. & Virginia St.)

Phone:	510-841-8783	Mon – Thu 11:30am - 2pm & 5:30pm - 9pm
Fax:	510-559-3703	Fri – Sat 11:30am - 2pm & 5:30pm - 9:30pm
Web:	N/A	Closed Sun
Prices:	$$	

Sandwiched between trendy home furnishing stores in Berkeley's luxe 4th Street shopping district, O Chamé surprises as a Japanese restaurant. First of all, you'll find no typical Zen décor here; instead, sunny walls create a soothing tavern vibe and only Japanese lithographs here and there suggest the theme of the food.

Another surprise: they don't serve sushi. Grilled fish and a selection of noodles constitute the entrées on the short daily changing menu. Soba and udon noodles fill bowls of clear fish broth, embellished with toppings like roasted oysters, pork tenderloin, wakame seeweed and shiitake mushrooms. Order yourself a bowl and enjoy it outside on the little sidewalk terrace, a great place to soak up the neighborhood scene and perhaps ogle a fashion victim or two.

Oliveto

020

Italian ✗✗

5655 College Ave., Oakland (at Shafter Ave.)

Phone:	510-547-5356	Open daily 11:30am - 2:30pm & 5:30pm - 9:30pm
Fax:	510-547-4624	
Web:	www.oliveto.com	
Prices:	$$$	

Located in Market Hall in tony Rockridge, Oliveto manages to cover three meals a day between the casual cafe downstairs and the rustic upstairs dining room with its natural light and olive wood paneling.

Although founding chef and co-owner Paul Bertolli (formerly of Chez Panisse) recently left Oliveto's kitchen to start his own company making salumni in Berkeley, his artisanal cured meats and pâtés still figure prominently alongside dishes like spit-roasted loin and belly of Willis Farm pork, and pici with lamb sugo and pecorino cheese.

Theme dinners—tomato dinners in August, truffle dinners in November, the popular Whole Hog dinners (where the kitchen finds a novel way to use nearly every part of the hog) in February—spotlight the chef's favorite seasonal ingredients.

Olivia 😊

021

Californian ✗

1453 Dwight Way, Berkeley (at Sacramento St.)

Phone:	510-548-2322	Tue – Sat 5:30pm - 10pm
Fax:	510-548-2333	Closed Sun & Mon
Web:	www.oliviaeats.com	Closed January 1 - 12 & July 4 - 11
Prices:	$$	

You've got to love a chef who names his restaurant after his yellow lab, and that's what Nathan Peterson (formerly chef at Oakland's Bay Wolf) did when he opened Olivia in 2005. Despite the name, the cafe's design theme is Mediterranean, from the four-seat zinc bar to the bright, sunny colors and beehive fireplace.

The Cal-Med menu changes daily and is posted out front to inform regulars and tempt newcomers. Choosing is easy, since all the appetizers are one price, all the entrées are also one price, and the unpretentious desserts follow suit. Count on sensible combinations like grilled long-line Hawaiian swordfish with pan-fried potatoes, grilled asparagus, and subtle yet assertive garlic mayonnaise. Wines on the all-French list are carefully selected to pair with the dishes.

East of San Francisco

Pizzaiolo

022

5008 Telegraph Ave., Oakland (at 51st St.)

Phone:	510-652-4888	Tue – Sat 5:30pm - 10pm
Fax:	510-652-4848	Closed Sun & Mon
Web:	N/A	
Prices:	💰	

There's something to be said for the second time around. This 1870 hardware store now houses a hip new pizzeria, opened in 2005 by Charles Hallowell, who is taking his show on the road from his former gig at Chez Panisse.

Cool jazz plays in the dining room, as patrons crank up their voices to be heard above the music. All this creates quite a lively atmosphere, so if you don't mind the din or standing in line for a table (Pizzaiolo doesn't accept reservations), you'll be rewarded with thin, crispy, wood-fired pizza. Wild nettles, chanterelles and butterball potatoes make up a few of the more unique toppings; plainer palates may prefer sausage, ricotta, mozzarella or marinara. Just keep in mind that extras (prosciutto, anchovy, egg) can add up fast.

Rivoli

023

1539 Solano Ave., Berkeley (bet. Neilson St. & Peralta Ave.)

Phone:	510-526-2542	Mon – Thu 5:30pm - 9:30pm
Fax:	510-525-8412	Fri 5:30pm - 10pm
Web:	www.rivolirestaurant.com	Sat 5pm - 10pm
Prices:	$$	Sun 5pm - 9pm

Husband-and-wife team, Roscoe Skipper (the manager) and chef Wendy Brucker (the chef), embarked on their first solo venture in 1994, converting this erstwhile office building into a popular Berkeley boîte. Named for the Parisian rue where the couple spent their honeymoon, Rivoli reverberates with a steady stream of regulars who are not ashamed to take their doggy bags and unfinished bottles of wine to go.

The menu changes every three weeks or so to show off dishes that meld France and Italy in combinations like roast chicken roulade stuffed with sopressata and mozzarella, and slow-braised pot roast with apple and horseradish crème fraîche and winter vegetable tortino.

Best seat in the house? Along the window wall that affords views of the leafy garden.

East of San Francisco

Sea Salt

024

2512 San Pablo Ave., Berkeley (at Dwight Way)

Phone:	510-883-1720	Open daily 11:30am - 10pm
Fax:	N/A	Closed major holidays
Web:	www.seasaltrestaurant.com	
Prices:	$$	

A new venture by Haig and Cynthia Krikorian, owners of Lalime's and T-Rex BBQ in Berkeley, and Fonda Solana in Albany, Sea Salt goes nautical with its ocean-blue and green color scheme, picnic tables, and big wire fish hanging from the ceiling. You almost expect to see the ocean from the patio out back.

The food casts a line strictly to lovers of sustainable seafood; there are no meat dishes on the daily changing menu. At the raw bar you can net an assortment of littlenecks and oysters (come any day between 4pm and 6pm for $1 oysters). For lunch, many sandwiches (oyster po' boy, lobster roll, tuna confit) come with divine chips made fresh in-house. Prices are easy on the wallet, with most of the dinner entrées (Quinault River sturgeon, Alaskan cod, yellowfin tuna) running $20 or less.

Soi Four

025

5421 College Ave., Oakland (bet. Kales & Manila Sts.)

Phone:	510-655-0889	Mon – Fri 11:30am - 2:30pm & 5:30pm - 10pm
Fax:	510-655-0889	Sat 5:30pm - 10pm
Web:	www.soifour.com	Closed Sun
Prices:	⊜	

At Soi Four Bangkok Eatery, sophisticated Thai cuisine comes customized for Westerners, with small plates for sharing, and mild spices that don't cause a three-alarm fire in your mouth (unless you request it that way). At lunch, mix and match your meal from the wok-fried dishes and curries that come with a choice of soup or salad. For dinner, you can choose among skewers, soups, noodles, and entrées that range from braised Australian lamb chop in sweet cumin mutsamun curry to tofu, shiitake mushrooms, baby bok choy and glass noodles baked in a clay pot.

Soi means "street" in Thai, and this addition to College Avenue's restaurant row dishes up Thai street food in a contemporary atmosphere, lit by floor-to-ceiling windows and featuring a mezzanine for more intimate dining.

East of San Francisco

Soizic

026

300 Broadway St., Oakland (at 3rd St.)

Phone:	510-251-8100	Tue – Thu 11:30am - 2pm & 5:30pm - 9pm
Fax:	N/A	Fri 11:30am - 2pm & 5:30pm - 10pm
Web:	www.soizicbistro.com	Sat 5:30pm - 10pm
Prices:	$$	Sun 5:30pm - 9pm
		Closed Mon

Located two blocks from the waterfront and Jack London Square, this attractive bistro sits in the middle of a district where old warehouses and Asian eateries are slowly being overtaken by modern office buildings and coffee shops. Soizic's name pays tribute to a French friend of Korean chef/owner Sanju Dong.

Dishes in the spacious dining room, with its baroque décor, respect French techniques and California products. Copious combinations include warm duck confit salad with bacon red wine vinaigrette, grilled lamb filet mignon with Madeira sauce, and creamy ginger custard served with crunchy almond cookies.

Tip: If you're a guy who's trying to impress his date, avoid the low banquettes, where you could end up feeling like a schoolboy struggling to see over the top of the table.

Tacubaya

027

1788 4th St., Berkeley (bet. Hearst Ave. & Virginia St.)

Phone:	510-525-5160	Mon 10am - 9pm
Fax:	510-525-3782	Tue 10am - 4pm
Web:	www.tacubaya.net	Wed – Fri 10am - 9pm
Prices:	🥜	Sat – Sun 9am - 9pm

So, you're shopping on 4th Street and can't decide between those two designer outfits? Take a lunch break and mull it over at Tacubaya. Here you'll be faced with more decisions: will it be homemade tacos folded over Niman Ranch beef, *fideo* (a home-style Mexican dish of angel hair pasta and tomato sauce heated up by the addition of chiles), or, perhaps, *chilaquiles* (eggs, onions and cheese over a bed of spicy tortilla chips). Sure, this is a breakfast dish, but *desayuno* is available weekdays from 10am to noon and on weekends until 4pm.

Once you've narrowed down your selection, place your order at the counter, grab a seat and enjoy a glass of sangria while you wait for your meal. Now that you've made that choice, deciding on that outfit should be a piece of cake.

Trattoria La Siciliana

028

2993 College Ave., Berkeley (at Ashby Ave.)

Phone:	510-704-1474	Open daily 11:30am - 2:30pm & 5:30pm - 10pm
Fax:	N/A	
Web:	N/A	
Prices:	$$	

You'll recognize this trattoria by the line stretching out the door at dinnertime. It seems that family-run La Siciliana has built quite a fan base among Berkeley residents and students, who are willing to wait 30 minutes or more and endure the cramped tables for generous plates of southern Italian food served in a festive atmosphere.

A meal here starts with fresh-baked bread and fruity olive oil for dipping. Then it's on to the likes of *bucatini chi Finucchiede*, an authentic Sicilian dish made with a sauce of fresh sardines, imported anchovies, pine nuts, olive oil, raisins, onion, saffron, fennel and toasted breadcrumbs.

Have some extra time before dinner? Take a walk around the neighborhood to admire the lovely Craftsman-style bungalows that line Webster and Prince streets.

Uzen

029

5415 College Ave., Oakland (bet. Hudson St. & Kales Ave.)

Phone:	510-654-7753	Mon – Fri 11:30am - 2pm & 5:30pm - 10pm
Fax:	N/A	Sat 5:30pm - 10pm
Web:	N/A	Closed Sun
Prices:	$$	

You'll find the atmosphere at Uzen outside, along hip College Avenue in Oakland's thriving Rockridge neighborhood. Inside the restaurant, there's a tiny sushi bar (10 seats), a small, spare dining room (24 seats) and no décor to speak of, save an orchid or two.

But you've come here for the sushi, not the ambience, and in this regard you won't be disappointed. The quality of the fish is superior, the rice is steamed perfectly, and the artfully presented dishes are prepared with indisputable savoir faire. Sure, the menu is short and has no surprises (it cites sushi, maki, udon and teriyaki), but the kitchen only orders enough fish for each day, so you can be sure you're getting the freshest products from the sea.

East of San Francisco

Venus

030

Californian

2327 Shattuck Ave., Berkeley (at Durant Ave.)

Phone:	510-540-5950	Open daily 11am - 2:30pm
Fax:	510-540-5878	& 5pm - 9:30pm
Web:	www.venusrestaurant.net	
Prices:	$$	

Near the U.C. Berkeley campus sits this discreet eatery, where an enthusiastic clientele crowds the bare-wood tables for breakfast, lunch, dinner and the popular weekend brunch. Inside, exposed brick walls are built with charred bricks left behind after the 1906 earthquake, and a changing collection of work by local artists enhances the simple décor. Sliding-glass windows along the façade open in summer.

Chef/partner Amy Murray, who opened Venus in 2000, hones in on a slow-food-based philosophy of wholesome food and growing practices. She supports area organic farmers by frequenting the Berkeley farmers' market every week, bringing back heirloom tomatoes, baby lettuces, Bloomsdale spinach, and artisan cheeses to incorporate into her globally accented California cuisine.

Zachary's Chicago Pizza

031

Pizza

5801 College Ave., Oakland (at Oak Grove Ave.)

Phone:	510-655-6385	Sun – Thu 11am - 10pm
Fax:	N/A	Fri – Sat 11am - 10:30pm
Web:	www.zacharys.com	
Prices:		

The Windy City's signature dish has been enjoying success in Oakland since 1983 at this no-frills pizzeria (check out their other location at 1853 Solano Avenue in nearby Berkeley). Zachary's specializes in stuffed pizza: a satisfying deep-dish concoction made with a layer of dough on the bottom of the pan, filled with a copious helping of cheese and your choice among 19 ingredients, and topped by another layer of crust and flavorful fresh tomato sauce.

A few caveats: Zachary's doesn't deliver, they don't accept credit cards, and they don't accept reservations. In any case, you should be prepared to wait—it takes 20 to 40 minutes to prepare a pizza to order here. Otherwise, you can opt to pick up one of Zachary's half-baked pies, take it home and serve it hot from your own oven.

East of San Francisco

Zax Tavern

Californian ✗✗

032

2826 Telegraph Ave., Berkeley (bet. Oregon & Stuart Sts.)

Phone:	510-848-9299	Tue – Thu 5:30pm - 9pm
Fax:	N/A	Fri – Sat 5pm - 10pm
Web:	www.zaxtavern.com	Sun 5pm - 9pm
Prices:	$$	Closed Mon

Riding on the success of their former North Beach restaurant (called Zax), chefs Mark Drazek ("Zax" to his friends) and Barbara Mulas have taken their two toques over the line (and the Bay Bridge) to bring their California-style cooking to Oakland. The Telegraph Avenue digs are bigger than the space they had in the city, accommodating a lively mix of business people and couples.

Twice-baked goat cheese soufflé or house-cured gravlax make good places to start, before digging into seasonal fare like grilled double-cut pork chops, mostaccioli pasta with baby spinach and asparagus tossed in mascarpone cream, or Asian-accented pepper-seared tuna.

Cherry wood and Carrera marble turn the interior into a cool, classy cafe where you get a lot—both portion- and quality-wise—for your money.

East of San Francisco

North
of San Francisco

Golden Gate Bridge

North of San Francisco
Marin County

Introduced by the windswept ridges, sheltered valleys and sandy coves of the Marin Headlands, Marin County lies just over the Golden Gate Bridge from San Francisco. Here, surrounded on three sides by water, you'll find unparalleled natural sites such as the wave-lashed sands of Point Reyes National Seashore, the lofty peak (2,571 feet) of Mount Tamalpais, and the majestic stands of redwoods at Muir Woods National Monument. All this natural beauty, coupled with the laid-back atmosphere of the county's rural towns, provides a welcome break from the dynamism of the city. Not to mention the fact that this area makes a great jumping-off point for exploring the wineries of Sonoma Valley.

A favorite excursion for both residents and visitors, sophisticated **Sausalito** lies a short drive or ferry ride across the bay from San Francisco. Indeed, the most appealing way to get here—on a nice day—is to hop aboard a ferry from the city. Once you disembark, it's easy walking along Bridgeway Boulevard, the community's commercial spine. Here you'll find upscale shops, gorgeous views and eateries galore. What better place to enjoy seafood than in a restaurant by the water, enjoying vistas that stretch across the blue bay to Tiburon and Angel Island? On the land side, tiers of pricey private residences climb down the steep slopes to the bay.

Keep going north on Highway 101 and you'll discover charming towns like peaceful, chi-chi **Mill Valley** and lovely **Larkspur**, whereas a detour along the coast will bring you to tiny **Inverness** and **Tomales Bay**.

Tiburon

Dennis Anderson/Marin County Visitors Bureau

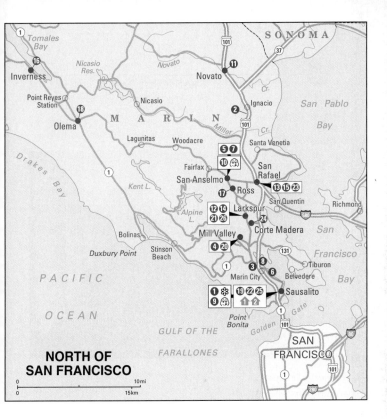

**NORTH OF
SAN FRANCISCO**

Exuding the quaint feel of a European village, Mill Valley's lush hilly landscape sits in the shadow of Mt. Tamalpais. The action here centers on Lytton Square, surrounded by stylish boutiques and good restaurants. Queen Anne Victorians distinguish the architecture of **Larkspur**, a place whose entire downtown is listed on the National Register of Historic Places as a model turn-of-the-20th-century town. Antiques buffs should head for the historic railroad town of **San Anselmo**.

Marin County's northernmost city, **Novato** is located about 29 miles north of San Francisco. Downtown's restored Grant Avenue beckons with shops and restaurants, and nearby sites that preserve Novato's past. **San Rafael** wins the prize as Marin's oldest and largest city. It grew up around the Mission San Rafael Arcangel, established in 1817. Today San Rafael's downtown shopping district is a mix of retail, ethnic restaurants and Victorian architecture.

Sushi Ran ✿

001

Japanese ✗

107 Caledonia St., Sausalito (bet. Pine & Turney Sts.)

Phone:	415-332-3620
Fax:	415-332-3940
Web:	www.sushiran.com
Prices:	$$

Mon – Fri 11:45am - 2:30pm
& 5:30pm - 11pm
Sat – Sun 5:30pm - 11pm

Sushi Ran/Cavan Clark

Sushi Ran lives up to its reputation as one of the best sushi restaurants in the Bay Area. From the smiling hostess to the well-managed dining room with its attentive, efficient staff, this establishment is a winner. The restaurant occupies two spaces: the original sushi bar and dining room, and the wine and sake bar next door, which was added in 2000. If you end up having to wait for a table, the wine bar will placate you with a daily changing list of some 30 limited-production wines and premium sakes by the glass.

Executive chef Scott Whitman and his team of professional sushi chefs create original Japanese dishes, from sushi to more contemporary recipes, turning extraordinarily fresh products into works of art. On the list of dinner specials, corn coconut soup, scallop-chive dumplings, and lemongrass broiled butterfish represent the chef's idea of "Something Different."

Owner Yoshi Tome, who hails from Okinawa, Japan, enjoys educating his guests about sake. Thus, the 300-bottle wine list offers a large selection of sakes, organized by category: fragrant, rich, aged, and light and smooth.

APPETIZERS

Kobe Beef Carpaccio with Gochujang Chile Miso Paste, Wasabi Oil, Tumble of Iced Onions, Arugula and Kaiware

Kaffir Lime Lobster Sticks with Sauce of Kaffir Lime Leaves, Lemongrass and Garlic, served with Crispy Noodle Cake and Tamarind Vinaigrette and Snow Pea Salad.

Scallop-Chive Dumplings with Water Spinach and Soy-Vinegar Sauce

ENTRÉES

Today's "Omakase" Sushi Plate: Toro, Shima Aji, Kasugodai (fresh daily from the Tokyo fish market) plus four more chef's choices and 7 pieces of Nigiri Sushi served with our Signature Soy Sauce

Nori-wrapped Seared Ahi Tuna with Tomato-Ginger Relish and Soy-Mustard Sauce

Roasted Rack of Lamb with Macadamia Nut Crust and Hoisin Jus

DESSERTS

Green-Tea and Sour-Cherry Brioche Bread Pudding presented with Whipped Cream and Cherry Caramel

House-made Mascarpone Ice Cream with Fresh Berries

Chocolate Bombe with Toffee Crunch and Hazelnut Crème Anglaise

begin vertical sidebar

North of San Francisco

Boca

002

steak

Steakhouse ✗✗

340 Ignacio Blvd., Novato
(bet. Alameda Del Prado & Enfrente Rd.)

Phone:	415-883-0901	Mon – Thu 11:30am - 2:30pm & 5pm - 9:30pm
Fax:	415-883-0802	Fri 11:30am - 2:30pm & 5pm - 10pm
Web:	www.bocasteak.com	Sat 5pm - 10pm
Prices:	$$	Sun 5pm - 9:30pm
		Closed Christmas Day

Boca is a Northern California restaurant with a South American twist. Chef George Morrone (whose credits include Tartare, Aqua and Fifth Floor in San Francisco) moves north and pays homage to his heritage with his latest concept: an Argentinean steakhouse. Amid an atmosphere of natural wood paneling, brick walls and wrought-iron accents designed to recall a South American ranch, the kitchen team grills grass- and corn-fed beef over hardwood fires. From skirt steak to tournedos of tenderloin, meats are served with a baked potato and two kinds of chimichurri sauces. The Boca brownie sundae, served tableside for two, makes a sweet end to any day on the range.

Go Tuesday for half-price bottles of wine, including a selection from Argentina.

Buckeye Roadhouse

003

American ✗✗

15 Shoreline Hwy., Mill Valley (west of Hwy. 101)

Phone:	415-331-2600	Mon – Thu 11:30am - 10:30pm
Fax:	415-331-6067	Fri – Sat 11:30am - 11pm
Web:	www.buckeyeroadhouse.com	Sun 10:30am - 10pm
Prices:	$$	Closed Christmas Day

Just after you cross the Golden Gate Bridge on Highway 101, keep an eye out for Buckeye Roadhouse. When it's cool outside, this charming 1937 lodge makes the ideal place to cozy up to the stone fireplace and gaze out at the woods from the warmth of the vaulted, wood-paneled room. It's also a good place for contemporary American cuisine.

Basic all-American burgers (turkey and beef) and sautéed calf's liver share the bill with more modernized fare such as barbecued curried Dungeness crab, and a Mongolian spiced pork chop. The wood-burning smoker, set outside near the terrace, turns out succulent smoked chicken wings, slow-smoked spicy pork, and barbecued baby back ribs.

A meal here wouldn't be complete without a taste of the sinfully rich S'mores pie.

Bungalow 44

44 E. Blithedale Ave., Mill Valley (at Sunnyside Ave.)

Phone:	415-381-2500	Sun – Thu 5pm - 10pm
Fax:	415-381-1476	Fri – Sat 5pm - 11pm
Web:	www.bungalow44.com	Closed major holidays
Prices:	$$	

The Real Restaurants group, the same folks that brought the Buckeye Roadhouse (located just a few miles away) to Mill Valley, score another hit with Bungalow 44. True to its name, which conjures images of plush booths and a warming fireplace, the restaurant provides a cozy setting for a meal at any time of year. The second dining room, the one with the fireplace, morphs into an outside patio on warm days.

The open kitchen reveals a serious team of chefs, hustling to plate combinations like mussels steamed in rioja with spicy chorizo; butternut squash soup with apples, walnuts and blue cheese; braised pork shank with gigante beans; and a grilled hamburger made with no less than Kobe beef. Roughly 95 percent of the bottles on the appealing wine list hail from California vineyards.

Cucina

Italian X

510 San Anselmo Ave., San Anselmo (at Tunstead Ave.)

Phone:	415-454-2942	Tue – Thu 5:30pm - 9:30pm
Fax:	415-454-1768	Fri – Sat 5:30pm - 10pm
Web:	N/A	Sun 5:30pm - 9pm
Prices:	$$	Closed Mon

The second time is clearly the charm for chef/owner Jack Krietzman's Cucina, which shortened its name from Cucina Jackson Fillmore and moved down the street to a smaller space. Yellow walls, tile floors, and a wood-burning oven near the semi-open kitchen form a simple setting for this family-friendly neighborhood trattoria in downtown San Anselmo.

The nightly changing menu presents a generous selection of Italian dishes, including pasta and gnocchi, and entrées such as mahi mahi Fra Diavolo, *salsicce* (spicy sausage with cannellini beans), and *pollo alla Siciliana*. If you're primed for pizza, don't come here on Friday or Saturday night, because on those nights you won't find it on the menu. Any night of the week, you will find 150 different entries on the wine list, most of them Italian.

North of San Francisco

Fish

006

Seafood ✗

350 Harbor Dr., Sausalito (at Bridgeway)

Phone:	415-331-3474	Open daily 11:30am - 4:30pm & 5:30pm - 8:30pm
Fax:	415-331-3421	Closed New Year's Day & Christmas Day
Web:	www.331fish.com	
Prices:	$$	

Housed in a former bait and tackle shop on the harbor, Fish is where the cognoscenti go in Sausalito for the day's freshest catch. There are no frills to this seafood shack, only a counter for placing your order, and picnic tables and benches for chowing down on fish that's right off the boat.

Barbecued local oysters are a Marin specialty, grill-poached and napped with the house sauce. Chowder comes in New England white and Portuguese red styles, while the Dungeness crab roll is a West Coast version of that Maine staple, served here with Clover butter, salt and pepper on an Acme sweet torpedo roll, with fries on the side.

Don't have time to eat in? Buy your fresh fish at the counter and take it home to cook. Just be sure to bring your cash or checkbook, because they don't accept credit cards.

Fork

007

Californian ✗✗

198 Sir Francis Drake Blvd., San Anselmo (bet. Bank St. & Tunstead Ave.)

Phone:	415-453-9898	Tue – Sat 11:45am - 2:30pm & 5:30pm - 9:30pm
Fax:	N/A	Closed Sun & Mon
Web:	www.marinfork.com	Closed January 1 - 8 & July 1 - 9
Prices:	$$	

Simplicity rules at Fork, beginning with the name of the restaurant and carrying through to the décor and the cooking. This is a classic food tale: choice local ingredients meet classic technique, and their marriage is a happy one. The relationship is not complicated; a few select products are paired together to highlight the freshness and flavor of each one. The chef proposes dishes like scallop ceviche, Ahi tuna carpaccio, Tai snapper with corn and sweet Italian pepper, and Colorado lamb loin with crispy potatoes.

At lunch and dinner, you'll have a choice between a fixed-price and an à la carte menu (the fixed-price dinner—a fantastic value at less than $25—is offered only from 5:30pm to 6:15pm).

Frantoio

008

152 Shoreline Hwy., Mill Valley
(Stinson Beach exit off Hwy. 101)

Phone:	415-289-5777	Open daily 4:30pm - 10pm
Fax:	415-289-5775	Closed major holidays
Web:	www.frantoio.com	
Prices:	$$	

Next to Holiday Inn Express, Frantoio (Italian for "olive press") is a rare find among Italian restaurants. They make their own state-certified extra virgin olive oil in an on-site facility. The highlight of the spacious dining room lies at the back, behind a large window. There you'll see the actual press, a contraption with two large granite stone wheels used to crush the olives. The first thing the waiter will bring to your table is a bottle of golden olive oil and some bread to dip in it. As wonderful as the oil is, save room for wood-oven-fired pizzas, house-made pastas, grilled fish, and roasted meats from Niman Ranch.

The wheels are in motion—literally—between December and February, so go then if you want to watch the machine in action while you linger over dinner—that is, unless you're pressed for time.

Gaylord

009

201 Bridgeway, Sausalito (on 2nd St. at Main St.)

Phone:	415-339-0172	Mon 5pm - 10pm
Fax:	415-331-8849	Tue – Thu noon - 2:30pm & 5pm - 10pm
Web:	www.gaylords.com	Fri – Sat noon - 2:30pm & 5pm - 10:30pm
Prices:	$$	Sun noon - 2:30pm & 5pm - 10pm

Gaylord has been in San Francisco since 1976, but it wasn't until October 2005 that the restaurant branched out to Sausalito. None of its other locations *(1 Embarcadero Center, and in Menlo Park at 1706 El Camino Real)* can boast the scenery that this one does. Large windows afford fabulous views of the bay and Angel Island and Tiburon. In the distance rises San Francisco's skyline.

Indian traditions sparkle in aromatic tandooris, biryanis, kebabs and curries that come from the kitchen. Abundance is the theme here, from the multipage menu to the copious but moderately priced prix-fixe meals, offered at both lunch and dinner. Go for the latter if you want to sample an array of different dishes.

At the bar, you can order small plates and naan pizzas, but you'll miss the great view.

North of San Francisco

Insalata's

010

Mediterranean ✕✕

120 Sir Francis Drake Blvd., San Anselmo (at Barber Ave.)

Phone: 415-457-7700
Fax: 415-457-8375
Web: www.insalatas.com
Prices: $$

Mon – Thu 11:30am - 2:30pm & 5:30pm - 9pm
Fri – Sat 11:30am - 2:30pm & 5:30pm - 10pm
Sun 11am - 2:30pm & 5:30pm - 9pm

Tastes of the Mediterranean sparkle inside the sunny vine-covered façade of Insalata's, where chef/owner Heidi Krahling takes inspiration from Italy, Provence, Spain, Portugal, Greece, Morocco and the Middle East.

Set in downtown San Anselmo, this attractive spot with its larger-than-life paintings of fruit and vegetables is a local favorite, and for good reason. Middle Eastern couscous heaped with lemony lentils, roasted acorn squash, spinach, Moroccan spiced onions, Turkish yogurt and tomato-pistachio relish; and braised beef short ribs spiked with sherry, orange and chocolate, and served over Yukon Gold mashed potatoes are just a couple of the draws.

If time is an issue, you can order your meal to go from the full take-out menu.

Kitchen at 868 Grant

011

Contemporary ✕

868 Grant Ave., Novato (bet. Machin & Reichert Aves.)

Phone: 415-892-6100
Fax: 415-892-4322
Web: www.kitchen868.com
Prices: $$

Tue – Sun 5pm - 9pm
Closed Mon & major holidays

In January 2005 three Bay Area business partners opened this little bistro in Novato's old town. Since then, Kitchen at 868 Grant has raised the bar on the town's culinary offerings with its nightly changing menu of fresh, local ingredients.

Chef/partner Christopher Douglas (whose experience includes the kitchens at LuLu and Rose Pistola) bases his short bill of fare around the market, incorporating locally raised meats and vegetables in dishes like seared day boat scallops, house-cured pork chops with cheddar-cheese polenta, a salad of organic heirloom tomatoes and watercress, and grilled Monterey calamari with spicy aioli.

Framed mirrors and photographs decorate the gold and claret-colored walls of the 45-seat dining room.

Lark Creek Inn

XXX

234 Magnolia Ave., Larkspur (at Madrone Ave.)

Phone: 415-924-7766

Fax: 415-924-7117

Web: www.larkcreek.com

Prices: $$$

Mon – Fri 11:30am - 2pm & 5:30pm - 10pm
Sat 5pm - 10pm
Sun 10am - 2pm & 5pm - 10pm

Venerable redwoods shade this yellow 1888 Victorian, located a half-hour north of San Francisco. Opened in 1989, Lark Creek Inn was the first star in a constellation of restaurants owned by the Lark Creek Restaurant Group, headed by restaurateur Michael Dellar and chef Bradley Ogden.

A commitment to a local network of organic farmers and producers of all-natural meats and seafood sets the tone for the market-driven menu. The chef improvises sophisticated American fare from the likes of Liberty Farms duck breast, Star Route arugula, and Hobbs smoked ham hock. Of course, good food deserves good wine, and that's something you'll have no trouble finding on a list offering some 250 selections, including many California producers.

Sunday brunchers favor the cool—as in shady—patio in summer.

Las Camelias

X

912 Lincoln Ave., San Rafael (bet. 3rd & 4th Sts.)

Phone: 415-453-5850

Fax: N/A

Web: www.lascameliasrestaurant.com

Prices: $$

Open daily 11am - 9pm
Closed major holidays

Behind the colorful façade that marks Las Camelias, lies a love story. It's the story of chef/owner Gabriel Fregoso and his wife, Carol, and of their love of fine food and art. The couple opened their own restaurant in 1978, after Gabriel honed his skills at the Lark Creek Inn.

The chef pays homage to his Mexican roots, as well as to his mother and grandmother whose recipes inspired him, by showcasing real Mexican home cooking. Specialties include shrimp burritos, pork loin fajitas, and naturally raised chicken in spicy, chocolate-infused mole sauce. Save your calories for the main course, since desserts and wine selection are limited.

And the art? It's all around you in the dining room in the form of original sculptures by Carol Fregoso (yes, they are for sale).

North of San Francisco

Left Bank

French French ✗✗

 014

507 Magnolia Ave., Larkspur (at Ward St.)

Phone:	415-927-3331
Fax:	415-927-3034
Web:	www.leftbank.com
Prices:	$$

Mon 11:30am - 10pm
Tue – Sat 11:30am - 11pm
Sun 10am - 10pm
Closed Christmas Day

The name of this restaurant leaves no guessing as to the type of cuisine they serve. Its location in the historic Blue Rock Inn in downtown Larkspur may be a far cry from the Rive Gauche in Paris, but French comfort food such as bouillabaisse, coq au vin, blanquette de veau, and tarte au citron stay as true to tradition as any you'll find in St. Germain des Près. And domestic and French wines are reasonably priced.

Chef Roland Passot (of La Folie) started this venture with partner Ed Levine in 1994. Since then, they've added four more branches in the Bay Area (Menlo Park, Pleasant Hill, San Jose and San Mateo). Echoing the atmosphere found in brasseries in Passot's hometown of Lyon, Left Bank is outfitted with French advertising posters, a cherry wood bar and a stone fireplace.

Lotus of India

Indian ✗

015

704 4th St., San Rafael (at Tamalpais Ave.)

Phone:	415-456-5808
Fax:	415-456-5874
Web:	www.lotusrestaurant.com
Prices:	⊜⊜

Mon – Sat 11:30am - 2:30pm
& 5pm - 9:30pm
Sun 5pm - 9pm

While its location near the entrance of Highway 101 isn't particularly appealing, Lotus of India manages to pack the house for its bargain-priced all-you-can-eat lunch buffet. Traditional à la carte entrées at dinner run the gamut from curries (meat, fish and vegetarian) to biriyani dishes and tandoori specialties. The kitchen happily accommodates special requests, so feel free to specify your dietary needs (more or less spice, no oil, a vegan dish). Save room for sweet endings such as rice pudding perfumed with saffron and cardamom, or *gulab jamun*, a light milk pastry served with hot honey syrup.

On warm, sunny days, the roof over the main dining room retracts so you can enjoy a sky-blue view.

Manka's Inverness Lodge

016

30 Callendar Way, Inverness (at Argyle St.)

Phone:	415-669-1034
Fax:	415-669-1598
Web:	www.mankas.com
Prices:	$$$$

Mon & Thu – Sat 7pm - closing
Sun 4pm - closing
Closed Tue & Wed
Closed January 1 - February 14

Rustic charm oozes out of every inch of this 1917 hunting lodge, sheltered in the woods just steps from Tomales Bay (there's no sign; take Argyle St. off Sir Francis Drake Blvd.) with Point Reyes National Seashore as its backyard.

In the Arts and Crafts parlor, you'll be greeted—if it's cold out—by a blazing wood fire. Diners (only one seating; reservations required) proceed to a cozy wood-paneled room whose windows look out on the trees. In this romantic setting you'll revel in a set five-course menu prepared with fresh local ingredients and as much loving care as your Cordon Bleu-trained grandmother would employ.

It's so relaxing here, you'll want to stay, so go ahead and reserve one of the 14 bewitching rooms, spread among the lodge and its annex, as well as the outlying cabins and 1911 boathouse.

Marché aux Fleurs

017

23 Ross Common, Ross (off Lagunitas Rd.)

Phone:	415-925-9200
Fax:	N/A
Web:	www.marcheauxfleursrestaurant.com
Prices:	$$$

Tue – Thu 5:30pm - 8:30pm
Fri – Sat 5:30pm - 9pm
Closed Sun & Mon

Named for farmers' markets in the south of France, Marché aux Fleurs borders the green of Ross Common in the sleepy town center. Chef Dan Baker presides over the kitchen, while his wife, Holly, manages the small but pleasant dining room, done in pastel tones with rustic furnishings and tiled floors.

Baker's food philosophy is simple: serve the freshest seasonal produces, free-range meats and sustainable seafood garnered from Marin County markets, and local farms and waters. This practice results in outstanding preparations such as wild California white Corniva bass and Duroc pork chop milanese. Boutique family-run wineries—whether from California, Alsace, Burgundy or Piemonte—take the fore on the informative and lengthy wine list.

North of San Francisco

Olema Inn

018

Californian

10000 Sir Francis Drake Blvd., Olema (at Hwy. 1)

Phone:	415-663-9559
Fax:	415-663-8783
Web:	www.theolemainn.com
Prices:	$$$

Mon & Wed – Fri 5pm - 9pm
Sat – Sun 11am - 3pm & 5pm - 9pm
Closed Tue

Opened in 1876 to serve the area's loggers, ranchers and farmers, the Olema Inn sits above the junction of Highway 1 and Sir Francis Drake Boulevard. Owners Dana and Jennifer Sulprizio restored the farmhouse-style building in the late 1990s with a 100-year-old pine floor; today it operates anew as a hostelry.

Three sparkling white dining rooms, simply decorated with small paintings and white linens, don't detract from California cuisine that plays up the talents of chef Edward Vigil. Local and sustainable products, such as Star Route Farms greens, Hog Island oysters, Cowgirl Creamery cheeses, wild foraged mushrooms, and Niman Ranch meats, make his food special.

Upstairs, six antique-furnished bedrooms make a good jumping-off point for exploring the wilds of Point Reyes National Seashore.

Paradise Bay

019

Seafood

1200 Bridgeway, Sausalito (at Turney St.)

Phone:	415-331-3226
Fax:	415-332-2532
Web:	www.paradisebaysausalito.com
Prices:	$$

Mon – Fri 11:30am - 3:30pm & 5pm - 10:30pm
Sat – Sun 10:30am - 3:30pm & 5pm - 10:30pm
Closed Christmas Day

You can't beat the breezy waterfront terrace at Paradise Bay on a warm evening. While the chef and his team prepare your meal, you can settle back with a glass of wine and watch the boats sail by.

Island accents spike dishes such as grilled freshwater sturgeon with tangerine-ginger vinaigrette, coconut prawns, and favorites like the fish and chips, served with malt vinegar tartar sauce and house-made cocktail sauce. For meat lovers, tamarind-glazed double-cut pork chop with pickled ginger demi-glace, lemongrass-marinated chicken breast, and filet mignon will certainly fill the bill.

If you're staying in the area on Sunday, come on over for some ginger-blueberry pancakes or Island Benedict (Dungeness crab cakes, grilled pineapple and spicy hollandaise).

Piazza D'Angelo

Italian ✗✗

020

22 Miller Ave., Mill Valley
(bet. Sunnyside & Throckmorton Aves.)

Phone:	415-388-2000	Mon – Fri 11:30am - 11pm
Fax:	415-388-2126	Sat – Sun 10:30am - 11pm
Web:	www.piazzadangelo.com	Closed major holidays
Prices:	$$	

Looking for a lively Italian restaurant in Marin County? Look no further than Piazza D'Angelo. Between its valet parking and moneyed clientele, this local institution fits right in with its setting in downtown Mill Valley. In winter, a large fireplace sets the tone in the airy main room, while in fair weather, two terraces invite outdoor dining.

The menu ranges across tortelloni della casa (homemade pasta stuffed with ricotta, spinach and parmesan) and pizza with Calabrese sausage, mozzarella and goat cheese to milk-fed veal scallopini with artichokes and lemon. Desserts are made fresh daily; chocoholics will go for the rich, dark-chocolate pâté. Many Italian appellations number among the selections on the wine list, which includes a section of limited-production wines.

Picco

Contemporary ✗✗

021

320 Magnolia Ave., Larkspur (at King St.)

Phone:	415-924-0300	Mon – Thu 5:30pm - 10pm
Fax:	415-924-0306	Fri 5:30pm - 11pm
Web:	www.restaurantpicco.com	Sat 5pm - 11pm
Prices:	$$	Sun 5pm - 10pm

"Taste more—dare to share" is the motto at this Larkspur newcomer. In an atmosphere of exposed rafters, brick walls and earth tones, chef Bruce Hill (of San Francisco's Bix) crafts an eclectic menu of small plates that reads like a world tour. Recipes mix flavors from California, Asia, Italy, France and Morocco, resulting in an innovative contemporary cuisine.

The intriguing wine list is a roster of some 300 selections, grouped under such fun-to-read headings as It's School Night (wines with a low percentage of alcohol), Wacky Wines (made using biodynamic agricultural practices), and Wine Geeks to Gurus (favorite beverages of the wine pros).

If you're in the mood for a quick bite, adjoining Pizzeria Picco can satisfy your craving with wood-fired pizzas and fresh organic salads.

North of San Francisco

Poggio

022

Italian XX

777 Bridgeway, Sausalito (at Bay St.)

Phone: 415-332-7771
Fax: 415-332-6847
Web: www.poggiotrattoria.com
Prices: $$

Sun – Thu 11:30am - 10pm
Fri – Sat 11:30am - 11pm
Closed Christmas Day

You'll find this large, modern, trattoria-style restaurant on the ground floor of the historic Casa Madrona Hotel *(see hotel listings)*. It's conveniently located on Bridgeway, Sausalito's main thoroughfare, where you can best appreciate the views of the yacht harbor from the sidewalk tables out front. The interior is comfortable and classy, with soft red banquettes, arched doorways and a floor-to-ceiling dark-wood wine cabinet along the back wall.

The generous menu changes its offerings of pastas, fish and spit-roasted meats daily. Regional Italian fare (polpettone braised in savory tomato sauce, bucatini with veal and green-olive meatballs) abounds, but the menu also cites a number of American-style dishes such as local Petrale sole with lemon-caper sauce, and grilled bone-in ribeye.

Sabor of Spain

023

Spanish X

1301 4th St., San Rafael (at C St.)

Phone: 415-457-8466
Fax: 415-457-1719
Web: www.saborofspain.com
Prices: $$

Tue – Thu 5pm - 9:30pm
Fri – Sat 5pm - 11pm
Sun 5pm - 9pm
Closed Mon

At this vinoteca, you'll be immersed in the sights, sounds and, of course, sabors (flavors) of Spain, even though you're sitting in the center of San Rafael. Lunch features tapas portions of Spanish tortillas, Serrano ham, and seafood-stuffed piquillo peppers, along with salads and *bocadillos* (sandwiches). At dinner, the menu adds more elaborate *raciones*, or main dishes, such as honey-roasted quail with chorizo-cornmeal filling, or pistachio-almond snapper with salsa verde and black figs.

All the wines here—more than 100 selections—come from Spain. You can order by the glass (more than 30 choices), by the bottle or by the flight; the latter is a good option if you're interested in discovering the regional vintages of Spain.

Simmer

024

60 Corte Madera Ave., Corte Madera (near Redwood Ave.)

Phone:	415-927-2332	Tue – Thu 6pm - 9:30pm
Fax:	415-927-2335	Fri – Sat 6pm - 10pm
Web:	www.simmerrestaurantmarin.com	Sun 10am - 2pm
Prices:	$$	Closed Mon

You could easily miss this tiny neighborhood restaurant, if you don't keep your eyes peeled for the single-story green house on Corte Madera Avenue, set in a town sandwiched between Mill Valley and Larkspur about 12 miles north of San Francisco.

It's worth watching for Simmer, though, to enjoy a meal in the cozy mustard-yellow dining room, whose focal point is a whimsical black fork and spoon hanging near the large windows that look out on the street. On the plate, Mediterranean sensibilities pepper California products such as Sonoma County duck, golden trout, and locally gathered greens. Owner Ken Harris intentionally keeps his menu short in order to underscore the best of each season. Of the handful of offerings on the wine list, all of them are available by the glass.

Spinnaker

025

100 Spinnaker Dr., Sausalito (at Anchor St.)

Phone:	415-332-1500	Open daily 11am - 11pm
Fax:	415-332-7062	Closed January 1 - 8 & December 24 - 25
Web:	www.thespinnaker.com	
Prices:	$$	

One of Sausalito's first restaurants, this dowager has presided over the bay for more than 45 years. The view's the thing in the large dining room, surrounded on three sides by picture windows. Built on a pier right over the water, Spinnaker enjoys a panorama that takes in the glittering bay waters, the city skyline, Angel Island, and Alcatraz, with the Sausalito hills rising on the other side.

The menu is long and ambitious, listing everything fishy from New England clam chowder, shrimp Louis, and Dungeness crab cakes at lunch to bouillabaisse, seafood pastas, and paella at dinner. After your meal, generous desserts and coffee are served from rolling carts.

Since the ferry dock is a short walk away, this place gets its share of the tourist trade along with a mix of stalwart locals.

North of San Francisco

Yankee Pier

026

Seafood

286 Magnolia Ave., Larkspur
(bet. King St. & Madrone Ave.)

Phone: 415-924-7676
Fax: 415-924-7117
Web: www.yankeepier.com
Prices: $$

Mon – Fri 11:30am - 2:30pm & 5pm - 9pm
Sat – Sun 11:30am - 9pm
Closed major holidays

To the port side of the Lark Creek Inn lies Yankee Pier, part of the fleet of restaurants operated by chef Bradley Ogden. Atlantic meets Pacific in this nautical-themed eatery where, from Maine lobster to Dungeness crab, the menu nets the best of both coasts. The likes of fresh-caught Pacific red snapper, Petrale sole, catfish and mahi mahi are served grilled, sautéed or blackened and topped with either spicy homemade red bell pepper sauce or cilantro vinaigrette. Your selection comes with oven-roasted potatoes and a choice of veggies.

If you're floating around, visit one of Yankee Pier's other locations: in San Jose *(358 Santana Row)*, in San Francisco's new Westfield shopping center *(865 Market St.)*, and in Terminal 3 of San Francisco International Airport.

Not every atlas comes with a legend like this.

We put the same quality and reliability into our atlases that we put into our tires. The innovative design makes for easy navigation, allowing you to travel with confidence. To learn more, visit michelintravel.com.

MICHELIN
A better way forward

©RobertHaynes

South
of San Francisco

Plaza de Cesar Chavez, San José

South of San Francisco

Charming in their own right, the Bay Area bedroom communities south of San Francisco range down the east side of the Santa Cruz Mountains, sandwiched between US-101 and I-280. From north to south, Millbrae, Burlingame, San Mateo, Redwood City, Palo Alto, Mountain View, Los Altos and Santa Clara stretch down toward San Jose, California's third-largest city. Self-styled "capital of Silicon Valley," and "Gateway to the Bay Area," San Jose was founded at the southern tip of San Francisco Bay (50 miles south of present-day San Francisco) in 1777 as El Pueblo San José de Guadalupe—the first civilian settlement in Alta California.

Silicon Valley – Agriculture remained the city's chief industry from the mid-19th to the mid-20th century, at which point electronics industries began to supplant the orchards. Beginning with the development of the semiconductor industry in the 1950s, innovative new enterprises arose in the Bay Area to fill the growing demand for electronic products. By the 1970s, "Silicon Valley," which included such computer giants as Hewlett-Packard, Apple Computer, Intel, and a host of semiconductor laboratories, had encompassed San Jose and its neighboring communities.

In the late 1990s, these companies were joined by a new breed of Internet-based companies (Yahoo, Amazon.com, eBay, etc.) that came to be known as "dot-coms." The stock prices of these companies rocketed in the short term, making millionaires of many investors until the bubble finally burst in 2001. Today San Jose boasts the largest concentration of technology expertise in the world. With a population hovering around 945,000, the city ranks as the 10th-largest in the United States.

Stanford University, Palo Alto

©Robert Holmes

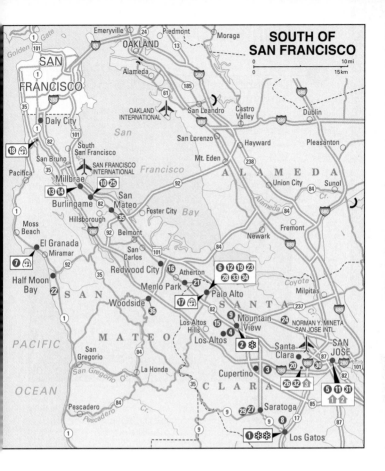

The local braintrust includes **Stanford University** in Palo Alto, with its lovely Richardsonian Romanesque-style buildings roofed with red tile and surrounded by eucalyptus, bay and palm trees. Established by railroad magnate Leland Stanford in 1891, the university boasts a distinguished faculty of 1,771, whose members include 16 Nobel laureates, 4 Pulitzer Prize winners, and 21 recipients of the National Medal of Science. In the early 1960s, Frederick Terman, provost of Stanford from 1955 to 1965, had a large hand in helping engineer the university-industry partnerships that led to the establishment of many key high-tech companies in the area.

Cutting-edge technology is far from the only reason to visit this area today. Here you'll find a wealth of cultural attractions and good eating, too, offering an array of cuisines from Chinese to Californian, and almost everything in between.

Manresa ✿✿

Contemporary 🍴🍴🍴

320 Village Lane, Los Gatos (bet. N. Santa Cruz & University Aves.)

Phone:	408-354-4330	Tue – Sat 5:30pm - 9pm
Fax:	408-354-0134	Sun 5pm - 8:30pm
Web:	www.manresarestaurant.com	Closed Mon
Prices:	$$$$	

Manresa/Pim Techamuanvivit

Hidden away on a narrow lane in a trendy shopping area of this Bay Area bedroom community, Manresa resides inside a renovated brick ranch-style house. The modern original style of the elegant dining room, with its beamed ceilings, Oriental area rugs, and mosaic-tiled fireplace, takes a back seat to chef David Kinch's fabulous contemporary cuisine.

In the kitchen, with its custom-made island cooktop, Kinch works his culinary magic. The show starts with a series of amuse-bouches, miniature bites that might include a red-chile pâte de fruit, a delicate beggar's purse wrapped around Dungeness crabmeat, or a sumptuous hollowed-out brown eggshell layered with soft-cooked egg, chives, Tahitian vanilla and sherry vinegar. Not to divert your attention from the main attraction, like the chef's signature local abalone—couched in a creamy avocado mousse and served atop a milk-skin "ravioli" filled with braised pigs' trotters and drizzled with brown butter.

This is no hocus-pocus; this is imaginative cooking with European inspiration. It's no coincidence that the restaurant's name refers to a medieval town in the Catalonia region of northern Spain.

South of San Francisco

Appetizers

Sweet Onion-Brioche Soup, Slow Egg with Manchego Cheese

Duck Foie Gras grilled slowly over Mesquite with Meyer Lemon

Local Abalone, Meuniere-style, with Pig's Trotters and Avocado

Entrées

Roast Saddle of Rabbit with Prunes marinated in Black Tea

Shellfish with Exotic Indian Spices, Spinach perfumed with Citrus

Roast Suckling Pig and House-made Boudin Noir

Desserts

Warm Medjool Date Cake with Apple Caramel and Date Milkshake

Roast Blenheim Apricot with Pain Perdu and Sweet-Corn Ice Cream

Chocolate Pudding Steamed in a Jar with Condensed-Milk and Cocoa-Nib Ice Cream

Chez TJ ❀

002

Contemporary French ✗✗✗

938 Villa St., Mountain View (bet. Bryant & Franklin Sts.)

Phone:	650-964-7466	Tue – Sat 5:30pm - 9:30pm
Fax:	650-964-9647	Closed Sun & Mon
Web:	www.cheztj.com	
Prices:	$$$$	

Mark Leet Photography

Chez TJ cossets diners in a series of intimate rooms inside a Victorian-era house off the main street in downtown Mountain View. Built in 1894, this former residence was the town's only fine-dining restaurant when founders George Aviet and the late Thomas McCombie served their first meal here in 1982. Now the place is a local institution and a favorite for birthdays, anniversaries and other special occasions.

Chef Christopher Kostow, a former sous-chef at Campton Place under Daniel Humm, took over the kitchen at Chez TJ in early 2006. Here young Kostow crafts a nightly prix-fixe, nine-course tasting menu and a four-course menu gastronomique, both available with wine pairings. His talented and playful touch updates French classics by matching foie gras au torchon with oysters en gelée, filling ravioli with a mousse made from frogs' legs sparked by lemon zest, and slow-poaching beef tenderloin and serving it with pearl barley, earthy glazed porcini and oxtail consommé.

Feel free to ask the well-informed waitstaff about any of the dishes, which they describe in detail as each course is served. To ensure that everyone is happy, the chef himself makes the rounds in the dining room.

South of San Francisco

Appetizers

Butter-poached Crayfish with Roasted-Corn Sabayon, Wood Ear Mushrooms and Vanilla

Chilled Broccoli Soup with Poached Egg, Black Truffles and Almond Oil

Seared Foie Gras and Cherries with White Balsamic, Green Almonds and Crispy Pancetta

Entrées

Roasted Sonoma Squab with Berberé, Heirloom Carrots and Candied Kumquat

Slow-roasted Turbot with Crispy Trotters, Caperberries and Olive Whipped Potatoes

Poached and Roasted Poussin with Cockles, Chorizo and Lime Thyme

Desserts

Strawberries and Fromage Blanc with Basil, Olive Oil and Black-Olive Confit

Artisan Cheese and Accompaniments: One Cow, One Sheep, One Goat

A Tasting of Seasonal Sorbets: Black Currant, Mango, Peach, Tangerine

Alexander's Steakhouse

003

Steakhouse XXX

10330 N. Wolfe Rd., Cupertino (at I-280)

Phone:	408-446-2222	Mon – Thu 11:30am - 3pm & 5:30pm - 10pm
Fax:	408-446-2242	Fri – Sat 5:30pm - 11pm
Web:	www.alexanderssteakhouse.com	Sun 5:30pm - 9pm
Prices:	$$$$	Closed major holidays

Run by chef Jeffrey Stout and restaurateur J.C. Chen, this Silicon Valley staple puts a surprising Asian spin on traditional steakhouse fare. Lobster-shrimp dumplings and crab hand rolls may not be your usual preludes to a steak dinner, but they prove delicious starters here. For the main course, filet mignon, New York strip, and a 24-ounce Porterhouse come from cuts of corn-fed Angus beef dry-aged in the glass case near the entrance.

Order à la carte, or try one of the chef's menus, which encompass an 11-course seafood tasting (Ocean's Eleven), the 4-course Kobe Experience, or the 9-course Omakase menu. A seductive choice of red wines from French Bordeaux to California Cabernet perfectly complements the red meat. To create privacy, the dining space is divided into several separate rooms.

Amber India

004

Indian X

**2290 El Camino Real, Mountain View
(bet. Ortega & S. Rengstorff Aves.)**

Phone:	650-968-7511	Open daily 11:30am - 2:30pm & 5pm - 10pm
Fax:	650-968-1820	
Web:	www.amber-india.com	
Prices:	🥜	

Mountain View's Olive Tree shopping center holds this Indian restaurant. Brightened by Indian artwork and artifacts, Amber India appeals at lunchtime for its bargain-priced buffet. Loads of local families line up for a bounty of salads, lentil soup, tandoori chicken, *malai kofta* (deep-fried cheese and potato dumplings), and basmati rice perfumed with cinnamon. At dinner the menu expands its offerings to a wide range of regional Indian fare including kebabs, tandoori dishes, Kerala lamb curry, and vegetarian specialties. Breads—leavened naan, northern Indian kulcha, deep-fried whole-wheat poori—are baked daily on-site.

Striking contemporary graphics decorate Amber India's second and more comfortable location in San Jose's Santana Row neighborhood (*377 Santana Row, Suite 1140*).

Arcadia

005 100 W. San Carlos St., San Jose (at Market St.)

Phone:	408-278-4555	Sun – Thu 11:30am - 2pm & 5:30pm - 10pm
Fax:	408-278-4444	Fri – Sat 11:30am - 2pm & 5:30pm - 11pm
Web:	www.michaelmina.net/arcadia	
Prices:	$$$	

Airy and spacious with its exhibition kitchen and wall of windows, Arcadia falls under the umbrella of the Mina Group, managed by Michael Mina (whose eponymous restaurant graces San Francisco's Westin St. Francis Hotel). Its location off the lobby of the Marriott hotel in downtown San Jose is convenient to the McEnery Convention Center, right next door.

At lunch, the tasting menu best embodies the spirit of Arcadia's contemporary cuisine; two samplings of soup accompany four savory bites (as in an American Kobe burger and a Maine lobster corndog). Or craft your own salad from the extensive Market List. Dinner brings a selection of shellfish and hearty fare like steak Rossini, tapioca-crusted black bass, and Mina's signature lobster pot pie. A kids' menu caters to families staying at the hotel.

Bistro Elan

006 448 California Ave., Palo Alto (near El Camino Real)

Phone:	650-327-0284	Tue – Fri 11:30am - 1:30pm
Fax:	650-327-0188	& 5:30pm - 9:30pm
Web:	N/A	Sat 5:30pm - 9:30pm
Prices:	$$	Closed Sun & Mon

This well-established bistro boasts a professional and friendly staff who have been welcoming Silicon Valley gourmands for years. Inside, the relaxed vibe is reinforced with ceiling fans, banquette seating and tables spaced to foster privacy.

The kitchen puts a French spin on the ever-changing California cuisine. Chilled cucumber soup is creamy and light, and Niçoise salad, made with pan-seared albacore tuna, is a colorful mélange of boiled eggs, haricots vert, bright tomatoes and black olives over a bed of butter lettuce. Check out the display of the day's desserts at the counter, and be sure to reserve a slice of the delicious fruit tart before the end of your meal. The restaurant always seems to run out of this cream-cheese-filled pastry topped with fresh seasonal fruit.

South of San Francisco

Cafe Gibraltar

007

M e d i t e r r a n e a n ✗✗

425 Avenue Alhambra, El Granada (at Palma St.)

Phone:	650-560-9039	Tue – Thu & Sun 5pm - 9pm
Fax:	650-728-8620	Fri – Sat 5pm - 10pm
Web:	www.cafegibraltar.com	Closed Mon
Prices:	$$	

Located on the San Mateo County coast, about 25 miles south of San Francisco, Cafe Gibraltar makes a pleasant excursion from the city. From the cheery, sun-filled dining room, you'll have a view of the blue Pacific and of the open kitchen where chef/owner Jose Luis Ugalde holds sway.

Although Ugalde is Mexican, he realizes scrumptious dishes from around the Mediterranean (France, Italy, Spain, Morocco, Greece) with ease and expertise. You can see him working in the kitchen (unlike many chefs who concentrate on supervising the line) fashioning complex layers of flavor in combinations like lamb with pistou, or *cassola*, an herb-scented seafood stew.

Every week a new prix-fixe menu adds options to the à la carte fare, while pizza, pasta and couscous on the kids' menu whet young appetites.

Cafe Marcella

008

M e d i t e r r a n e a n ✗✗

368 Village Lane, Los Gatos
(bet. N. Santa Cruz & University Aves.)

Phone:	408-354-8006	Tue – Sat 11:30am - 2:30pm & 5pm - 10pm
Fax:	408-354-9086	Sun 5pm - 10pm
Web:	www.cafemarcella.com	Closed Mon
Prices:	$$	

With a self-proclaimed goal of serving food that suits a casual family meal as well as a special occasion, Alain Staebler and his wife, Martine, opened this downtown Los Gatos cafe in 1991. They accomplish their aim with a menu of Mediterranean-inspired dishes (penne with garlic sausage, pan-roasted monkfish with French lentils, mustard-herb-crusted rack of lamb) that they couple with a surprising wine list. Some 350 selections encompass an intriguing roster of wines from California's Santa Cruz Mountains as well as varietals from the renowned growing regions of France.

Recently refurbished, the restaurant's two dining rooms foster a friendly bistro atmosphere with colorful paintings, ceramics and wine bottles; service is equally amiable.

Cantankerous Fish

009

Seafood ✕✕

420 Castro St., Mountain View (bet. California & Mercy Sts.)

Phone: 650-966-8124
Fax: 650-966-8259
Web: www.thecantankerousfish.com
Prices: $$

Mon – Sat 11:30am - 10pm
Sun 4:30pm - 9pm

Cantankerous or not, fish is clearly king in this spin-off of Scott's Seafood (Palo Alto and San Jose) in downtown Mountain View. Luckily, the friendly staff doesn't share the seafood's apparent ill-temper; they handle the crowds at this often-packed place with good-natured smiles.

Things go swimmingly in the open kitchen, where chefs dish up a good variety of fruits of the sea—and several meat entrées for you carnivores. The kitchen casts seafood in a modern light, stuffing king salmon with spinach and mushroom duxelles, flavoring sea bass with chipotle marinade, and wrapping Dungeness crabmeat and fresh herbs inside spring rolls.

This is a place to kick back and relax—and come listen to live jazz every Wednesday and Sunday evening.

Ecco

010

Contemporary ✕✕

322 Lorton Ave., Burlingame (at Burlingame Ave.)

Phone: 650-342-7355
Fax: 650-342-7433
Web: www.eccorestaurant.com
Prices: $$

Mon – Fri 11:30am - 2:30pm & 5:30pm - 10:30pm
Sat 5:30pm - 10:30pm
Closed Sun and January 1 - 8 & July 1 - 8

If you find yourself in Burlingame at midday or at dinnertime, you can count on Ecco for a good meal. Located in a downtown shopping center, this 75-seat neighborhood establishment with its apricot-colored walls makes a pleasant setting for a business or social meal—and an audible conversation.

Chef/owner Tooraj Sharif, who opened Ecco in 1986, features dishes that combine Mediterranean and Asian touches in preparations like roasted rack of lamb with mustard crust, and Maine lobster with passion fruit-ginger sauce and enoki mushrooms. Those with a more patriotic palate may find the Dungeness crab cakes, American Kobe beef burger or New York-style cheesecake more appealing. In addition to the à la carte offerings, a prix-fixe tasting menu is available in the evening.

South of San Francisco

Emile's

French

 011

545 S. 2nd St., San Jose (bet. Reed & William Sts.)

Phone:	408-289-1960	Tue – Sat 5:30pm - 10pm
Fax:	408-998-1245	Closed Sun & Mon
Web:	www.emiles.com	
Prices:	$$$	

Emile's has been a San Jose fixture since 1973, a relative lifetime in the restaurant world. This is the kind of homey place that regulars love for its consistently good French food and old-fashioned charm.

Owner and chef Emile Mooser was born in Switzerland, so it's no surprise that specialties like émincée of veal with rösti, and Gruyère fondue with Kirschwasser appear on the menu. Otherwise, the food runs to French classics (foie gras au torchon, duck à l'orange, trout grenobloise); the one concession Emile makes to modernity is the addition of *petites assiettes,* or small plates. The ample wine list nods to the chef's homeland with Swiss varietals including a Merlot from Ticino.

Learn to make goodies such as a Grand Marnier soufflé at one of Emile's hands-on cooking classes.

Evvia

Contemporary Greek

 012

420 Emerson St., Palo Alto (bet. Lytton & University Aves.)

Phone:	650-326-0983	Mon – Thu 11:30am - 2pm & 5:30pm - 10pm
Fax:	650-326-9552	Fri 11:30am - 2pm & 5:30pm - 11pm
Web:	www.evvia.net	Sat 5pm - 11pm
Prices:	$$	Sun 5pm - 9pm

Ancient Greece meets its contemporary cousin in the Silicon Valley at Evvia. Designed, or so the myth goes, to sate the gods, ancient Hellenic dishes (moussaka, octopus salad, lamb souvlaki, and freshly made, grilled organic pita bread) are now available to mere mortals here. This cuisine takes on a modern spin in preparations like roasted Pacific halibut with Greek fava beans, morels and asparagus tapenade. Even the wine list is divided into Old World and New World.

Sister to Kokkari Estiatorio in downtown San Francisco, Evvia packs in a steady stream of Palo Alto diners for both lunch and dinner (be sure to make reservations in advance). Wine casks, wood beams and hand-thrown pottery lend a rustic touch to the lovely dining room.

Fook Yuen Seafood

195 El Camino Real, Millbrae (at Victoria Ave.)

Phone: 650-692-8600
Fax: 650-692-2833
Web: N/A
Prices: 🥜

Mon – Fri 11am - 2:30pm & 5:30pm - 9:30pm
Sat – Sun 10am - 2:30pm & 5:30pm - 9:30pm

Located 15 miles south of San Francisco and just south of San Francisco International Airport, the little burg of Millbrae occupies less than 3.5 square miles. While it's not exactly a dining destination, the city does have a few claims to culinary notoriety. One of these is Fook Yuen Seafood.

By day, the restaurant serves dim sum in the 1960s-style dining room, decorated with Chinese artwork and Oriental screens. These little bites are all freshly prepared, varied and tasty. The fact that waitresses alternately tempt diners with trays of savory and sweet items, with little respect for any order of the courses, doesn't seem to bother the mostly Chinese crowd. At dinnertime, the menu angles in on Hong-Kong-style seafood specialties.

Hong Kong Flower Lounge

Chinese ✕

51 Millbrae Ave., Millbrae (at El Camino Real)

Phone: 650-692-6666
Fax: 650-692-0522
Web: www.flowerlounge.net
Prices: $$

Mon – Fri 11am - 2:30pm & 5pm - 9:30pm
Sat – Sun 10:30am - 2:30pm & 5pm - 9:30pm

You can't miss the striking Disneyesque Chinese temple façade of the Hong Kong Flower Lounge. Decked out with traditional green-tile pagoda-style roofs, soaring pillars and a huge statue of Buddha, this Millbrae fixture (opened since 1995) is way more than a lounge. Two levels of airy dining space accommodate hosts of families, both Asian and otherwise, who frequent this local favorite.

Although the menu runs the gamut from noodles to vegetarian to meat dishes, seafood is the specialty here. You can get an idea of the offerings from the live lobsters, crabs, prawns and more swimming in the tanks in the first-floor dining room. Dim sum, from steamed chicken feet in black bean sauce to deep-fried shrimp dumplings, is available, too.

South of San Francisco

South of San Francisco - **227**

Hunan Home's

015

Chinese

4880 El Camino Real, Los Altos (at Showers Dr.)

Phone: 650-965-8888
Fax: 650-965-0877
Web: www.hunanhomes.com
Prices: ⊜⊝

Open daily 11:30am - 2:30pm & 5pm - 9:30pm

Bursting with character, Hunan Home's is a lively spot to enjoy traditional and tasty Chinese cuisine. Its infectious energy and large tables make this a perfect gathering place for groups, and Sunday lunch is often packed with Chinese families who flock to this Los Altos restaurant for good food and good conversation.

Expertly run by the Yuan family who also owns the original in San Francisco's Chinatown *(622 Jackson St.)*, the service here is efficient and prompt. The authentic Chinese menu offers a wide variety of traditional dishes prepared and presented with pride. Photographs of many of the dishes assist diners with their choices, while a special selection of gourmet menus with exceptional cuisine and extraordinary prices (up to $300) caters to gastronomes.

John Bentley's

016

Contemporary

**2915 El Camino Real, Redwood City
(bet. Berkshire Ave. & E. Selby Lane)**

Phone: 650-365-7777
Fax: 650-365-2294
Web: www.johnbentleys.com
Prices: $$$

Mon – Fri 11:30am - 4pm & 5pm - 9pm
Sat 5pm - 9pm
Closed Sun

Whereas the original John Bentley's in Woodside plays up its historic setting in a circa 1920s firehouse *(2991 Woodside Rd.)*, the newer location (opened in summer 2004) displays an urbane elegance. The large dining space here ranges across three sections—including one for private parties—enhanced by dark woods, subdued lighting and colorful artwork.

Chef/owner John Bentley renders classics with a creative, contemporary touch, in such preparations as crispy golden sweetbreads, covered with smoked bacon and served atop creamy Yukon Gold mashed potatoes with grain-mustard sauce. To go with your meal, there's a large selection of wines, which leans heavily on varietals from Northern California.

Downside—or upside, depending on your point of view: The full bar in back draws a boisterous local crowd at night.

Junnoon 👁️

017

150 University Ave., Palo Alto (at High St.)

Phone:	650-329-9644	Mon – Thu 11:30am - 2:30pm & 5:30pm - 10pm
Fax:	650-329-9401	Fri 11:30am - 2:30pm & 5:30pm - 10:30pm
Web:	www.junnoon.com	Sat 5:30pm - 10:30pm
Prices:	$$	Closed Sun

Passion, energy, obsession. That's how the kitchen staff at Junnoon approaches their cuisine, and that's also what the restaurant's name means in Hindi. The piquant flavors of modern India shine through here in eclectic dishes such as the minced beef patty (spicy ground beef wrapped in puff pastry and served with mint chutney) and tandoori prawns smothered in a yummy coconut and Bengali mustard sauce. If you're on a budget, go at noon for the Power Lunch, a real deal at two courses for only $15.

Opened in February 2006, Junnoon is a collaboration between consulting chef Floyd Cardoz (of New York City's Tabla) and executive chef Kirti Pant (formerly of Cinnamon Club in London and Tamarind in New York City). The décor blends the feel of a contemporary lounge with traditional Indian touches.

Koi Palace 👁️

018

365 Gellert Blvd., Daly City
(bet. Hickey & Serramonte Blvds.)

Phone:	650-992-9000	Mon – Fri 11am - 3pm & 5pm - 9:30pm
Fax:	N/A	Sat – Sun 11am - 3pm & 5pm - 10pm
Web:	www.koipalace.com	
Prices:	$$	

Don't let the sheer size of Koi Palace intimidate you. Sure, this restaurant in Serramonte Plaza seats 400 and it's always mobbed at lunch with an Asian crowd taking tickets and standing in line for a table, but the excellent dim sum is worth the hassle.

There's a staggering variety of these little bites, from savory (steamed fish maw and chicken, whole crabmeat Shanghai dumplings, suckling pig) to sweet (bird nest egg-custard tart). Indicate your order from the selections listed on the paper menu and wait for your food to be cooked to order and delivered to your table. In the meantime, servers circulate around the room with additional items on trays and carts.

Hint: If you're coming for dim sum at lunchtime, get here early; the lines only get longer closer to noon.

South of San Francisco

Lavanda

019

Mediterranean ✗✗

185 University Ave., Palo Alto (at Emerson St.)

Phone:	650-321-3514	Mon – Thu 11:30am - 3pm & 4pm - 10pm
Fax:	650-321-3517	Fri – Sat 11:30am - 3pm & 4pm - 11pm
Web:	www.lavandarestaurant.com	Sun 4pm - 10pm
Prices:	$$$	Closed major holidays

On a busy corner in the heart of Palo Alto you'll find a piece of the sun-drenched Mediterranean inside the angled façade of Lavanda. The open dining space, with its inviting granite bar and large mural of a field of lavender splashing across one wall, makes a perfect setting for a relaxing meal.

Chef Clyde Griesbach conjures up the cuisine of southern France, Spain and Italy with a light California touch. Ricotta gnocchi glazed in walnut pesto, pan-seared snapper with braised kale and puttanesca vinaigrette, and vanilla lavender crème brûlée are typical of his uncomplicated creations. To pair with your meal, more than 600 wines—all served in Riedel stemware—include all the major wine-growing regions of the world from California and Oregon to France and New Zealand.

Le Papillon

020

French ✗✗✗

410 Saratoga Ave., San Jose (at Kiely Blvd.)

Phone:	408-296-3730	Thu – Fri 11:30am - 2:30pm & 5pm - 9pm
Fax:	408-247-7812	Sat – Wed 5pm - 9pm
Web:	www.lepapillon.com	
Prices:	$$$$	

Silicon Valley didn't exist as such when Papillon opened its doors in 1977. As the area mushroomed into a haven for high-tech industry, the restaurant evolved along with it, tailoring its menu to the tastes of South Bay executives.

Despite changes over the years, Papillon (French for "butterfly") maintains the tradition of elegance and sophisticated French cuisine that is its hallmark. Lunch and dinner à la carte offerings are similar, but the prix-fixe tasting menu is more elaborate in the evening. If you choose the former, you might relish roasted pheasant breast with Cognac jus, black-currant-glazed rack of lamb, or slow-roasted salmon with flageolet-fennel-artichoke ragout, depending on the season.

Oenophiles will love the long list of French and California wines.

Marché

021

898 Santa Cruz Ave., Menlo Park (at University Dr.)

Phone: 650-324-9092
Fax: 650-324-9690
Web: www.restaurantmarche.com
Prices: $$$$

Tue – Sat 5:30pm - 10pm
Closed Sun & Mon

Looking for an elegant restaurant for dinner south of the city? Look no farther than Marché in downtown Menlo Park. A favorite with the local dot-com crowd, Marché is done in tones of caramel and chocolate-brown, with sleek contemporary furnishings.

In this refined atmosphere, chef/owner Howard Bulka proposes a crossover cuisine that reflects elements of French, Mediterranean, Asian and California cooking (Ahi tuna seared rare in coconut-curry broth perfumed with Thai herbs; butternut squash bisque with vanilla-bean crème fraiche; and pear tarte Tatin). The menu changes, item by item, each week; a four-course tasting menu is also available.

Expect knowledgeable and attentive service, and a wine list that spotlights French and California vintages.

Navio

022

1 Miramontes Point Rd., Half Moon Bay (at Hwy. 1)

Phone: 650-712-7040
Fax: 650-712-7070
Web: www.ritzcarlton.com
Prices: $$$$

Open daily 11:30am - 2:30pm & 6pm - 10pm

Couched within the sumptuous Ritz-Carlton Half Moon Bay, the hotel's signature dining room stares out at the stunning Pacific from atop a high bluff. Every detail here is designed to please, from the comfortable chairs with pillows for your back and the gorgeous wood-lined barrel-vaulted ceiling to the courteous and knowledgeable waitstaff.

The cuisine, too, spares no expense in the quality of the ingredients and the precision of the cooking: painstakingly selected organic lettuces are dressed with 50-year-old sherry vinegar and organic California olive oil; hand-picked Dungeness crab marries parsnip purée and Earl Grey-scented jicama in a light salad; and green spring garlic is enriched with cream in a decadent soup.

About the name? It's Portuguese for "ship."

South of San Francisco

Osteria

Italian 🍴

023

247 Hamilton Ave., Palo Alto (at Ramona St.)

Phone: 650-328-5700
Fax: 415-474-7611
Web: N/A
Prices: 🥜

Mon – Fri 11:30am - 2pm & 5pm - 10pm
Sat 5pm -10pm
Closed Sun

While downtown Palo Alto has grown to be sophisticated and pricey, this longtime local favorite has retained its unpretentious atmosphere. Osteria is a place to come for good old-fashioned Italian food: copious plates of house-made pastas, veal saltimbocca, and eggplant parmesan, not to mention calorie-dense but yummy desserts like the creamy tiramisu.

Set on a corner across from city hall, Osteria with its large picture windows provides diners with a good opportunity to take in the downtown street scene. Service is considerate and friendly; you'll feel like a regular after you've been here ten minutes.

If you're coming for dinner, be sure to make reservations—the reasonable prices at this restaurant make it popular with both the university and professional sets.

Parcel 104

Contemporary 🍴🍴🍴

024

2700 Mission College Blvd., Santa Clara
(off Great America Pkwy.)

Phone: 408-970-6104
Fax: 408-970-6190
Web: www.parcel104.com
Prices: $$$

Mon – Fri 11:30am - 2pm & 5:30pm - 9pm
Sat 5:30pm - 9pm
Closed Sun

Parcel 104's connection to the land begins with its name, a generic moniker that refers to the site's original land grant number. Once a pear orchard, this plot is now covered by Silicon Valley corporate buildings, including the Marriott Santa Clara. It's here that you'll find modern-day Parcel 104, a member of Bradley Ogden's Lark Creek Restaurant Group.

In this same spirit of staying close to the land, chef Bart Hosmer fixates on farm-fresh organic items like Coke Farms beets, Cowgirl Creamery organic cheeses, Broken Arrow Ranch venison and wild-caught white prawns in his evening tasting menus. The same sparkling products appear at midday, when the restaurant caters to the hurried business-lunch crowd. Seasonal wine flights round out the list of varietals from regions around the world.

Piazza Italia

025

321 Primrose Rd., Burlingame (near Burlingame Ave.)

Phone:	650-343-4444	Mon – Wed & Sat 8am - 3:15pm
Fax:	N/A	Thu – Fri 8am - 3:15pm & 5pm - 8pm
Web:	N/A	Closed Sun
Prices:	🍸	

At Piazza Italia, owners Mena Curci and Roberta Restani aim to share their version of the *la dolce vita*. In keeping with this goal, service at their casual place is welcoming and pleasant, and imported products from Italy (cured meats, cheeses, olives) are displayed in the tiny dining room.

A good selection of panini and salads are sure to satisfy those midday hunger pangs. Garlic, olive oil and tomato sauce predominate in the handful of hot dishes and in the house specialties, which encompass pasta, gnocchi, and crostino (Italian bread with various toppings). *Specialita del giorno* are spelled out on a board at the entrance. If you're exploring south of the city, stop by for a meal, or get a good start on the day with espresso and homemade biscotti.

Pizza Antica

026

334 Santana Row, Suite 1065, San Jose
(bet. Stevens Creek Blvd. & Tatum Lane)

Phone:	408-557-8373	Sun – Thu 11:30am - 10pm
Fax:	408-557-8738	Fri – Sat 11:30am - 11pm
Web:	www.pizzaantica.com	
Prices:	🍸	

Santana Row, a neighborhood complex of upscale shops, condominiums (and even a hotel), contains a whole host of restaurants, but Pizza Antica is the place to go for a good thin-crust pie. On the menu, pizza is divided into sections called "Ours" and "Yours." The former, as set combinations, run the gamut from tomato sauce, house-made mozzarella and fresh basil to Bartlett pear, sweet garlic and Mt. Tam triple-cream cheese. If you pick from the "Yours" column, you can customize your pie with any combination of 20 tempting toppings.

They don't take reservations, but call ahead to put your name on the waiting list for the bistro-style dining room. Check out Pizza Antica's other location in Mill Valley (*705 Strawberry Village, near Hwy. 101*).

South of San Francisco

The Plumed Horse

French   ✗✗✗

027

14555 Big Basin Way, Saratoga (at 4th St.)

Phone:	408-867-4711	Mon – Sat 5pm -10pm
Fax:	408-867-6919	Closed Sun
Web:	www.plumedhorse.com	
Prices:	$$$	

This local landmark set up shop in a 19th-century stable in the village of Saratoga in 1952, and it's been on track ever since. Klaus Pache and his wife, Yvonne, have owned the Plumed Horse since 1975; their son now holds the reins as general manager. In the comfortable wood-paneled dining room, warmed in winter by a stone fireplace, the tuxedo-clad waitstaff delivers plates of escargots in herbed garlic butter, pan-seared foie gras, seared Ahi tuna and other Cal-French dishes.

With more than 800 labels encompassing California vintages as well as varietals from around the world, the amazing wine list has galloped off with Wine Spectator awards every year for more than 15 years running.

The Crazy Horse Lounge rocks on Friday and Saturday nights with live music and dancing.

Saint Michael's Alley

Contemporary   ✗

028

806 Emerson St., Palo Alto (at Homer Ave.)

Phone:	650-326-2530	Tue – Fri 11:30am - 2pm & 5:30pm - 9:30pm
Fax:	650-326-1436	Sat 10am - 2pm & 5:30pm - 9:30pm
Web:	www.stmikes.com	Sun 10am - 2pm
Prices:	$$	Closed Mon

This café, a Palo Alto fixture since 1959, has seen its share of social change. In the 60s, the management at the time gave then-unknown singers like Joan Baez and Jerry Garcia a chance to entertain here. In its current incarnation, Saint Michael's Alley resides near the university on Emerson Street, where it's been spiffed up with a smart bistro décor, complete with tile floors and vintage chandeliers. It still draws lots of students, who, along with professors and longtime locals, come for kicked-up American cuisine.

If macadamia-crusted mahi mahi, cassoulet with duck confit, and baked gnocchi gratin sound good to you, join the crowd at this neighborhood favorite. The weekend brunch packs 'em in for blueberry pancakes, Belgian waffles and Italian frittatas.

South of San Francisco

Sent Sovi

029

14583 Big Basin Way, Saratoga (at 5th St.)

Phone:	408-867-3110
Fax:	408-705-2016
Web:	www.sentsovi.com
Prices:	$$$

Tue – Sun 5pm - 9:30pm
Closed Mon & January 1-10

In 2003 chef Josiah Slone took over the kitchen at Sent Sovi from founder David Kinch (who now presides over Manresa restaurant in Los Gatos). Kinch's footsteps were hard to fill, but Slone has hit his stride with seasonal preparations based on local ingredients and complemented by a list of wines from the nearby Santa Cruz Mountains and the Santa Clara Valley. Marinated hanger steak with black truffle mashed potatoes and fennel-marinated prawns on baked garlic gnocchi demonstrate a French flair, while "jerk" duck confit harks back to the chef's experience in the Caribbean.

Housed in a quaint little cottage in the picturesque village of Saratoga, the dining room spells cozy with warm copper wainscoting, cafe curtains, and bright flower arrangements enhancing the elegant table settings.

Seven

030

754 The Alameda, San Jose (at Bush St.)

Phone:	408-280-1644
Fax:	408-280-1818
Web:	www.7restaurant.com
Prices:	$$

Mon – Fri 11:30am - 2:30pm & 5pm - 10pm
Sat 5pm - 10pm
Closed Sun

Prepare to have double the gastronomic pleasure at the hands of identical twins Curtis and Russel Valdez, co-executive chefs who opened Seven in 2003. Their menu of contemporary American fare changes daily, but French technique consistently pervades the likes of crispy duck cassoulet, steamed mussels with andouille sausage, and slow-braised lamb shank.

Exposed ductwork, dark colors and an exhibition kitchen mark the industrial-chic design of this Silicon Valley hot spot. Seven stands on its own as a destination restaurant, but its location two blocks from HP Pavilion (the city's special-events venue and home ice to the San Jose Sharks) also makes it a great place to dine before a concert or a game. Or stop by the sleek, high-energy lounge for a cocktail afterwards.

South of San Francisco

71 Saint Peter

031

Mediterranean

71 N. San Pedro St., San Jose (bet. Santa Clara & St. John Sts.)

Phone:	408-971-8523	Mon – Fri 11:30am - 2pm & 5pm - closing
Fax:	408-938-3440	Sat 5pm - closing
Web:	www.71saintpeter.com	Closed Sun
Prices:	$$	

An English translation of its address on San Pedro Square in San Jose's historic core, 71 Saint Peter adds a Mediterranean note to downtown restaurant offerings. It's well located for sightseers, too, since the establishment is a few steps away from Peralto Adobe and Fallon House, two sites that preserve the city's Spanish Colonial past.

The waitstaff aims to please at 71 Saint Peter, which displays its rustic charm in exposed beams, brick walls and terra-cotta tile floors. In the kitchen, chef/owner Luis Rodriguez whips up his version of Mediterranean fare, peppered with California panache (crab cakes with tapenade aioli; dry-spiced seared lamb loin with blackberry marmalade).

Come weeknights for the seasonal prix-fixe tasting menu, a deal at less than $50 per person (with wine).

Sino

032

Chinese

377 Santana Row, Suite 1000, San Jose
(bet. Oline Ave. & Olsen Dr.)

Phone:	408-247-8880	Sun – Tue 11am - 10pm
Fax:	408-247-8881	Wed – Sat 11am - midnight
Web:	www.sinorestaurant.com	
Prices:	$$	

Santana Row is where you'll find this ultra-modern Chinese restaurant, which premiered in 2005. The interior design provides a feast for the eyes, with its fiery red and gold color scheme, Asian artwork and gossamer curtains that close to separate the different dining areas.

Belly up to the curving backlit bar and sample their drink "collections": Aphrodisiac Martinis, the Elements Cocktails, or Good Fortune Margaritas. Then it's on to the main course, which for lunch means a mouthwatering selection of dim sum, from potstickers to taro puffs. At dinner, Indochine hot and sour soup, garlic roasted Dungeness crab, and star anise- and soy-braised lamb shank number among the sophisticated dishes.

When the temperatures heat up, so does the scene on the outdoor terrace.

Spago Palo Alto

Californian ✗✗

265 Lytton Ave., Palo Alto (bet. Bryant & Ramona Sts.)

Phone:	650-833-1000	Mon – Thu 11:30am - 2pm & 5:30pm - 9pm
Fax:	650-325-9586	Fri 11:30am - 2pm & 5:30pm - 10pm
Web:	www.wolfgangpuck.com	Sat 5:30pm - 10pm
Prices:	$$$	Closed Sun

The Palo Alto outpost of Wolfgang Puck's flagship brings Los Angeles flash to this university town. Designed by Adam Tihany, the dining space recasts a historic structure with bold primary colors, marble surfaces, contemporary artwork—including a painting by Robert Rauschenberg—and a display kitchen. In addition to the main room, guests can dine on outdoor patios, in a casual pavilion with a retractable roof, or in a snug cottage warmed by a wood-burning fireplace.

The changing menu mixes California cuisine, including Puck's signature gourmet pizzas, with the chef's favorites from his childhood in Austria (Wiener Schnitzel and spicy beef goulash). As a prelude to your meal, the bread basket is an artful composition of crackers, cheese-spiked breadsticks and crispy flatbread.

Tamarine

Vietnamese ✗✗

546 University Ave., Palo Alto
(bet. Cowper & Webster Sts.)

Phone:	650-325-8500	Mon – Thu 11:30am - 2:30pm & 5pm - 9pm
Fax:	650-325-8504	Fri 11:30am - 2:30pm & 5pm - 10pm
Web:	www.tamarinerestaurant.com	Sat 5pm - 10pm
Prices:	$$	Sun 5pm - 9pm

You'll be treated to cheerful attentive service and refined Asian cuisine in this modern Vietnamese establishment on the edge of downtown. Like the food, the décor here is trendy and elegant without being overbearing; soft colors and dark woods are accented by changing exhibits of works by contemporary Vietnamese artists.

Chef/partner Tammy Huynh plays with the aromatic flavors of Southeast Asia, sparking dishes with tamarind, lemongrass, coconut, and ginger, instead of fiery spices. Small-plate entrées are meant to be paired with a selection of rice, infused with the likes of turmeric, ginger and cinnamon; tomato, garlic and butter; or coconut and vanilla.

Choose a seat at one of the two communal tables if you want to mingle with Silicon Valley techies.

South of San Francisco

231 Ellsworth

035

Contemporary 🍴🍴

231 S. Ellsworth Ave., San Mateo (bet. 2nd & 3rd Aves.)

Phone: 650-347-7231
Fax: 650-347-7329
Web: www.231ellsworth.com
Prices: $$$

Mon – Thu 11:30am - 2pm & 5:30pm - 9:30pm
Fri 11:30am - 2pm & 5:30pm - 10pm
Sat 5:30pm - 10pm
Closed Sun and July 3-5 & Thanksgiving

Special occasions seem tailor-made for this South Bay restaurant, where warm woods and a dark-blue barrel-vaulted ceiling set an elegant background for chef Tim Hilt's refined contemporary cuisine. Hilt blends French technique with the freshest California products in fragrant white bean and fennel soup, and pan-roasted salmon on a bed of creamy cauliflower purée.

The staff is adept at pairing food and wine, of which there's no lack on the 50-page wine list. Remember that cherry-wood day cellar you passed on your way in? Some 800 bottles of wine wait there in a temperature-controlled atmosphere, but there's more where that came from; the main cellar can hold up to 12,000 bottles.

For lunch, the inexpensive Express Lunch menu, with your choice of two or three courses, is the way to go.

The Village Pub

036

Contemporary 🍴🍴

2967 Woodside Rd., Woodside (off Whiskey Hill Rd.)

Phone: 650-851-9888
Fax: 650-851-6827
Web: www.thevillagepub.net
Prices: $$

Mon – Fri 11:30am - 2:30pm & 5pm - 10pm
Sat – Sun 5pm - 10pm

Although "pub" may conjure up images of dark musty rooms with dart boards and bare tables, at the Village Pub a mahogany bar, plush burgundy banquettes and well-spaced white-clothed tables distinguish this tavern from your local watering hole. Another standout: staffers here really know their stuff when it comes to the innovative wine list, which blends vintages from the Old World and the New. For the budget-conscious, a special section cites 40 wines under $40.

Unpretentious and well-prepared dishes coax bright flavors from fresh organic produce, (as in silky Chantenay carrot soup with cardamom crème fraîche), while foraged nettle and mascarpone ravioli shares menu space with house-cured salami and country pâté. Of course, the pub burger and Caesar salad are available any time of day.

South of San Francisco

A WATER THAT BELONGS ON THE WINE LIST.
ACQUA PANNA STILL FROM S.PELLEGRINO.

Wine Country

Vineyards

Wine Country
Napa Valley, Sonoma Valley, Russian River Valley

Picnicking on artisanal cheeses and fresh crusty bread amid acres of gnarled grapevines; sipping wine on a terrace above a hillside of silvery olive trees; touring caves heady with the sweet smell of fermenting grapes: this is northern California's Wine Country. Lying within an hour's drive north and northeast of San Francisco, the hills and vales of Sonoma County and Napa Valley thrive on the abundant sunshine and fertile soil that produce grapes for some of North America's finest wines.

Fruit of the Vine – Cuttings of Criollas grapevines traveled north with Franciscan padres from the Baja Peninsula during the late 17th century. Wines made from these "mission" grapes were used primarily for trade and for sacramental purposes. In the early 1830s, a French immigrant propitiously named Jean-Louis Vignes (*vigne* is French for "vine") established a large vineyard near Los Angeles using cuttings of European grapevines *(Vitis vinifera)*, and by the mid-19th century, winemaking had become one of southern California's principal industries.

In 1857 Hungarian immigrant Agoston Haraszthy purchased a 400-acre estate in Sonoma County, named it Buena Vista, and successfully cultivated Tokay vine cuttings imported from his homeland. In 1861, bolstered by promises of state funding, Haraszthy went to Europe to gather *vinifera* cuttings to plant in California soil. Upon his return, however, the state legislature reneged on their commitment. Undeterred, Haraszthy persisted in distributing some 100,000 cuttings and testing varieties in different soil types. Successful application of his discoveries created a boom in the local wine industry in the late 19th century.

The Tide Turns – As the 1800s drew to a close, northern California grapevines fell prey to phylloxera, a root louse that attacks susceptible *vinifera* plants. Entire vineyards were decimated. Eventually researchers discovered they could combat phylloxera by replanting vineyards with disease-resistant wild grape rootstocks from the midwestern U.S., onto which *vinifera* cuttings could be grafted. The wine industry had achieved a modicum of recovery by the early 20th century, only to be faced with the 18th Amendment to the Constitution, prohibiting the manufacture, sale, importation and transportation of intoxicating liquors in the U.S.

California's winemaking industry remained at a near-standstill until 1933, when Prohibition was repealed. The Great Depression slowed the reclamation of vineyards, and it wasn't until the early 1970s that California's wine industry was fully re-established. In 1976 California wines took top honors in a blind taste testing by French judges in Paris. These results helped open up a new world of respectability for California vineyards.

Coming of Age – As Napa and Sonoma wines have established their reputations, the importance of individual growing regions has increased. Many sub-regions have sought and acquired Federal regulation of their place names as American Viticultural Areas, or AVAs, in order to set the boundaries of wine-growing areas that are distinctive for their soil, microclimate and wine styles. Although this system is subject to debate, there is no doubt that an AVA such as Russian River Valley, Carneros or Spring Mountain can be very meaningful. The precise location of a vineyard relative to the Pacific Ocean or the San Pablo Bay, the elevation and slope of a vineyard, the soil type and moisture content, and even the proximity to a mountain gap can make essential differences.

Peju Province Winery, Napa Valley

Together, Sonoma and Napa have almost 30 registered appellations, which vary in size and sometimes overlap. Specific place names are becoming increasingly important as growers learn what to plant where and how to care for vines in each unique circumstance. The fact that more and more wines go to market with a specific AVA flies in the face of the worldwide trend to ever larger and less specific "branded" wines. Individual wineries and associations are working to promote the individuality of North Coast appellations and to preserve their integrity and viability as sustainable agriculture.

Destination Wine Country – In recent decades, the Napa and Sonoma valleys have experienced tremendous development. Besides significant increases in vineyard acreage, the late 20th century witnessed an explosion of small-scale operations. Meanwhile, the Russian River Valley remains less developed, retaining its rural feel with country roads winding past picturesque wineries, rolling vineyards, and stands of redwood trees.

With easy access to world-class wines, and organic produce and artisanal cheeses from local farms, residents of northern California's Wine Country enjoy an enviable quality of life. Happily for visitors, those same products supply the area's burgeoning number of restaurants, creating a culture of gourmet dining that stretches from the city of Napa north to Healdsburg and beyond.

Note that if you elect to bring your own wine, most restaurants charge a corkage fee (which can vary from $10 to $25 per bottle). Many restaurants waive this fee on one particular day, usually a weekday.

Which Food?	Which Wine?	Some Examples
Shellfish	Semi-dry White	Early harvest Riesling, Chenin Blanc, early harvest Gewürztraminer, Viognier
	Dry White	Lighter Chardonnay (less oak), Pinot Blanc, Sauvignon Blanc, dry Riesling, dry Chenin Blanc
	Sparkling Wine	Brut, Extra Dry, Brut Rosé
	Dry Rosé	Pinot Noir, Syrah, Cabernet
Fish	Dry White	Chardonnay (oaky or not) Sauvignon Blanc, dry Riesling, dry Chenin Blanc, Pinot Blanc
	Sparkling Wine	Brut, Blanc de Blancs, Brut Rosé
	Light Red	Pinot Noir, Pinot Meunier, light-bodied Zinfandel
	Dry Rosé	Pinot Noir, Syrah, Cabernet
Cured Meats/ Picnic Fare	Semi-dry White	Early harvest Riesling or early harvest Gewürztraminer
	Dry White	Chardonnay (less oak), Sauvignon Blanc, dry Riesling
	Sparkling Wine	Brut, Blanc de Blancs, Brut Rosé
	Light Red	Gamay, Pinot Noir, Zinfandel, Sangiovese
	Young Heavy Red	Syrah, Cabernet Sauvignon, Zinfandel, Cabernet Franc, Merlot
	Rosé	Any light Rosé
Red Meat	Dry Rosé	Pinot Noir, Cabernet, Syrah, Blends
	Light Red	Pinot Noir, Zinfandel, Gamay, Pinot Meunier
	Young Heavy Red	Cabernet Sauvignon, Cabernet Franc, Syrah, Grenache, Petite Sirah, Merlot, Blends, Pinot Noir, Cabernet Sauvignon
	Mature Red	Merlot, Syrah, Zinfandel, Meritage, Blends
Fowl	Semi-dry White	Early harvest Riesling, Chenin Blanc, Viognier
	Dry White	Sauvignon Blanc, Chardonnay, Pinot Blanc, dry Riesling
	Sparkling Wine	Extra Dry, Brut, Brut Rosé
	Rosé	Any light Rosé
	Light Red	Pinot Noir, Zinfandel, Blends, Gamay
	Mature Red	Pinot Noir, Cabernet Sauvignon, Merlot, Syrah, Zinfandel, Meritage, Blends
Cheese	Semi-dry White	Riesling, Gewürztraminer, Chenin Blanc
	Dry White	Sauvignon Blanc, Chardonnay, Pinot Blanc, dry Riesling
	Sparkling Wine	Extra Dry, Brut
	Rosé	Pinot Noir, Cabernet, Grenache
	Light Red	Pinot Noir, Zinfandel, Blends, Gamay
	Young Heavy Red	Cabernet Sauvignon, Cabernet Franc, Syrah, Grenache, Petite Sirah, Merlot, Blends
Dessert	Sweet White	Any late harvest White
	Semi-dry White	Riesling, Gewürztraminer, Chenin Blanc, Muscat
	Sparkling Wine	Extra Dry, Brut, Rosé, Rouge
	Dessert Reds	Late harvest Zinfandel, Port

Vintage	2004	2003	2002	2001	2000	1999	1998	1997	1996	1995	1994
Chardonnay **Carneros**											
Chardonnay **Russian River**											
Chardonnay **Napa Valley**											
Sauvignon Blanc **Napa Valley**											
Sauvignon Blanc **Sonoma County**											
Pinot Noir **Carneros**											
Pinot Noir **Russian River**											
Merlot **Napa Valley**											
Merlot **Sonoma County**											
Cabernet Sauvignon **Napa Valley**											
Cabernet Sauvignon **Southern Sonoma**											
Cabernet Sauvignon **Northern Sonoma**											
Zinfandel **Napa Valley**											
Zinfandel **Southern Sonoma**											
Zinfandel **Northern Sonoma**											

= Outstanding   = Above Average   = Average

Napa Valley

©Brent Miller/winecountry.com

Napa Valley

Cradled between two elongated mountain ranges, the Mayacamas on the west and the Vaca on the east, Napa Valley extends about 35 miles in a northerly direction from San Pablo Bay to Mount St. Helena. The valley is home to some of California's most prestigious wineries, many of which cluster thickly along the main artery of **Route 29**. This road runs straight up the western side of the mountains, passing through the famous little wine towns of Napa, Yountville, Oakville, Rutherford, St. Helena and Calistoga. Other wineries dot the tranquil **Silverado Trail**, which hugs the foothills of the eastern range and gives a distinctly more pastoral view of this rural county. Throughout the valley you'll spot mountains, knolls, canyons, dry creek beds and broad stretches of valley floor, all of which afford varying microclimates and soil types for growing wine.

San Pablo Bay has a considerable moderating effect on temperatures, while the influence of the Pacific Ocean (40 miles west) is lessened by the mountains. Thus as you head north up Napa Valley, you tend to encounter greater extremes; summer highs are higher and winter and spring lows are lower as the influence of the bay diminishes with distance. The Napa River, a trickle in most seasons, wanders the length of the valley floor, culminating in the historic shipping center of **Napa**—the largest and southernmost population center in the valley.

Napa Valley first flourished in the wine trade in the late 1800s. Reclaimed stone wineries and Victorian houses dot the landscape, reminding the traveler that there were over 140 wineries here prior to 1890. Today, you can appreciate the area's history while wondering at the explosion of the last 40 years.

Oakville Winery

©Brent Miller/winecountry.com

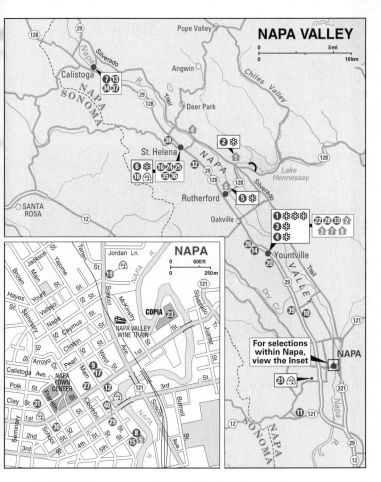

Napa Valley boasts more than 250 wineries today, up from a post-Prohibition low of perhaps a dozen. Along with the boom in wine production has come a special kind of food-and-wine tourism. Tasting rooms, tours and haute cuisine abound.

Napa's success with premium wine (the valley hardly deals in any other kind) has fostered a special pride of place. American Viticultural Areas (AVAs) regulate the boundaries for sub-regions such as Carneros, Stags Leap, Rutherford and Spring Mountain. For now, there are 14 in all. As these sub-regions within the county are becoming better understood, more wineries are giving labeling prominence to specific sources of grapes, even down to the level of a specific vineyard within an AVA. Certain sections are gaining reputations for specific grape types and even wine styles, and sophisticated consumers are beginning to look for the provenance of a certain vineyard or region rather than simply a grape type.

The French Laundry ✿✿✿

001

Contemporary ✗✗✗✗

6640 Washington St., Yountville (at Creek St.)

Phone:	707-944-2380	Mon – Thu 5:30pm - 9pm
Fax:	N/A	Fri – Sun 11am - 1pm & 5:30pm - 9pm
Web:	www.frenchlaundry.com	Closed January 1 - 14
Prices:	$$$$	

French Laundry/Deborah Jones

Lodged in a century-old stone laundry, Thomas Keller's famed restaurant opened in 1994 and remains one of the country's most sought-after reservations. It requires patience to book a table here—start two months ahead and steel yourself for long waits on the phone—but once you do, you'll have a table for the evening. And an epic evening it promises to be.

Keller's exquisite dishes amount to sheer poetry on the plate. Beginning with a series of amuse-bouches, a parade of tiny, artful courses appear as succinct odes to the chef's expertise. Organic canaroli risotto marries regally with Castelmagno cheese and shavings of perfumed black truffles, while a meltingly tender ribeye of nature-fed veal is presented beside a small cake of arrowleaf spinach crowned with slivers of fried Jambugo ham and a rich Périgueux sauce. To complement such lyric cuisine, the superb wine list recites some of the finest labels from France and the U.S.

The sophisticated waitstaff will explain the three tasting menus, which change nightly and all come at the same price. So, although a dinner at French Laundry may set you back a pretty penny, it will, like a well-written poem, long resonate in your memory.

Appetizers

Oysters and Pearls: Sabayon of Pearl Tapioca with Beau Soleil Oysters and Russian Sevruga Caviar

White Truffle Egg Custard with a Ragoût of Black Périgord Truffles

Santa Barbara Sea Urchin "Tongues" with Apple Farm Orchard Green-Apple Granité

Entrées

Beets and Leeks: Maine Lobster Tail, *Cuite Sous Vide au Beurre Doux* with King Richard Leeks, *Pommes Maxim's* and Red Beet Essence

Turbotin Rôti sur l'Arête, with Glazed Sunchokes, Toasted Almonds, Jacobsen's Farm Vine-Ripe Tomato Marmalade and Niçoise-Olive Emulsion

Snake River Farm *Calotte de Bœuf Grillée* with Yukon Gold Potato-Black Truffle Millefeuille, French Laundry Garden Onions, Crispy Bone Marrow and Sauce Périgourdine

Desserts

Coffee and Doughnuts: Cinnamon-Sugared Doughnuts with Cappuccino Semifreddo

Soufflé aux Noyaux d'Abricots with Marshall Farm Wildflower-Honey Ice Cream

Warm Bittersweet Chocolate Tart

Auberge du Soleil ✿

002

Californian ✕✕✕

180 Rutherford Hill Rd., Rutherford
(off the Silverado Trail)

Phone: 707-963-1211   Open daily 11:30am - 2:30pm & 6pm - 9:30pm
Fax: 707-963-8764
Web: www.aubergedusoleil.com
Prices: $$$$

Auberge du Soleil

The year 1981 was a good one for Napa Valley. That was the year that San Francisco restaurateur Claude Rouas opened Auberge du Soleil restaurant (it pre-dated the inn—*see Wine Country hotel listings*—by four years).

Perched above the Silverado Trail about halfway down the valley, Auberge is an idyllic place to take a midday break between winery visits. At lunch, there's a short à la carte menu; at dinner two prix-fixe meals are featured, a four- and a six-course. The latter is a tasting proposed nightly by executive chef Robert Curry, a Los Angeles native, who on any given night might pair crispy skate wing with apples, fennel and glazed pork belly; pan-seared foie gras with peach marmalade; or roasted lamb loin with ratatouille and potato gnocchi. The superb wine list cites some 1,300 selections, including 35 wines by the glass; the selection may span the globe, but its heart rests in the Napa Valley.

Although the recently refurbished dining room envelopes guests in rich earth tones and abstract art, the most sought-after tables are outside on the terrace. Here, shaded by a vine-covered arbor, you can sip a glass of the valley's finest and watch the sun sink below the hills.

Appetizers

Seared Scallops, Veal Sweetbreads, Curried Sunchokes, Tarragon

Pan-seared Foie Gras, Poached Rhubarb, Baby Fennel, Red-Wine Vanilla Jus

Poached Lobster, Avocado, Brioche, Orange Vanilla Vinaigrette

Entrées

Herb-crusted Rabbit, Wild Mushroom Millefeuille, Thyme Jus

John Dory, White Asparagus Purée, Mizuna, Glazed Pork Belly

Roasted Lamb, Potato Gnocchi, Niçoise Olives, Green-Garlic Red-Wine Jus

Desserts

Crisp Filo-wrapped Chocolate Dumplings, Tarragon Ice Cream, Arbequina Olive Oil

Vanilla-scented Chiboust, Trailside Strawberries, Lemon Chiffon

Fromage Blanc Cheesecake, Charbay Nostalgie, Sweet and Sour Toy Box Carrots, Walnut Streusel

Bistro Jeanty ✿

6510 Washington St., Yountville (at Mulberry St.)

Phone:	707-944-0103	Open daily 11:30am - 10:30pm
Fax:	707-944-0370	
Web:	www.bistrojeanty.com	
Prices:	$$	

Bistro Jeanty

Look for the cheery red-and-white-striped awnings to point you to Bistro Jeanty on tiny Yountville's main street. You can feel comfortable wearing jeans to dinner in this casual bistro, the brainchild of Philippe Jeanty (of Jeanty at Jack's in San Francisco). Chef/owner Jeanty was born in the Champagne region of France, where his father worked for Moët & Chandon. In 1977, Jeanty came to Napa Valley to open Chandon Restaurant at the winery across the highway. Restless for something new, he opened Bistro Jeanty on Washington Street in 1998.

The bar is the focal point of the front room, where neighbors and tourists mingle over a glass of wine, eau de vie, or single-malt scotch. Sunny yellow walls line the back room, decorated with lace cafe curtains, rustic copper pots, and French advertising posters from the 1950s.

As for the food, authentic regional French fare here is crafted from top-notch products. House specialties such as cassoulet, house-smoked trout, mussels in red wine, daube de boeuf, and tarte citron will have your taste buds clamoring for more.

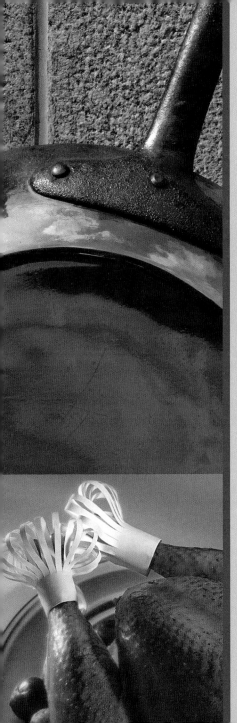

Appetizers

Crème de Tomate en Croûte (tomato soup in puff pastry)

Escargots with Garlic-Pastis Butter

Croûtons de Foie Blond, (duck foie gras pâté with port-poached pear)

Entrées

Moules au Vin Rouge (mussels steamed in red wine)

Cassoulet (baked beans with sausage and duck confit)

Daube de Bœuf (beef stew with mashed potatoes, peas and carrots)

Desserts

Mousse au Chocolat Brûlée (chocolate mousse crème brûlée)

Crêpe Suzette (warm crèpe with orange butter)

Tarte Tatin (caramelized apple tart with crème fraîche)

FRENCH

Bouchon ❀

004

6534 Washington St., Yountville (at Yount St.)

Phone:	707-944-8037	Open daily 11:30am - 2:30pm & 5:30pm - 10:45pm
Fax:	N/A	
Web:	www.bouchonbistro.com	
Prices:	$$$	

French Laundry/Deborah Jones

Set within a late-19th-century stagecoach stop on Yountville's main street, Thomas Keller's Bouchon captures the spirit of the distinctive style of cafe (called a *bouchon*) in Lyon for which it's named. The bright burgundy façade and awning catch your eye, while, inside, designer Adam Tihany has re-created a traditional French bouchon, complete with a zinc bar, mosaic floor, red velvet banquettes and a hand-painted mural.

If you've never been to France, Bouchon is as close as you can get to an authentic bistro on this side of the ocean. Under executive chef Jeffrey Cerciello's watchful eye, perfectly prepared boudin noir is served with sautéed apples and creamy mashed potatoes tinged with flavor from the boudin's jus; salmon rillettes appeal to the eye and the palate as a vivid mélange of fresh and smoked salmon that melt on your tongue.

If you're staying in town, let the tantalizing aromas of fresh-baked breads and pastries guide you to Bouchon Bakery (next to Bouchon) for a cup of coffee and a memorable breakfast. Although it's difficult to choose between buttery scones, French *macarons*, and the signature chocolate bouchons, when in doubt, go for the wonderfully flaky chocolate-almond croissants.

Wine Country Napa Valley

Appetizers

Rillettes aux Deux Saumons (fresh and smoked salmon rillettes with toasted croutons)

Beignets de Brandade de Morue (cod brandade with tomato confit and fried sage)

Pâté de Campagne (country-style pâté with watercress, cornichons and radishes)

Entrées

Poulet Rôti (roasted chicken with a ragoût of fingerling potatoes and garden arugula)

Gigot d'Agneau (roasted leg of lamb with coco beans, piquillo peppers and garden sorrel in a thyme jus)

Steak Frites (a pan-seared Prime flatiron served with maître d'hôtel butter and French fries)

Desserts

Tarte au Citron (lemon tart)

Profiteroles with Vanilla Ice Cream and Chocolate Sauce

Pot de Crème (infused custard)

FRENCH

La Toque ✿

005

C o n t e m p o r a r y   F r e n c h ✕✕✕

1140 Rutherford Rd., Rutherford (east of Hwy. 29)

Phone:	707-963-9770	Wed – Sun 5:30pm - 9:30pm
Fax:	707-963-9072	Closed Mon & Tue
Web:	www.latoque.com	
Prices:	$$$$	

La Toque

Located in, but operated independently of, the Rancho Caymus Inn *(see Wine Country hotel listings)*, La Toque turns dinner into an evening-long event. It all starts with a warm welcome from the maitre d', and the knowledgeable servers whose passion for this place beams from their faces. In the softly lit French-country atmosphere, Bernadaud china, Riedel and Spiegelau crystal, and sparkling white linens set the stage for a meal to remember.

Enter chef Ken Frank, who stars in this culinary production. Each week he designs a different five-act prix-fixe tasting. Sublime flavors and textures, in such courses as pan-roasted boneless quail with potato-chorizo risotto, American wagyu beef with cheddar tapioca and cabernet foie gras sauce, and black cod atop cucumber vermicelli with fragrant Kaffir lime broth, illustrate Frank's talent and French training. As the pièce de résistance, wine pairings are recommended with each course, and the sommelier will present each bottle for reference.

Dishes are all exquisitely seasoned, down to the sprinkling of fleur de sel on the chocolate mousse dome. Such attention to detail is what raises La Toque a notch above many other Napa Valley restaurants.

Appetizers

Barely Scrambled Farmhouse Egg with Fresh Black Truffle

Pickled Japanese Vegetable Salad with Spanish Bluefin Tuna

Seared Artisan Foie Gras with "Fresh" Corn Polenta and Chanterelles

Entrées

North Sea Turbot as a "T-Bone" with Lobster Crushed Potatoes and Lobster Red-Wine Sauce

American Wagyu Beef Served Rare with Irish Cheddar Tapioca and Cabernet Foie Gras Sauce

Ballotine of Pennsylvania Guinea Hen with Morels

Dessert

Crêpes with Sautéed Napa Valley Strawberries and Balsamic Crème Fraîche Sherbet

Roasted-Pineapple Fritter with Hot Buttered-Rum Sauce

Chocolate Concorde Cake

Terra ✿

006

1345 Railroad Ave., St. Helena (bet. Adams & Hunt Sts.)

Phone:	707-963-8931
Fax:	707-963-0818
Web:	www.terrarestaurant.com
Prices:	$$$

Wed – Mon 6pm - 10pm
Closed Tue & January 1 - 14

Terra/Faith Echtemeyer

Since Terra posts only the most discreet of signs outside, you'll need to look for the rustic 1884 fieldstone foundry with its arched windows and doors, located off Main Street in St. Helena. A romantic air hits you once you step inside, where exposed rough-hewn wood beams and stone walls, low lighting and soft music strike an intimate note.

Chef Hiro Sone met his wife, pastry chef Lissa Doumani, at Spago in Los Angeles, where they both worked in the early 1980s. The couple launched Terra, their first opus together, in 1988. As maestro in the kitchen, Sone orchestrates a menu that reflects his Japanese heritage, his world travels and his passion for food. Spaghettini with a stew of tripe, tomatoes, butter beans and basil, or the signature broiled sake-marinated Alaskan black cod with shrimp dumplings in shiso sauce epitomize the exquisite harmonies of flavors and premium products that sets this chef apart.

Such a lovely symphony wouldn't be complete without a finale, and under Lissa Doumani's direction, chocolate may express itself in a warm truffle cake or a pudding parfait, while just-picked strawberries sing in a sauce of Cabernet Sauvignon sparked with black pepper.

Appetizers

Radicchio Salad with Parmesan Balsamico Vinaigrette

Capellini with Home-smoked Salmon, Sterling Caviar and Lemon-Caper Vinaigrette

Fried Miyagi Oysters on Pork Belly "Kakuni" in Black-Vinegar Sauce

Entrées

Broiled Alaskan Black Cod and Shrimp Dumplings in Shiso Broth

Medallions of Lamb with Fried Artichokes and Anchovy Black-Olive Sauce

Grilled Squab on Sweet Corn and local Cheddar Cheese Bread Pudding with Foie Gras Sauce

Dessert

Orange Risotto in Ginger Snap with Passion Fruit Sauce

Sautéed Strawberries in Black Pepper-Cabernet Sauvignon Sauce with Vanilla-Bean Ice Cream

Chocolate Mousseline on a Pecan Sablé with Coffee Granité

CONTEMPORARY

All Seasons Cafe

Californian ✗✗

1400 Lincoln Ave., Calistoga (at Washington St.)

Phone:	707-942-9111
Fax:	707-942-9420
Web:	N/A
Prices:	$$

Tue – Thu 6pm - 9pm
Fri – Sun noon - 2:30pm & 6pm - 9pm
Closed Mon

This Calistoga bistro fills a sunny room with small tables, hand-painted transom windows and colorful artwork from a local gallery. An eclectic collection of wine auction paddles decorates the wall behind the long bar, a reference to the wine shop in back of the cafe.

At lunch the seasonal menu features a good selection of salads and sandwiches for tourists looking to take a lunch break. Dinner brings a more sophisticated and adventurous list of entrées such as pan-roasted Alaskan halibut with sweet pea flan, pea shoots and snow pea confetti, or smoked Liberty duck breast with a Pinot-cherry sauce.

Weekly wine tastings highlight some of the unique Californian, French and Italian vintages available for sale in the little wine shop (open Thursday to Sunday from 3pm to 10pm).

Angèle

008

French ✗✗

540 Main St., Napa (at 5th St.)

Phone:	707-252-8115
Fax:	707-252-8239
Web:	www.angelerestaurant.com
Prices:	$$

Open daily 11:30am - 10pm

Napa Valley's commercial hub is finally coming of age in terms of its restaurants, thanks to places like Angèle. Located in the restored 1893 Napa Mill complex, Angèle sits at the end of the Hatt Building, overlooking the Napa River. Exposed wood beams of the vaulted ceiling recall the building's erstwhile use as a boathouse for the mill.

Refined French food prepared from market-fresh ingredients keeps diners coming back for more. Pot au feu, rillettes de canard, croque monsieur, steak Bordelaise, and coquilles St. Jacques are just a taste of what you'll find on the menu. Local winemakers enjoy this casual, family-friendly restaurant, with its bistro-style furnishings and impeccable white tablecloths. At lunchtime, the wine bar vies with the little waterfront terrace as the place to be.

Wine Country Napa Valley

Annalien

Vietnamese ✗

009

1142 Main St., Napa (bet. 1st & Pearl Sts.)

Phone:	707-224-8319	Tue – Sat 11:30am - 2:30pm & 5pm - 9pm
Fax:	707-224-5708	Closed Sun & Mon
Web:	N/A	
Prices:	$$	

Vietnamese cuisine is hard to come by in the Napa Valley, and Napa residents are glad to finally have a good Asian restaurant in their midst. This recent addition to Napa's downtown restaurant scene sits right on Main Street, near the Napa Opera House. Inside, two large recessed skylights flood the room with natural light, while floor lamps, shaded sconces and whimsical twinkling strands light the night.

Service is friendly and knowledgeable, and the food is prepared in the best Vietnamese tradition. Dalat spicy beef salad and Hue sea bass (laid over a bed of cellophane noodles, wrapped in a banana leaf and steamed) typify the dishes here. Annalien provides locals with a nice alternative to Wine Country fare; you'll have to travel far to find better Vietnamese food in the valley.

Bistro Don Giovanni

Italian ✗✗

010

4110 Howard Lane, Napa (bet. Oak Knoll & Salvador Aves.)

Phone:	707-224-3300	Sun – Thu 11:30am - 10pm
Fax:	707-224-3395	Fri – Sat 11:30am - 11pm
Web:	www.bistrodongiovanni.com	
Prices:	$$	

All the trappings of Tuscany envelope you at this rustic restaurant, located on Highway 29, about three miles north of downtown Napa. Reserve a seat on the spacious outdoor terrace, surrounded by vineyards and olive trees, and you'll understand why this place is such a favorite among local vintners.

Decorated with copper pots, fresh flowers and a wood-burning fireplace, the dining room boasts its own Mediterranean character. Here, the culinary traditions of Liguria inspires a daily changing roster of antipasti, pizza, pasta, risotto and wood-oven-roasted meats and fish (think risotto with meltingly soft Cabernet-braised short ribs, or roasted Napa Valley lamb with Tuscan farro, artichokes and gremolata).

Expect amiable and attentive service—and don't forget to make reservations.

Wine Country Napa Valley

Wine Country - **261**

Boon Fly Café

Californian

011

4048 Sonoma Hwy., Napa (at Los Carneros Ave.)

Phone: 707-299-4870
Fax: 707-299-4969
Web: www.thecarnerosinn.com
Prices: $$

Open daily 7am - 10pm

Tucked away amid 27 acres of grapevines and apple orchards off the Old Sonoma Highway, the Boon Fly Café is part of the PlumpJack group's Carneros Inn. The more casual of the inn's two restaurants, this roadhouse-style cafe dishes up three squares a day.

Stop by for breakfast, which could be as simple as a cup of coffee and a couple of the cafe's signature homemade donuts, or as elaborate as Boon Fly Benedict with Hobbs ham and jalapeno hollandaise. For lunch, sandwiches and flatbreads (the house version of pizza) satisfy locals as well as inn guests. The dinner menu adds a couple of pasta dishes plus a handful of hearty entrées (grilled Black Angus ribeye, pan-roasted chicken breast).

If you have to wait for a table, stake out one of the swings or rocking chairs on the front porch.

Bounty Hunter

American

012

975 First St., Napa (at Main St.)

Phone: 707-226-3976
Fax: 707-257-2202
Web: www.bountyhunterwine.com
Prices: $$

Sun – Thu 11am - 10pm
Fri – Sat 11am - 1am

Worn wooden floors, exposed brick walls and pressed-copper ceilings suggest the old age (1888) of this former grocery store. In its present incarnation, Bounty Hunter and its knowledgeable blue-jean-clad wine professionals, headed by owner Mark Pope, take pride in supplying rare wines and provisions.

Although wine forms the raison d'être of this place, you can also get some good down-home food here. Pull up a saddle stool and dig into American favorites like house-smoked ribs, pulled-pork sandwiches, and the fantastic beer can chicken (local Rocky Jr. chicken rubbed with Cajun spices and cooked with Tecate beer and lime). As for wines, 40 are available by the glass (in 2- or 5-ounce pours), and the voluminous wine list cites 400 hard-to-find selections by the bottle.

Brannan's Grill

1374 Lincoln Ave., Calistoga (at Washington St.)

Phone: 707-942-2233   Open daily 11:30am - 9:15pm
Fax: 707-942-2299
Web: www.brannansgrill.com
Prices: $$

If you're shopping or wine-tasting in the Calistoga area, Brannan's makes a great place to stop for lunch or dinner. Large screened windows let in the mountain breezes during the summer months, while a blazing fire in the stone fireplace warms the lodge-like dining room in winter.

For lunch, big salads, sandwiches and a few main plates satisfy a mixed clientele of locals and tourists, while dinner adds grilled meats and fish (thick-cut pork Porterhouse, Harris Ranch ribeye), as well as specialties like caramelized sweet-potato gnocchi and braised rabbit Bolognese. A generous wine list plus a selection of locally produced micro-brews are on hand to quench any thirst, and friendly servers are as happy to answer menu questions as they are to provide visitors with information about the area.

Brix

7377 St. Helena Hwy., Yountville (at Washington St.)

Phone: 707-944-2749   Open daily 11am - 10pm
Fax: 707-944-8320
Web: www.brix.com
Prices: $$$

In winemaking, the term "brix" refers to the measure used to estimate the amount of sugar in a given volume of wine (the measure honors its 19th-century inventor, German chemist Aldolf Brix). It makes a cute name for this restaurant, which sits on the grounds of its own vineyard just north of Yountville.

The pergola-covered patio lures diners with its views of the surrounding mountains, groves and gardens. When it's cold out, the stone fireplace warms guests in the dining room, where the same views are visible through the picture windows. Many of the entrées are grilled or roasted in the remodeled kitchen's wood-burning oven; fresh herbs are plucked from the on-site garden.

Before you leave, browse the wine shop at the entrance for linens, ceramics, glassware and other Wine Country gifts.

Wine Country Napa Valley

Celadon

015

500 Main St., Napa (at 5th St.)

Phone:	707-254-9690	Mon – Fri 11:30am - 2:30pm & 5pm - 9pm
Fax:	707-254-9692	Sat 5pm - 10pm
Web:	www.celadonnapa.com	Sun 5pm - 9pm
Prices:	$$	Closed January 9 - 14

Around the corner from the Napa River Inn, Celadon occupies part of the same historic mill complex by the river. Inside, the walls are bathed in—what else?—celadon green, and hung with vintage French posters. Outside, the brick courtyard with its vaulted roof is the place to sit in warm weather; when it's chilly out, guests can warm themselves by the raised brick fireplace. Tables nestle close together, encouraging friendly banter and promoting a neighborhood-restaurant feel.

The changing menu of "global comfort food" comprises small plates, green plates (salads), and big plates (generous portions). Products, from salad greens to sea scallops, are impeccably selected by chef/owner Greg Cole. A popular local gathering place, the bar offers an interesting list of specialty cocktails.

Cindy's Backstreet Kitchen

016

1327 Railroad Ave., St. Helena (bet. Adams & Hunt Sts.)

Phone:	707-963-1200	Sun – Thu 11:30am - 9pm
Fax:	707-963-1207	Fri – Sat 11:30am - 10pm
Web:	www.cindysbackstreetkitchen.com	
Prices:	$$	

Cindy Pawlcyn has put a lot of herself in this little charmer. Located one block off Main Street in the center of St. Helena, Cindy's Backstreet Kitchen occupies a pretty 1829 white clapboard house, brightened by flower-filled window boxes outside, and an airy, tasteful décor inside.

In this relaxed ambience chef Cindy (owner of longtime Napa favorite Mustards Grill) dishes up seasonal home-style American cuisine, ranging from meatloaf with horseradish barbecue sauce to grilled chicken BLT. Modern makeovers like mushroom tamales with Yucatecan salsa, and rabbit tostada are thrown in for good measure. You'll want to be sure to leave room for dessert here; the warm pineapple upside-down cake with homemade vanilla ice cream, rum-caramel and pecans is a must.

Cole's Chop House

017

Steakhouse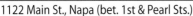

1122 Main St., Napa (bet. 1st & Pearl Sts.)

Phone:	707-224-6328	Sun – Thu 5pm - 9pm
Fax:	707-254-9692	Fri – Sat 5pm - 10pm
Web:	www.coleschophouse.com	
Prices:	$$$$	

Sibling of Celadon, this downtown Napa steakhouse, opened in spring of 2000, is chef Greg Cole's second venture (Celadon was his first). You can look forward to charming, efficient service, USDA Prime dry-aged steaks, and wonderful wine in the handsome bi-level dining space, with its Honduran mahogany bar and original (1886) stone walls. Quality is high and so are the prices of Midwestern corn-fed beef, Iowa pork, Wisconsin veal and New Zealand lamb at Cole's. As in most chop houses, sides and sauces will run you extra.

What better to pair with your steak than a full-bodied Cabernet Sauvignon? Cole's award-winning wine list hones in on Napa Cabernets from each of the valley's subappellations, carefully explaining the distinguishing features of each.

Cook St. Helena 😊

018

Italian ✗

1310 Main St., St. Helena (at Hunt Ave.)

Phone:	707-963-7088	Tue – Sat 11:30am - 10pm
Fax:	N/A	Closed Sun & Mon and January 15 - 30
Web:	N/A	
Prices:	$$	

Jude Wilmoth took over the Green Valley Café when it closed in 2004, reopening as Cook. He completely renovated the matchbox-size restaurant with a contemporary décor highlighted by dark wood, modern paintings, and a marble-topped bar.

Read the blackboard for selections of wines by the glass before perusing the menu and its short list of dishes made from farm-fresh products, including locally crafted mozzarella and prosciutto. Choose your entrée among braised meats, grilled fish, and pastas such as farfalle Bolognaise, in a hearty tomato sauce with meatballs and aged parmesan.

Along with his young staff, Wilmoth provides casual, friendly service in the crowded dining room. This is the ideal place to schmooze with locals and visitors, both of whom are seduced by this alluring bistro.

Cuvée

019

1650 Soscol Ave., Napa (at River Terrace Dr.)

Phone:	707-224-2330
Fax:	707-265-0969
Web:	www.cuveenapa.com
Prices:	$$

Sun – Wed 11:30am - 9:30pm
Thu 11:30am - 10pm
Fri – Sat 11:30am - midnight
Closed major holidays

Opened in May 2006, Cuvée is located adjacent to The River Terrace Inn with (despite its name) no wineries in sight. The elegant restaurant fills the space formerly occupied by Restaurant Budo with deep red hues and warm woods.

The classy bar/lounge includes seating for those wishing to dine in this area, as well as comfy leather couches for patrons who desire a cocktail before dinner. A unique concept normally reserved for wineries allows Cuvée's customers to sample wines poured straight from the barrel.

Modernized comfort food shines here in harmonious preparations like Ahi tuna tartare with tangy Asian cabbage slaw, and potato-wrapped salmon served with herbed orzo in a light citrus-butter sauce. On a warm day, the secluded tree-lined courtyard makes the perfect place for lunch.

Domaine Chandon

020

1 California Dr., Yountville (off Hwy. 29)

Phone:	707-204-7529
Fax:	707-944-1123
Web:	www.chandon.com
Prices:	$$$$

Thu – Mon 11:30am - 2:30pm & 6pm - 9:30pm
Closed Tue & Wed

Domaine Chandon is the ultimate Wine Country experience. As you walk up to the winery past a landscape dotted with ponds and contemporary sculptures, you'll know you're in for a treat.

Founded in Yountville in 1977 by the famed French champagne house Moët & Chandon, Domaine Chandon stands out both for its sparkling wines and for its restaurant. Set off the tasting room, the restaurant is wrapped in serene neutral colors brightened by pieces of contemporary artwork under a wood-lined, barrel-vaulted ceiling—a visual reference to the oak barrels in which wine is aged. Here, chef Chris Manning improvises a vibrant cuisine designed to pair perfectly with the house wines.

On a warm, sunny day, take a loved one to lunch on the stone terrace, where you can gaze out over the rolling grounds.

Foothill Cafe 👻

021

2766 Old Sonoma Rd., Napa (at Foothill Blvd.)

Phone:	707-252-6178	Wed – Thu 5pm - 9:30pm
Fax:	707-252-2818	Fri – Sat 5pm - 10pm
Web:	N/A	Sun 8am - 1pm & 4pm - 8pm
Prices:	$$	Closed Mon & Tue

In spite of its bland strip-mall setting, the Foothill Cafe furnishes good food and friendly service off the traditional tourist route. Celery-green walls with chocolate-brown trim highlight the trendy décor inside this popular neighborhood bistro and grill, and butcher paper covers the square tables that crowd close together.

From the kitchen chef/owner Mari Jennings and her team send out their versions of American favorites. Jerry's "famous" slow-roasted baby back ribs are tender and flavorful and coated with piquant barbecue sauce; preserved lemon and glazed shallots kick up Sonoma Country free-range chicken (show up Friday or Saturday night for oak-roasted prime rib). For brunch, locals chow down on omelets or the special scrambles. Small plates for kids accommodate families.

Hurley's

Californian ☓☓

022

6518 Washington St., Yountville (at Yount St.)

Phone:	707-944-2345	Open daily 11:30am - 10pm
Fax:	707-944-2386	
Web:	www.hurleysrestaurant.com	
Prices:	$$	

Competing with a handful of other renowned restaurants that line Yountville's main street, Hurley's holds its own with consistently steady and friendly service, Mediterranean spirit and healthful California cuisine.

Bob Hurley, owner and executive chef, favors local artisanal ingredients, typified by the fruity olive oil and crusty country bread. He features an all-day menu and a late-night version, which kicks in at 9pm and goes until midnight. While the former encompasses salads, pastas and more hearty entrées, the latter lightens things up with a short selection of appetizers, sandwiches and desserts.

Locals like to gather at the lively bar—with its good selection of wine by the glass—and on the large patio when the weather heats up.

Wine Country Napa Valley

Wine Country - **267**

Julia's Kitchen

023

Californian XX

500 1st St., Napa (bet. Silverado Trail & Soscol Ave.)

Phone:	707-265-5700	Mon & Wed 11:30am - 3pm
Fax:	707-265-5703	Thu – Sun 11:30am - 3pm & 5:30pm - 9pm
Web:	www.copia.org	Closed Tue
Prices:	$$$	

Although Julia Child, the beloved chef who introduced America to French cuisine in the 1960s, died in 2004, her indomitable spirit lives on in the Napa restaurant named for her. Couched within COPIA, the American Center for Food, Wine and the Arts—worth a visit in itself for its food-and-wine-related exhibits, tastings and cultural events—Julia's Kitchen displays a contemporary design enlivened by vibrant colors, an exhibition kitchen, and an oil portrait of Julia herself dominating one wall.

Inspired by Julia's recipes, chef Victor Scargle's seasonal menu includes distinctively fresh ingredients, cooked, of course, with a French twist. The roasted apple and huckleberry tart for two, topped with Tahitian vanilla-bean ice cream, requires a few extra minutes, but it's worth the wait.

Market

024

American X

1347 Main St., St. Helena (bet. Adam & Spring Sts.)

Phone:	707-963-3799	Open daily 11:30am - 10pm
Fax:	707-963-3889	
Web:	www.marketsthelena.com	
Prices:	⏎	

Chef Douglas Keane and maître d' Nick Peyton, the same team who recently opened Cyrus in Healdsburg, started their ensemble ventures in downtown St. Helena with Market. Local love this low-key place, where they can catch up with their neighbors while they tuck into generous portions of good, old-fashioned American comfort food.

If Prime rib, meatloaf, macaroni and cheese, and butterscotch pudding sound good to you, you won't be disappointed at Market. Prices are reasonable, and the set lunch menu is a steal for less than $15. The California wine list has prices to suit most every budget.

With its lofty ceilings, exposed stone walls and impeccably dressed tables, the dining room centers on the massive wooden bar, which adorned the Palace Hotel in San Francisco in the early 20th century.

Wine Country Napa Valley

Martini House

025

1245 Spring St., St. Helena (bet. Main & Oak Sts.)

Phone:	707-963-2233	Mon – Thu 5:30pm - 10pm
Fax:	707-967-9237	Fri – Sun 11:30am - 3pm
Web:	www.martinihouse.com	& 5:30pm - 10pm
Prices:	$$$	

Pat Kuleto transformed this 1923 Craftsman-style bungalow into a rustic scene, where stained-glass lanterns, Native-American textiles, and exposed wood beams describe a Frank Lloyd Wright-meets-the-Old West vibe. Fireplaces warm the room, and a rough-hewn log inset with candles hangs from the ceiling. Downstairs, the cozy bar carries on the hunting-lodge feel with its natural rock fireplace.

Against the back wall of the main room, wooden cupboards frame the open kitchen where a team led by chef/partner Todd Humphries turns out refined California cuisine that changes with the market (as in a salad of fresh chanterelle mushrooms; or ravioli stuffed with diced lobster and ginger-and-tarragon mousseline).

Forget your glasses? Never fear; the staff keeps a tray of reading glasses at the ready.

Mustards Grill

026

7399 St. Helena Hwy. (Hwy. 29), Yountville

Phone:	707-944-2424	Sun – Thu 11:30am - 9pm
Fax:	707-944-0828	Fri – Sat 11:30am - 10pm
Web:	www.mustardsgrill.com	
Prices:	$$	

In 1983, long before there was a restaurant scene to speak of in the Napa Valley, chef Cindy Pawlcyn premiered her roadside restaurant just north of Yountville. Now a local institution, Mustards draws winemakers and visitors alike to its laid-back ranch-style space for welcoming service, impeccable Wine Country comfort food, and a top-notch wine list (or "way too many wines," as the staff refers to it).

From the wood-burning grill and oven, and the oak-wood smoker come the likes of slow-smoked barbecue pork, tea-smoked duck, grilled hanger steak, and lemon and garlic chicken. The menu changes constantly to incorporate the freshest vegetables, fish, and meat from area ranches. Don't leave without sampling the sublimely crispy onion rings, served with tangy house-made ketchup.

Wine Country Napa Valley

N.V.

Californian 🍴🍴

027

1106 1st St., Napa (at Main St.)

Phone:	707-265-6400	Mon – Wed 11:30am - midnight
Fax:	707-265-7545	Thu – Sat 11:30am - 2am
Web:	N/A	Closed Sun & January 1 - 14
Prices:	$$$	

In September 2005 chef Peter Halikas opened N.V. in downtown Napa's Clock Tower Plaza after cooking in such Bay Area kitchens as Dean & Deluca, Gary Danko and Domaine Chandon. A chic urban feel permeates the dining room, where tap water is poured from ribbed glass bottles, and presentations (a Caesar salad composed of upright sections of romaine hearts garnished with toasted basil croutons and shaved parmesan, or a stacked goat cheese and roasted beet Napoleon) tower on the plates.

The lounge, with its circular banquette and polished river-rock-lined fireplace, stays open until 2am on weekends, luring sophisticated night owls with eclectic cocktails and creative light fare. Guests need not worry about noise, though, since the dining room is well separated from the boisterous bar.

Napa Valley Grill

Californian 🍴🍴

028

6795 Washington St., Yountville (at Madison St.)

Phone:	707-944-8686	Mon – Thu 11:30am - 9:30pm
Fax:	707-944-2870	Fri – Sat 11:30am - 10pm
Web:	www.napavalleygrille.com	Sun 11am - 9:30pm
Prices:	$$$	

Part of a small chain with locations across the U.S., Napa Valley Grille occupies a small complex of Tuscan-style buildings, all but one of which is devoted to banquets and group functions. Inside, the Wine Country theme continues with warm colors and a large open kitchen.

California cuisine here is rustic and unpretentious, but copious and carefully prepared. The all-day menu features seasonal main courses such as Broken Arrow Ranch antelope filet, and California white sturgeon and smoked sea scallop mouse; from the oakwood grill come the likes of organic pork chops and Fulton Valley free-range chicken breast. Round up some friends and try the Harvest Platter, a bounteous tasting of treats from air-cured beef and Coppa ham to salmon tartare and Vella cheese from Sonoma.

Pilar

029

Contemporary ✕✕

807 Main St., Napa (at 3rd St.)

Phone:	707-252-4474
Fax:	N/A
Web:	www.pilarnapa.com
Prices:	$$

Tue – Thu 11:30am - 2:30pm & 5:30pm - 9pm
Fri – Sat 11:30am - 2:30pm & 5:30pm - 10pm
Closed Mon & Sun

Pilar Sanchez and her husband Didier Lenders act as chefs, proprietors, and hosts at this chic downtown Napa restaurant. In fact, chef Pilar often greets guests at the door, making them feel truly welcome. Shades of green—celery, sage and celadon—color the uncluttered 49-seat dining room, where a long black-leather banquette strewn with green throw pillows lines one wall.

The menu is short and to the point, listing only a dozen or so dishes dictated by the market, where this team shops daily. In winter, a crisp-skinned salmon might be served with silky leek fondue, while the first rhubarb of spring could share billing with fresh-picked strawberries in an airy crostata.

If you live nearby, chef Pilar offers periodic cooking classes for those who wish to expand their culinary repertoire.

Pizza Azzuro

030

Pizza ✕

1400 2nd St., Napa (at Franklin St.)

Phone:	707-255-5552
Fax:	707-255-2522
Web:	N/A
Prices:	🥜

Mon – Fri 11:30am - 9pm
Sat 5pm - 9pm
Closed Sun

While so many of Napa Valley's restaurants boast lavish designs in their dining rooms, there's something to be said for plain and simple. Located in Napa's commercial downtown, this tiny pizza joint is certainly nothing to look at, but locals know to come here for some of the best wood-fired pizza in town.

Thin crusts and fresh toppings mark the hand-tossed pies of chef/owner Michael Gyetvan, who learned a thing or two about Italian cooking at Tra Vigne. Funghi, for instance, comes topped with taleggio cheese, fragrant thyme and earthy roasted mushrooms, while for the signature Manciata, just-baked pizza dough is strewn with fresh greens tossed with olive oil and citrus vinaigrette (fold it up and eat it like a sandwich). All the labels on the short wine list are available by the glass.

Posticino

031

Italian

1408 Clay St., Napa (at Franklin St.)

Phone:	707-255-0110	Mon – Thu 11am - 9pm
Fax:	707-255-9470	Fri 11am - 10pm
Web:	www.posticinonapa.com	Sat noon - 10pm
Prices:	$$	Closed Sun

A Napa newcomer, Posticino is a jewel box of a restaurant, with only nine tables. In nice weather, this scattering of inside seats is augmented by a wonderful outdoor patio, adorned with white columns and potted olive trees, and shaded by a wooden pergola.

Pastas gleam amid the many facets of the menu; they are made fresh daily and express Northern Italian influences in delicate tortelloni alla fonduta, filled with fontina cheese, garlic, toasted almonds and nutmeg, or hearty lasagna Bolognese, made with wide layers of spinach pasta. Secondi range from a parmesan-and-porcini-crusted chicken breast to a 10-ounce beef tenderloin topped with foie gras.

The wine list see-saws between the Napa Valley and regions of Italy, and cites a good selection of reasonably priced wines by the glass.

Press

032

Steakhouse

587 St. Helena Hwy. South, St. Helena

Phone:	707-967-0550	Open daily 5pm - 10pm
Fax:	707-967-0440	
Web:	www.presssthelena.com	
Prices:	$$$$	

Set off Highway 29 in a white farmhouse-style structure overlooking prim rows of grapevines, Press is the brainchild of Leslie Rudd (owner of Rudd Winery and Dean & DeLuca) and his two Napa partners. The simple exterior belies the comfortable luxury of the airy space inside, where light filters in through the greenhouse glass panels and reflects off immaculate white paneling.

Moulard duck breast, whole farm-raised chicken, and double-cut Colorado lamb chops are roasted on the fruitwood-fired rotisserie, which, along with the oversized fireplace, is the focal point of the room. USDA Prime Black Angus beef, from an 8-ounce tenderloin to a 32-ounce Porterhouse for two, comes with a choice of house-made sauces. Select among some of Napa's finest vintages on the impressive 500-label wine list.

Redd

033

Contemporary ✗✗

6480 Washington St., Yountville (at Oak Cir.)

Phone:	707-944-2222
Fax:	707-945-0447
Web:	www.reddnapavalley.com
Prices:	$$$

Mon – Thu 11:30am - 2:30pm & 5:30pm - 9:30pm
Fri – Sat 11:30am - 2:30pm & 5:30pm - 10pm
Sun 10am - 3pm & 5:30m - 9:30pm

A new addition (November 2005) to Yountville's quiet main street, Redd shows off the culinary savoir faire of former Auberge du Soleil chef Richard Reddington. The little bungalow, subtly illuminated at night with strings of tiny white lights, gives off an urbane vibe with its minimalist décor and tables teeming with stylishly dressed diners.

Whether you order à la carte or trust your dinner to one of the chef's tasting menus (four or six courses), you'll delight in knowledgeable service and flavorful dishes that meander the globe from Asia (tuna and hamachi tartare) to Europe (duck confit tartine; butternut squash ravioli) and back to California (Wolfe Ranch quail with lentils).

Redd is a difficult reservation to get these days, so be sure to call in advance.

Stomp

034

Contemporary ✗✗

1457 Lincoln Ave., Calistoga
(bet. Fair Way & Washington St.)

Phone:	707-942-8272
Fax:	707-942-6846
Web:	www.stomprestaurant.com
Prices:	$$$

Tue – Fri 6pm - 9:30pm
Sat 5:30pm - 10pm
Sun 5:30pm - 9pm
Closed Mon

Inventive cuisine, artful presentations, and a warm welcome are the calling cards of this much-lauded restaurant located in the historic Mount View Hotel. Soothing earth tones and sleek furnishings create an inviting space, while the chef and his wife, both trained by Roland Passot of San Francisco's La Folie, deliver exemplary food and service from start to finish.

Stomp prevails with its sophisticated presentations of French-accented contemporary cuisine. Seafood, meat, and poultry are equally represented in the seasonal plates here. The wine list is a love letter to the Napa Valley, specializing in verticals, and small-batch and experimental lots.

Look for Stomp to move to Main Street in St. Helena by the end of 2006.

Taylor's Automatic Refresher

A m e r i c a n

035

933 Main St., St. Helena (at Charter Oak Ave.)

Phone:	707-963-3486	Open daily 10:30am - 8:30pm (7:30pm in winter)
Fax:	707-286-2624	
Web:	www.taylorsrefresher.com	
Prices:		

This St. Helena stalwart, opened in 1949, was here long before anyone came to Napa Valley for the wine. A piece of American pop culture, Taylor's was remodeled in 1999 but it still looks the part of the classic roadside drive-in.

A trip to Taylor's provides a welcome break from the valley's ubiquitous haute cuisine. Here you'll find no fancy fare with foam or jus; basic burgers, garlic fries and hot dogs are the mainstay of this menu. Of course, you can get wine at Taylor's, but you might find a thick chocolate milkshake a more satisfying accompaniment. Bring the family and enjoy a casual meal at one of the umbrella-shaded picnic tables on the lush green lawn.

Taylor's younger sibling in the Ferry Building in San Francisco features the same menu and enjoys a following of its own.

Tra Vigne

I t a l i a n

036

1050 Charter Oak Ave., St. Helena (off Hwy. 29)

Phone:	707-963-4444	Sun – Thu 11:30am - 9pm
Fax:	707-963-1233	Fri – Sat 11:30am - 10pm
Web:	www.travignerestaurant.com	Closed major holidays
Prices:	$$$	

Italian for "among the vines," Tra Vigne reflects founder Michael Chiarello's desire to bring southern Italy to northern California. Although Chiarello has moved on, Tra Vigne continues his tradition of serving refined Italian cuisine in a Tuscan-style complex that includes the Cantinetta wine bar, and the Pizzeria, which turns out crispy pies from its brick oven.

Step inside the velvet drapes that frame the soft-gray dining room, and you'll discover an elegant space where large arched windows reveal a brick courtyard shaded by mulberry trees. In this setting, the likes of pan-roasted John Dory with pancetta and chanterelles, and milk-braised pork with toasted semolina pasta are made from California and imported Italian products. The wine list changes weekly to incorporate new finds.

Wappo Bar Bistro

037

1226 Washington St., Calistoga (at Lincoln Ave.)

Phone: 707-942-4712   Open daily 11:30am - 2:30pm & 6pm - 10pm
Fax: 707-942-4741
Web: www.wappobar.com
Prices: $$

Follow Highway 29 to the north end of Napa Valley and you'll come to Calistoga, famed for the healing properties of its mineral-rich mud. Before you take that mud bath, though, head for this wine bar and bistro.

"Eclectic" is the best way to categorize Wappo's globe-trotting cuisine, which roams from India to Thailand, Brazil to Singapore, skirts the Mediterranean and ends up back in California. It's challenging to keep up with all these different flavors, but the kitchen in this redwood-lined dining space manages it well. Products are well selected and the execution is serious for such dishes as tandoori chicken, Thai coconut curry with prawns, and *vatapa* (Brazilian seafood stew).

Try to snag a table on the adorable patio.

Wine Spectator Greystone

California ✗✗

038

2555 Main St., St. Helena (at Deer Park Rd.)

Phone: 707-967-1010   Mon – Thu 11:15am - 4pm & 5pm - 8:45pm
Fax: 707-967-2375   Fri – Sun 11:15am - 4pm & 5pm - 9:45pm
Web: www.ciachef.edu   Closed major holidays
Prices: $$$

Erected in 1889 as Greystone Cellars winery, this impressive stone building set on Highway 29 just north of downtown St. Helena now houses the West Coast campus of the Culinary Institute of America (CIA) and its Greystone restaurant. From any of the handcrafted tables in the main room, you can watch the chefs at work in three open kitchens; hardcore foodies can pull up a stool at the counter for a ringside seat. Or, on a sunny Napa day, try the outdoor terrace with its vineyard view.

The menu proposes two different bills of fare. The à la carte menu offers seasonal fare, while "Today's Temptations," crafted from the fresh offerings of local farmers and food artisans, suggests a sampling of small bites to share. Don't pass up the impressive and well-classified regional wine list.

Wine Country Napa Valley

Zaré

Mediterranean ✗✗

039

5091 Solano Ave., Napa (bet. Oak Knoll Ave. & Hwy. 29)

Phone: 707-257-3318   Open daily 11:30am - 9:30pm
Fax: 707-257-1825
Web: www.zarenapa.com
Prices: $$

The sprawling red farmhouse that holds Zaré sits just off busy Highway 29 amid rows of vines. This is where you'll find chef Hoss Zaré dishing up Mediterranean cuisine with his own Persian flair. The tasty trio of dolmas (spiced ground lamb and rice, roasted Japanese eggplant and lentils, and roasted red bell pepper, mozzarella and pine nuts), and main dishes such as an open-faced salmon *koofteh* or lime-and-Chardonnary-marinated Dungeness crab linguine with grilled prawns capture the essence of this sun-drenched fare.

With its outdoor fireplaces and fresh Wine Country air, the pleasant patio offers the best atmosphere. If the weather isn't conducive to sitting outside, windows aplenty in the dining room reveal the same majestic mountain and vineyard views.

Zuzu ☺

Spanish ✗

040

829 Main St., Napa (bet. 2nd & 3rd Sts.)

Phone: 707-224-8555   Mon – Thu 11:30am - 10pm
Fax: 707-224-5885   Fri 11:30am - 11pm
Web: www.zuzunapa.com   Sat 4pm - 11pm
Prices: ☺☺   Sun 4pm - 9:30pm

For a good time and good food at attractive prices, round up some friends and hurry on over to Zuzu. One of the few tapas bars in the valley, Zuzu nestles on Main Street in Napa's up-and-coming Old Town. With its lively Latin beats and convivial atmosphere, Zuzu exudes a festive vibe any time of day.

Start the party with a round of the house-blend sangria or a bottle of wine from a list carefully chosen to match the tapas. Order a selection of carefully prepared hot and cold small plates (halibut ceviche, queso frito, Catalan cabbage rolls, and mashed boniato sweet potatoes with fried yucca chips) to share around the table, and—voilà—instant celebration.

Zuzu doesn't take reservations, but if the line is long, riverside Veterans Park across the street makes a pleasant spot to wait.

Show the locals around.

Michelin® Green Guides will introduce you to a world of information on the history, culture, art, and architecture of a destination. You'll be so well informed, they'll never suspect you're a tourist. To learn more, visit michelintravel.com.

Russian River Valley and Northern Sonoma County

Healdsburg Chamber of Commerce

Healdsburg Plaza

Little more than an hour north of San Francisco, the northern reaches of Sonoma County offer splendid landscapes, gourmet dining and increasingly famous wines. Seven distinct wine appellations (AVAs) have been assigned in the part of the county north of Santa Rosa, the region's biggest metropolis.

The **Russian River Valley** AVA, inclusive of **Green Valley**, borders the river named for early Russian trading outposts along the coast. This is often the coolest growing region in Sonoma, as the river basin offers a conduit for cool coastal air. On the hottest days of the year, the air rising from interior valleys is replaced by cool moisture-laden breezes from the chilly Pacific. A blanket of fog is a regular feature until late morning throughout the growing season. This effect is moderated by distance from the coast and—in the area of **Chalk Hill**, for example—elevation above the valley floor. Elegant Pinot Noir and Chardonnay are the headliners in this part of the county.

The lower end of **Dry Creek Valley** abuts the Russian River and yields fabulous Pinot Noir and Chardonnay. As one heads north up the valley, Cabernet Sauvignon, Merlot, and especially Zinfandel take over. Among the white varietals that thrive in the Dry Creek Valley, Sauvignon Blanc predominates. Seemingly minor elevation changes make an extreme difference here. Cold air sinks to the floor of this inland valley, and spring nights can threaten low-lying parcels with frost. Early flowering varieties may fail in one spot and succeed on a hillside 50 yards away, so that winery visits in Dry Creek are a study in contrasts. Palatial modern wineries rise up along the same country roads that have been home to independents for generations, and carefully trained young vineyards arranged in laser-straightened rows are broken up with dark, gnarly old vines.

The inlandmost AVAs of Sonoma County are Knights Valley and Alexander Valley, two warm regions. The southern end of **Knights Valley** abuts Napa's warmest vineyards at Calistoga. To

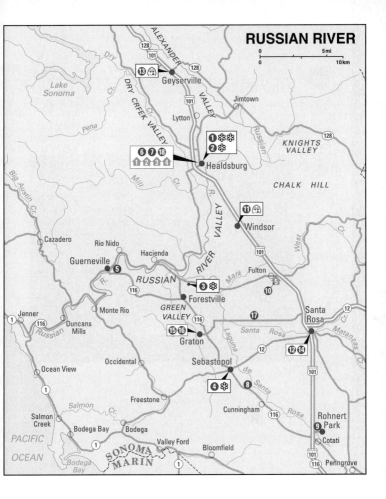

the north, Knights Valley reaches up to Alexander Valley, but is shielded from the influence of the Russian River by significant hills. Cabernet and its red cousins shine here. Named for Cyrus Alexander, who planted the region's first vineyard in 1846, **Alexander Valley** is also known for its Cabernet and yields a unique, mellow version of this often herbal variety. The Russian River runs along the western side of the valley, which is conducive to growing a Chardonnay that is more mellow and rich than fine Chardonnay from cooler climes.

While Sonoma County offers ample opportunity to ramble along rural roads and taste the produce of independent farmers, it is also home to sophisticated wineries and fine restaurants. The Russian River Valley may be a bit more rustic than Napa Valley, but it's never lacking in comforts.

Cyrus ✿ ✿

Contemporary 🍴🍴🍴🍴

29 North St., Healdsburg (bet. Foss St. & Healdsburg Ave.)

Phone:	707-433-3311	Open daily 5:30pm - 9:30pm
Fax:	707-433-6633	
Web:	www.cyrusrestaurant.com	
Prices:	$$$$	

Cyrus/Andy Katz

A wonderful experience awaits you at Cyrus, in Healdsburg's Les Mars Hotel *(see Wine Country hotel listings)*. It all starts as the hostess escorts you to the dining room, where she calls the chef on an antique phone to announce your arrival.

When they wheel up the champagne cart, begin your evening-long affair with fine food and wine with a glass of bubbly, and take in the sumptuous surroundings accented by warm woods, shirred cream-colored window shades and an arched and vaulted Venetian-plaster ceiling. Then surrender yourself to the masterful hands of chef Douglas Keane and his seven-course tasting menu, or craft your own multicourse meal from a list organized by type of product (vegetables, foie gras, fish and shellfish, meat). Either way, you won't go wrong with the likes of seared foie gras on a bed of pear coulis with a gastrique of meat jus, vinegar and vanilla; or delicate braised artichokes à la barigoule, sprinkled with diced vegetables.

Thanks to partner and consummate maitre d' Nick Peyton, service is flawless, from the waiter who explains that portions can be adjusted to your appetite, to the hostess who walks you to the door when you are, reluctantly, ready to leave.

Wine Country Russian River Valley

Appetizers

Thai Marinated Lobster with Avocado, Mango and Fresh Hearts of Palm

Billi-Bi Soup with Tempura Mussel and Olive Oil Potato Purée

Salt-cured "Torchon" of Foie Gras with Macadamias and Pineapple Compote, Lychee Gelée

Entrées

Sea Bream with Shiitakes, Bay Scallops and Pickled Watermelon Rind

Truffled Red Wine Risotto, Parmesan Broth

Striploin of Beef with Fingerling Potato and Shortrib Hash

Desserts

Three Custards: Chocolate Pot de Crème, Mousse of Crème Brûlée and Huckleberry Pain Perdu

Caramel Soup with Kettle Corn Sorbet and Chocolate Filigree

Pistachio Napoleon with Hibiscus-Rose and Honey Sorbet

Dry Creek Kitchen ✿

002

317 Healdsburg Ave., Healdsburg
(bet. Matheson & Plaza Sts.)

Phone:	707-431-0330	Mon – Thu 5:30pm - 9pm
Fax:	707-431-8990	Fri – Sat noon - 2:30pm & 5:30pm - 9:30pm
Web:	www.charliepalmer.com	Sun noon - 2:30pm & 5:30pm - 9pm
Prices:	$$$	

Dry Creek Kitchen/Cesar Rubio

With the spiffing up of the downtown plaza and the recent additions of snazzy hotels like the Hotel Healdsburg *(see Wine Country hotel listings)* and its restaurant, Dry Creek Kitchen, this little burg has now come into its own as a destination.

Another notch in the belt of the Charlie Palmer Group, run by and named for the distinguished chef, Dry Creek Kitchen brings sophistication to the town's historic plaza. The restaurant's elegant dining space echoes the colors of the vineyards, while many of the well-spaced tables look out onto the plaza through large windows in the façade.

Palmer's cuisine respects meats, cheeses and seasonal produce from local purveyors—even the superb wine list gathers only Sonoma Country vintages. He leaves the management of the kitchen to chef Michael Voltaggio, formerly at The Greenbrier in West Virginia. Although an à la carte menu is offered, the best way to appreciate the chef's talent is to experience the six-course tasting menu, on which a tart grapefruit-sumac sorbet can provide an icy foil for "chopped" tuna and hamachi, while vanilla pear and Belgian endive might harmonize with farm-raised venison loin drizzled with espresso oil.

Appetizers

Pan-seared Foie Gras with Fuji Apple Tarte Tatin and Red-Wine Star-Anise Jus

Hog Island Sweetwater Oysters broiled with Shallot-Chive Butter, Fleur de Sel

White Crane Watercress with Point Reyes Blue Cheese Vinaigrette, Candied Walnuts and Bosc Pears

Entrées

Porcini-crusted Niman Ranch Lamb with braised Lamb Brik, Sweet Potato Purée, Black Olive Jus

Snake River Farms Beef Culotte with German Butterball Boulangere, Haricots Verts and Oxtail Jus

Alaskan Halibut with Artichokes, Baby Fennel, Tomato Confit, Boquerones and Taggiasca Olives

Desserts

Valrhona Bombe – Chocolate & Caramel Mousse, Vanilla-bean Bavarian, Cocoa-Nib Ice Cream and Cinnamon Milk Gelée

Warm Pineapple Cake stacked with Pineapple Mango Salad, Coconut and Lime Foam and local Meyer Lemon Milk Sorbet

Raspberry Sponge Mousse with Pistachio Anglaise, warm Chocolate Croquettes and Chocolate Sorbet

Farmhouse Inn & Restaurant ✿

003

7871 River Rd., Forestville (at Wohler Rd.)

Phone:	707-887-3300	Thu – Mon 5:30pm - midnight
Fax:	707-887-3311	Closed Tue & Wed
Web:	www.farmhouseinn.com	
Prices:	$$$	

The Farmhouse Inn & Restaurant/Andy Katz

If your idea of an idyllic meal is dining in a little yellow farmhouse set amid acres of vineyards, make a beeline for the Farmhouse Inn. San Francisco will seem far away (it's only an hour and a half) as you settle into the tastefully decorated high-ceilinged dining room with its wrought-iron chandeliers, marble fireplace, and classical music playing softly in the background.

Picture yourself being cosseted by a knowledgeable waitstaff, who are happy to go the extra mile (as in bringing out tastes of the two different desserts you're trying to decide between) to make your experience here a memorable one.

Imagine that you're cutting into chef Steve Litke's succulent breast of Liberty Farms duck fanned out over a mound of nutty quinoa laced with toasted Marcona almonds and a dice of carrots and celery. Or perhaps a salad of spring asparagus, frisée and red beets topped with a truffled egg. For dessert, consider an airy chocolate soufflé, with vanilla-scented crème anglaise on the side.

Of course, you won't want the evening to end here—and it doesn't have to. Simply reserve one of the inn's eight luxurious cottages so you can saunter back to your room after dinner.

Appetizers

Salt-roasted Pear and Parmesan Ravioli (thin sheets of housemade pasta in sauce fonduta)

Parmesan Flan with Early Spring Asparagus, Black Truffle Beurre Fondue and Parmesan Tuile

Maine Lobster Sausage with Wild Ramp-Saffron Potato Salad and Piquillo Pepper Aioli

Entrées

Rabbit Rabbit Rabbit: Applewood-Smoked-Bacon-wrapped Loin, Roasted Rack, Confit of Leg, Whole-grain Mustard Sauce and Fingerling Potato

Roasted Wild Northern California Halibut with warm Meyer Lemon-Heirloom Tomato Vinaigrette, Crispy Rock Shrimp and Fourchette of German Butterball Potato

Grilled Noisette of Lamb with Fennel Ratatouille, Crispy Polenta, and Niçoise-olive-infused Lamb Jus

Desserts

Soufflé of Michel Cluizel Chocolate with Bourbon Crème Anglaise

Peach Leaf Crème Brûlée with Turbinado Sugar

Bellwether Farms Ricotta Cheesecake en Croûte with Wild Mountain Huckleberry Sauce

K & L Bistro ✿

004

119 South Main St., Sebastopol
(bet. Burnett St. and Hwy. 12)

Phone:	707-823-6614	Mon – Thu 11:30am - 3pm & 5pm - 9pm
Fax:	707-523-2067	Fri 11:30am - 3pm & 5pm - 10pm
Web:	N/A	Sat 5pm - 10pm
Prices:	$$	Closed Sun

♿

K & L Bistro

The name of this local favorite pays homage to its chef/owners, husband-and-wife team Lucas and Karen Martin, who left Hayes Street Grill in San Francisco for a more pastoral locale in wine country. And pastoral it is, tucked away in a little redbrick building on the main street of Sebastopol, at the intersection of highways 12 and 116.

French flair dominates this simple bistro, from the original paintings of Paris street scenes that fill the walls to the late-19th-century-style bistro furnishings. All things Gallic rule the cuisine, too. A chalkboard listing the day's special cheeses, desserts and wine augments the likes of house-made boudin blanc, chanterelle mushroom risotto and superbly fresh pan-roasted halibut on the à la carte menu. And don't forget classics such as steak frites, duck confit and French onion soup gratinée.

As for wine, there are good offerings from the region as well as from Europe. Service is pleasant, efficient and attentive to details, as in offering customers a taste of several different wines before they make their final choice.

Wine Country Russian River Valley

Appetizers

Warm Rabbit Terrine with Cornichons and Grilled Bread

Caramelized Onion Tart with Gravenstein Apples, Blue Cheese, Watercress, and Balsamic Reduction

Grilled Asparagus with Prosciutto, Shaved Parmesan, and Tomato-Olive Relish

Entrées

K & L Cassoulet, made with Duck Confit, Two Sausages, Hobb's Bacon and Corona Beans

Roasted Halibut with Baby Artichokes, Fava Beans, Tomato Confit, Fingerlings and Rosemary

Pepper-crusted Yellowfin Tuna with Lyonnaise Potatoes, Spinach, and Au Poivre Sauce

Desserts

Apricot-Cherry Galette with Crème Fraîche

Warm Chocolate Cake with House-made Vanilla-Bean Ice Cream

Strawberry Trifle with Champagne Custard

FRENCH

Applewood

005

Californian

13555 Hwy. 116, Guerneville

Phone:	707-869-9093	Tue – Sat 6pm - 8:45pm
Fax:	707-869-9170	Closed Sun & Mon
Web:	www.applewoodinn.com	
Prices:	$$$	

The Applewood Inn tucks into a wooded backdrop a mile from Guerneville. This Wine Country B&B also welcomes guests for dinner in its barn-like dining room, complete with a vaulted and beamed ceiling and a soaring stone fireplace at either end of the room.

Interpreted with French techniques and Italian accents, the California cuisine here fills the à la carte menu with the likes of seared foie gras with pain d'épice (spiced bread) French toast and red wine cherries, and grilled filet of beef with a fricassée of trumpet royal mushrooms. Lighter fare highlights the bistro menu, offered Tuesday through Thursday.

If you want to make a weekend of it, 19 individually decorated rooms are outfitted with such amenities as Italian linens, down comforters, and Wi-Fi Internet access.

Barndiva

006

Contemporary

231 Center St., Healdsburg (bet. Matheson & Mills Sts.)

Phone:	707-431-0100	Wed – Thu noon - 11pm
Fax:	707-431-0658	Fri – Sat noon - midnight
Web:	www.barndiva.com	Sun noon - 11pm
Prices:	$$	Closed Mon & Tue

"Country" takes on new meaning at Barndiva, just off Healdsburg's main plaza. Designed by co-owners Jil and Geoffrey Hales, the soaring mahogany barn houses a chic urban boîte with a pastoral soul, embodied by the tranquil outdoor terrace.

Lunch brings a short list of salads, sandwiches and savory pies, while the menu at dinner breaks down into "light" (goat cheese croquettes with house-made tomato jam), "spicy" (braised short ribs with horseradish mashed potatoes), or "comfort" (duck shepherds pie with root vegetables). Ingredients are sourced as close to home as possible, from artisanal producers or local growers.

Beverages run the gamut from a list of whimsically named "divatinis" using house-made syrups and fresh organic juices, to the wine list that stars rare Sonoma County vintages.

Bistro Ralph

Californian 🍴

109 Plaza St., Healdsburg (bet. Center St. & Healdsburg Ave.)

Phone: 707-433-1380
Fax: 707-433-1974
Web: N/A
Prices: $$

Mon - Sat 11:30am - 2:30pm & 5:30pm - 9:30pm
Closed Sun

Tucked away on Healdsburg's grassy town square, surrounded by chic shops and tasting rooms, this diminutive bistro showcases the California cuisine of chef Ralph Tingle. The chef apprenticed in Paris at renowned restaurants including Taillevent, so it's no surprise that his short, frequently changing menu adds a French finesse to such entrées as chicken paillard with brown butter, lemon and capers, and grilled lamb loin chops with rosemary jus and flageolet beans. Tingle returns to California with the wine list, which highlights local productions from the Russian River region.

In the little dining room, white brick walls, a pressed aluminum ceiling, and original artwork create a casual and contemporary bistro feel.

Bistro V

French 🍴🍴

2295 Gravenstein Hwy./ Hwy. 116, Sebastopol

Phone: 707-823-1262
Fax: 707-780-6361
Web: www.bistro-v.com
Prices: $$

Mon & Wed – Sat 11:30am - 2:30pm & 5pm - 10pm
Sun 10am - 2pm & 4:30pm - 10pm
Closed Tue

Couched in a quaint country house alongside Gravenstein Highway, about two miles southeast of Sebastopol, Bistro V takes full advantage of its location amid the fertile farmland of Sonoma County. Local artisanal ingredients, including vegetables, cheeses, organic meats, and varieties of honey, all contribute to the French-inspired bistro fare.

Chef Rick Vargas, who comes from a family of restaurateurs, trained in France as well as in some of San Francisco's better restaurants before embarking on his venture in the Russian River Valley. Organic chicken cooked under a brick, house-made spinach ravioli, and natural Angus ribeye represent the dishes here, while made-from-scratch desserts will tempt you with the likes of apple strudel, tiramisu and classic Spanish flan.

Hana

Japanese ✗

009

101 Golf Course Dr., Rohnert Park (at Roberts Lake Rd.)

Phone: 707-586-0270
Fax: 707-537-1653
Web: www.hanajapanese.com
Prices: $$

Tue – Thu 11:30am - 2:30pm & 5pm - 9pm
Fri – Sat 11:30am - 2:30pm & 5pm - 9:30pm
Sun 5pm - 9pm
Closed Mon & January 1 - 8

Just off Highway 101 in Rohnert Park Hana is hidden away in the DoubleTree Plaza. Since it opened in the early 1990s, chef/owner Ken Tominaga, a native of Tokyo, has been displaying his craft using fresh California products.

A large choice of sushi is available, along with noodles, teriyaki and tempura. More creative recipes include foie gras wonton soup, Ahi tuna with grated wasabi Chardonnay sauce, and pan-seared black Angus rib eye in chile-soy sauce. If you can't decide, the Bento Box Dinner is a modestly priced way to sample several different dishes. There's even a children's plate, composed of chicken teriyaki, shrimp tempura, mashed potatoes, rice and fruit.

Miniature plates and bowls filled with condiments act as table art with the Japanese pickles and complimentary edamame.

John Ash & Co.

Californian ✗✗

010

4330 Barnes Rd., Santa Rosa (at River Rd.)

Phone: 707-527-7687
Fax: 707-527-1202
Web: www.vintnersinn.com
Prices: $$$

Mon – Thu 11:30am - 9pm
Fri 11:30am - 9:30pm
Sat 5pm - 9:30pm
Sun 11am - 9pm

Whether or not you're staying at the Vintners Inn *(see Wine Country hotel listings)*, where John Ash & Co. has been located since 1987, it's worth planning a meal here. Launched by chef, cookbook author and now vineyard-owner John Ash, this rustic spot nestled amid the Ferrari-Carano vineyards suggests a Tuscan country house with its terra-cotta-colored walls, wood beams and wrought-iron chandeliers.

Executive chef Jeffrey Madura employs California products like Meyer lemon, Dungeness crab, Sonoma duck, Laura Chenel chevre, and produce from local farms to realize his Wine Country cuisine. To set it off, the well-selected wine list covers the globe and offers an appealing range of prices. After a dreamy meal on the terrace gazing out over the vines, you may just want to get a room.

Mirepoix

011

275 Windsor River Rd., Windsor (at Honsa Ave.)

Phone:	707-838-0162	Tue – Sun 11:30am - 9pm
Fax:	707-838-0191	Closed Mon
Web:	www.restaurantmirepoix.com	
Prices:	$$	

The medieval market town of Mirepoix in southern France lends its name to tiny, 28-seat place in Windsor's Old Downtown. While the city of Windsor is a far piece from Languedoc, a French spirit prevails in the kitchen at Mirepoix.

Chef Matthew Bousquet's gastronomic expertise sparkles in dishes like pan-roasted escolar with a fragrant emulsion marrying champagne and lavender. Although Bousquet's cooking credits cross the country from New York City to San Francisco, he stays close to home in terms of his ingredients, favoring locally grown vegetables and meats, and fish from nearby waters. The short menu changes daily, and a prix-fixe chef's tasting is also available.

Mixx Enoteca Luigi

012

135 4th St., Santa Rosa (at Davis St.)

Phone:	707-573-1344	Mon – Sat 11am - 10pm
Fax:	707-573-0631	Closed Sun
Web:	www.sterba.net/sro/mixx	
Prices:	$$	

Mixx has long (since it opened in 1989) been known as the showcase of founders Dan and Kathleen Berman. In 2005 they moved on to other things and sold their place to Luigi Lezzi.

Centerpiece of the restaurant, which is located in Santa Rosa's Historic Railroad Square neighborhood, the impressive late-19th-century bar was hand-carved in Italy. In 1904 the piece was shipped to this building, to be used in what was then the Silver Door Saloon. Under Luigi's ownership, the menu has turned Italian, replacing the Bermans' California cuisine with panini, pastas, and *secondi* such as *salmone alla Livornese* (salmon baked in Sauvignon Blanc with Kalamata olives, capers, tomatoes and extra virgin olive oil). The frequently updated wine list features a generous selection by the glass.

Wine Country Russian River Valley

Santi

013

Italian ✗✗

21047 Geyserville Ave., Geyserville

Phone:	707-857-1790	Mon – Wed 5:30pm - 9pm
Fax:	707-857-1793	Thu 11:30am - 2pm & 5:30pm - 9pm
Web:	www.tavernasanti.com	Fri 11:30am - 2pm & 6pm - 9:30pm
Prices:	$$	Sat 11:30am - 2pm & 5:30pm - 9:30pm
		Sun 11:30am - 2pm & 5pm - 9pm

It's worth the short drive north from Healdsburg to discover the quaint little wine village of Geyserville. On its main street you'll find Santi, couched inside a landmark 1902 building.

Farmers' markets dictate the menu at this Alexander Valley tavern, where both the décor and the food clearly express the concept of "country." House-made sausages join fragrant fennel and raw asparagus in the antipasto misto, while a hearty sauce of beef and pork ribs paired with tomatoes and herbs tops gemelli (again, house-made). Florentine-style braised tripe and a boneless half-chicken cooked under a brick further illustrate Santi's rustic Italian fare.

On a sunny day, the charming vine-shaded patio is the place to linger over lunch and savor hard-to-find vintages from local wineries.

Syrah

014

Californian ✗✗

205 5th St., Santa Rosa (at Davis St.)

Phone:	707-568-4002	Tue – Sat 11:30am - 2pm & 5:30pm - 9pm
Fax:	707-568-5137	Sun – Mon 5:30pm - 9pm
Web:	www.syrahbistro.com	
Prices:	$$$	

A warm vibe greets you in this 30-seat bistro, set in downtown Santa Rosa. Done with wood rafters and colorful artwork, Syrah blends a contemporary look with Cal-French cuisine executed by chef/proprietor Josh Silvers, former sous-chef at Napa Valley's Mustards Grill. The restaurant's name honors the rich Rhone Valley red that enjoys a prominent place on the wine list (though the majority of the Syrahs here come from California instead of France).

For dinner, you can order à la carte, or sample a four- or seven-course chef's tasting. Just don't overlook the selection of California artisan cheeses; your choice of three cheeses is served with black pepper, membrillo and a drizzle of local honey.

After your meal, stop in next door at the Silvers' wine shop, wittily named Petite Syrah.

Underwood

015 · Mediterranean ✗
9113 Graton Rd., Graton (at Edison St.)

Phone:	707-823-7023	Tue – Thu 11:30am - 2:30pm & 5pm - 10pm
Fax:	707-823-8094	Fri – Sat 11:30am - 2:30pm & 5pm - 11pm
Web:	www.underwoodgraton.com	Sun 5pm - 10pm
Prices:	$$	Closed Mon

A detour along Graton Road, just north of Sebastopol off Route 116, will reward you with not only serene landscapes, but with this laid-back bistro. Tucked away in the quiet village of Graton, Underwood is hard to miss with its red façade. Inside, Art Deco-inspired light fixtures, wood paneling, yellow walls, red banquettes, and copper-topped tables create a charming bistro atmosphere, complete with friendly service.

At lunch and dinner, the menu remains essentially the same. Both meals offer tapas, a selection of fresh oysters, an array of local artisan cheeses and a few salads to start. At dinner, the likes of harissa roasted chicken, Catalan fish stew and grilled lamb sirloin replace the noontime sandwiches. Of course, the Hereford Ranch beef hamburger is available all day.

Willow Wood Market Cafe

016 · Californian ✗
9020 Graton Rd., Graton (at Edison St.)

Phone:	707-823-0233	Mon – Sat 8am - 9:30pm
Fax:	707-823-7491	Sun 9am - 3pm
Web:	www.willowwoodgraton.com	
Prices:	$$	

The same folks who run Underwood own this funky market-cafe across the street. Willow Wood Market is open for breakfast, lunch and dinner, so you can stop by almost any time of day for regional California cuisine served in an old-fashioned country store.

Place your order at the counter and stake out one of the handful of tables inside, or one of the few tables scattered in the small garden out back. In this laid-back setting, you can dig into comforting dishes like pork tenderloin ragout, the Market Plate sampler, or a bowl of their locally renowned polenta. And speaking of polenta, the moist polenta-gingerbread cake is sure to please your sweet tooth.

Before you leave, browse the grocery shelves for local wines, preserves, and crafts by area artists.

Wine Country Russian River Valley

zazu

017

American

3535 Guerneville Rd., Santa Rosa (at Willowside Rd.)

Phone: 707-523-4814
Fax: 707-887-0416
Web: www.zazurestaurant.com
Prices: $$$

Wed – Mon 5:30pm - 9:30pm
Closed Tue

A cheerful aura envelopes you as you enter this roadhouse-style restaurant housed in an inviting red barn a few miles outside Santa Rosa. The room hums with the conversations of patrons at copper-topped tables or seated along the wine-themed banquette that lines one wall.

Husband-and-wife-team John Stewart and Duskie Estes serve as chefs and co-owners here, and their cuisine emphasizes house-cured meats and products raised within a 50-mile radius of zazu. Uncomplicated seasonal dishes could include anything from spicy tomato soup with a grilled Bellweather Farms Carmody cheese sandwich to steamed Bodega Bay Dungeness crab.

It's no wonder that this great viticultural area dominates the wine list in a place that is surrounded by 150 of the Russian River Valley's finest wineries.

Zin

018

American

344 Center St., Healdsburg (at North St.)

Phone: 707-473-0946
Fax: N/A
Web: www.zinrestaurant.com
Prices: $$

Mon – Fri 11:30am - 2pm & 5:30pm - 9pm
Sat – Sun 5:30pm - 9pm

The name of this Wine Country restaurant, with its cork-covered tables and cubbies filled with wine bottles, nods to Zinfandel, a grape that thrives in the soil of the surrounding Dry Creek Valley and the varietal that accounts for half the offerings on the changing wine list.

Located a block north of Healdsburg's plaza, Zin is a partnership between chef Jeff Mall and restaurateur Scott Silva, who both grew up on California farms. Mall's menu, which takes advantage of Sonoma County's agricultural bounty as well as organic vegetables from his own garden, speaks with a Southern accent in the likes of crispy duck leg jambalaya, and New Orleans red bean "cassoulet." Not surprisingly, most of the American comfort food here is designed to pair well with Zinfandel.

Wine Country Russian River Valley

EVERYTHING YOU GET FROM MICHELIN TIRES NOW
IN A NEW RANGE OF AUTOMOTIVE ACCESSORIES.

TAKE THEM FOR A TEST DRIVE TODAY.

For over a hundred years, Michelin has developed products and services to make life on the road safer, more efficient and more enjoyable. And now Michelin offers an innovative collection of automotive accessories which epitomize its long-standing values of performance, dependability and safety. The collection includes inflation and pressure monitoring products, air compressors and air tools, emergency/breakdown assistance products, wiper blades, wheel and tire change equipment, wheel and tire care products, pressure washers, floor mats and air fresheners. **The Michelin Automotive Accessories Collection is on the road right now.**

A better way forward

Sonoma Valley

Nestled between the Mayacamas and Sonoma mountain ranges, the 17-mile-long Sonoma Valley dominates the southern portion of Sonoma County, centering on the town of **Sonoma**, site of California's northernmost and final mission (San Francisco Solano Mission, founded in 1823). The historic eight-acre plaza at the town's heart is still surrounded by historic adobe buildings, most of them now occupied by shops, restaurants and inns.

Northern California's first premium winery, **Buena Vista**, was founded just outside the town of Sonoma in 1857 by Agoston Haraszthy. Situated on a rolling site amid eucalyptus, oak and bay laurel trees, Buena Vista's original site is now a California Historic Landmark that offers tours and daily tastings. The Gundlach-Bundschu and Sebastiani wineries are near neighbors to this historic cultural center of the county. Just below the town lies Sonoma's portion of the **Carneros** district, named for the herds of sheep (*carneros* in Spanish) that once roamed its hillsides. Carneros is now best known for its "cool climate" grapes, notably Pinot Noir and Chardonnay. North of Sonoma, the upper parts of the valley grow steadily warmer, with **Bennett Valley** and **Sonoma Mountain** providing varying topography, soil types and microclimates favorable to a host of different varietals. These three are the official AVAs that subdivide Sonoma Valley (itself an official AVA). However, Moon Mountain, Kenwood and Glen Ellen are examples of other important and distinctive sources for unique wines.

All along Highway 12 headed towards Santa Rosa, there are tempting byroads leading to out-of-the-way wineries, each with its own special stamp on the business of winemaking. In addition

Sonoma Plaza

©Robert Holmes

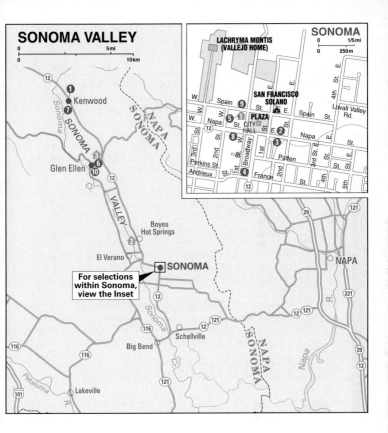

to the obvious differences of soil, sun, temperature, moisture and elevation, vineyards vary in the maturity of their vines, clonal selections, pruning and vineyard management. The so-called "boutique" bottlings of Sonoma Valley distinguish themselves in a thousand ways.

Although it is home to several substantial enterprises, and it struggles with signs of urbanization, Sonoma Valley still displays rural independence at its most intriguing, with a different wine around every bend. "Freeholds" still abound and vineyards and wineries rub shoulders with orchards and farms producing everything from apples and olives to organic eggs and artisanal cheeses. Be sure to spend some time here foraging at local farmers' markets for picnic supplies—to pair, of course, with some of Sonoma Valley's excellent wines. Sonoma Valley restaurateurs feature local foods and wines as a part of their culture, rather than as part of a dining trend.

Cafe Citti

001

Italian

9049 Sonoma Hwy., Kenwood (at Shaw Ave.)

Phone: 707-833-2690
Fax: N/A
Web: N/A
Prices: $$

Sun – Thu 11am - 3:30pm & 5pm - 8:30pm
Fri – Sat 11am - 3:30pm & 5pm - 9pm

A great stop in between visiting the surrounding wineries, this modest bungalow on Highway 12 provides a casual setting for a quick but tasty bite. Locals know the drill here: come in, claim a table, and place your order at the counter. A waiter will deliver your meal and take orders for additional drinks or dessert (the owner is a pastry chef, so don't skimp on the sweet course).

Pizzas and sandwiches are offered only at lunch, along with combination salad plates, polenta and roasted rotisserie chicken. Homemade specialty pastas include ravioli filled with meat, Swiss chard and fresh herbs in a tomato-basil cream, or potato gnocchi tossed in your choice of meat, marinara or pesto sauce.

Planning a Wine Country picnic? Many of the items at Cafe Citti are available to go.

Cafe La Haye

002

Contemporary

140 E. Napa St., Sonoma (bet. 1st St. E. & 2nd St. E.)

Phone: 707-935-5994
Fax: N/A
Web: www.cafelahaye.com
Prices: $$$

Tue – Sat 5:30pm - 9pm
Closed Sun & Mon

Locals love this little bi-level restaurant, set just off the central plaza in sleepy downtown Sonoma. Open only for dinner, the cafe fancies itself part restaurant, part art gallery; indeed, large canvasses by local artists adorn the dining room walls. It's a pleasant, albeit somewhat cramped, setting for a casual meal.

The cafe's kitchen is miniscule, and the changing menu stays purposely small so as not to overwhelm chef/owner John McReynolds and his staff. The surrounding valleys provide many of the ingredients for dishes such as the signature house-smoked salmon with crisp potato-scallion pancake, and seared black pepper lavender filet mignon with gorgonzola-potato gratin. Like the menu, the well-selected wine list is short and concentrates on local labels.

Della Santina's

003

133 E. Napa St., Sonoma (bet. 1st & 2nd Sts.)

Phone: 707-935-0576
Fax: 707-935-7046
Web: www.dellasantinas.com
Prices: $$

Open daily 11:30am - 3pm & 5pm - 9:30pm
Closed major holidays

A petit piece of Tuscany in downtown Sonoma, this family-run trattoria lies just off the square in an attractive gray stone building. A clientele of tourists and regulars seems to find Della Santina's equally appealing.

On a sunny day, the best seat in the house is on the brick patio, shaded by a vine-covered trellis. Here, a fountain happily burbles and the bustle of Sonoma center fades away as you tuck into generous plates of rabbit—a house specialty, as well as spit-roasted chicken, tripe with polenta, homemade gnocchi, and other simple Tuscan fare. No matter whether you sit inside or out, service is professional and smiling.

Be sure to save room for the excellent homemade tiramisu, rich and creamy, and scented with liquor.

Deuce

004

691 Broadway, Sonoma (at Andrieux St.)

Phone: 707-933-3823
Fax: 707-933-9002
Web: www.dine-at-deuce.com
Prices: $$

Sun – Thu 11:30am - 2:30pm & 5pm - 9pm
Fri – Sat 11:30am - 2:30pm & 5pm - 9:30pm

Alumni of Masa in downtown San Francisco, Peter and Kirsten Stewart converted this attractive 19th-century house, a couple of blocks from Sonoma Plaza, into a romantic dining spot. With its arched openings and wrought-iron accents, the dining room acts as a gallery for rotating shows of local artwork. In warm weather, a patio extends the dining space.

Uncomplicated American fare like a barbecue pork sandwich (the pork is smoked for 10 hours), hanger steak, or fresh fish of the day make up the lunch menu. If you're in a hurry, go for the bargain Express Lunch Box, three courses served at the same time. Dinner adds entrées like a brochette of prawns and seared diver scallops, and grilled Rosen Colorado lamb chops. For dessert, try the seasonal fruit cobbler, topped with vanilla ice cream.

El Dorado Kitchen

005

Californian ✗✗

405 1st St. W., Sonoma (at W. Spain St.)

Phone:	707-996-3030
Fax:	707-996-3148
Web:	www.eldoradosonoma.com
Prices:	$$

Open daily 11:30am - 9:30pm

Brought to you by the proprietors of Auberge du Soleil in Rutherford, El Dorado Kitchen premiered in June 2005 inside the El Dorado Hotel *(see Wine Country hotel listings)* on Sonoma's plaza. Country-casual meets contemporary-chic in the airy 226-seat dining space, where whitewashed walls contrast with dark woods. The room's focal point is a communal table fashioned from a single slab of 200-year-old wood.

Chef Ryan Fancher, formerly at The French Laundry, distills the essence of seasonal products in what he bills as "food of the sun." His short menu is just as likely to feature a forest-mushroom pizza from the oak-fired oven as it might wine-braised short ribs that literally melt in the mouth.

On a warm evening, the stone courtyard sets the scene for an intimate tête-à-tête.

Glen Ellen Inn

006

Californian ✗✗

13670 Arnold Dr., Glen Ellen (at Warm Springs Rd.)

Phone:	707-996-6409
Fax:	707-996-1634
Web:	www.glenelleninn.com
Prices:	$$

Fri – Tue 11:30am - 9pm
Wed – Thu 5:30pm - 9pm

Located just down the road from Jack London State Historic Park, Glen Ellen Inn offers both lodging and dining. As far as the latter goes, lunch bring salads, soups and sandwiches that tend to be on the light side, while dinner adds more substantial main courses (fire-grilled filet mignon, duck breast, grilled salmon, house-made pastas).

Of course, any place that bills itself as an "oyster grill and martini bar" has to serve oysters. Here, they offer three different types of oysters daily, depending on what's freshest. If you're a fan, go for the "Dirty Dozen," a sampling of four of each.

Sonoma ladies who lunch fill many of the tables at noontime, while at night the feminine room turns romantic with candlelight, flowers and windows that peek out on the garden.

Kenwood

Contemporary ✗✗

007

9900 Sonoma Hwy., Kenwood (at Warm Springs Blvd.)

Phone:	707-833-6326	Wed – Sun noon - 9pm
Fax:	707-833-2238	Closed Mon & Tue
Web:	www.kenwoodrestaurant.com	
Prices:	$$	

A pleasant stop for lunch while you're visiting Sonoma wineries, Kenwood is conveniently located on Highway 12. In cool weather, a fire greets you as you walk through the bar; in warm weather, the patio is the preferred place to dine. Year-round, the French doors in the main dining room give out onto a landscape of fields and vineyards.

Contemporary cuisine is seriously prepared here, and favors the French with steak tartare, mussels marinière, duck paté, escargots and beef Bourguignon appearing on the menu alongside house-smoked salmon and Ahi tuna sashimi. The wine list leans heavily toward Sonoma vintages, with some French and Italian labels rounding out the selection.

The well-organized waitstaff services a lively crowd of regulars and vineyard visitors.

Sonoma-Meritâge Martini Oyster Bar & Grill

International ✗✗

008

165 W. Napa St., Sonoma (bet. 1st & 2nd Sts.)

Phone:	707-938-9430	Mon, Wed – Fri 11:30am - 2pm
Fax:	707-938-9447	& 5:30pm - 9pm
Web:	www.sonomameritage.com	Sat – Sun 11am - 2pm & 5:30pm - 9pm
Prices:	$$	Closed Tue

Access to the bounty of Sonoma County's farms and vineyards is the main reason that chef/owner Carlo-Alessandro Cavallo chose Sonoma as the setting for his casual grill, which opened in 1999. Now in a new location closer to the plaza, Sonoma-Meritâge Martini Oyster Bar & Grill boasts a larger space smartly decorated with eye-catching Venetian-style light fixtures, custom-made by local artisan Frank Cavaz.

All of those farm-fresh products turn into delectable dishes in the chef's hands. Contemporary cuisine asserts Italian and French overtones in the likes of grilled free-range veal chop plated atop polenta, and vanilla-bean crème brûlée in a tulip-shaped tuile. True to its name, the restaurant offers a long list of specialty martinis to accompany a shellfish menu that goes well beyond oysters.

Wine Country Sonoma Valley

the girl & the fig

009

Californian ✗✗

110 W. Spain St., Sonoma (at 1st St. W.)

Phone: 707-938-3634
Fax: 707-938-2064
Web: www.thegirlandthefig.com
Prices: $$

Mon – Sat 11:30am - 10pm
Sun 10am - 10pm

This homey cafe sits on the northwest corner of Sonoma Plaza, inside the 1880 Sonoma Hotel *(see Wine Country hotel listings)*. Though the restaurant isn't nearly as old, it's every bit as charming, with its warm golden walls and sensuous paintings by local artist Julie Higgins.

What owner Sondra Bernstein calls "country food with a French passion" translates to a daily changing charcuterie platter, ribeye steak frites, and the signature fig salad, prepared in season with arugula, goat cheese, pancetta, pecans and grilled figs. The unusual wine selection focuses on Rhone Valley varietals (Roussanne, Carignane, Syrah, Marsanne) produced in California.

A sibling in nearby Glen Ellen, Fig Cafe *(13690 Arnold Dr. at Warm Springs Rd.)* caters to locals with inexpensive fare—and no corkage fee.

Wolf House

010

American ✗✗

13740 Arnold Dr., Glen Ellen (near London Ranch Rd.)

Phone: 707-996-4401
Fax: 707-996-0850
Web: www.jacklondonlodge.com
Prices: $$

Tue – Fri 11:30am - 3pm & 5:30pm - 9pm
Sat 11am - 3pm & 5:30pm - 9pm
Sun 10am - 3pm & 5:30pm - 9pm
Closed Mon

Named for the mansion of lava boulders and redwood logs that author Jack London and his wife began building in the hills above Glen Ellen in 1911, Wolf House restaurant rests on the wooded banks of Sonoma Creek. Nostalgia for that bygone era abounds as you enter through the adjacent Jack London Saloon, where you can imagine the dusty cowboys swaggering up to quench their thirst at the antique oak bar.

The ranch-style eatery makes a good stop before or after a visit to the historic ruins of the real Wolf House (which burned in 1913, just before the Londons were set to move in). Snag a seat on one of the two creekside decks and graze on American fare that incorporates ingredients like California sea bass, Liberty Farms duck breast, Dungeness crab and abundant produce from local markets.

Where to **stay**

Alphabetical list of Hotels

Where to stay

Alphabetical list of Hotels

Stanyan Park

750 Stanyan St. (at Waller St.)

Phone: 415-751-1000
Fax: 415-668-5454
Web: www.stanyanpark.com
Prices: rooms: $135 – $189 suites: $265 – $315

30
Rooms
6
Suites
&

Stanyan Park Hotel

Stanyan Park's handsome three-story Queen Anne-style turret marks the corner of Stanyan and Waller streets, overlooking Golden Gate Park to the west and the Haight-Ashbury neighborhood to the east.

Inside, its 30 well-kept rooms and 6 suites (all smoke-free) are quietly decorated in conventional Victorian style. Families and longer-term guests will appreciate the spacious suites (up to 900 square feet), fully equipped with kitchens and large living rooms. Free wireless Internet access and voice mail provide modern convenience in the historic atmosphere. The hotel's staff serves up a warm welcome, along with a complimentary breakfast and afternoon tea daily.

With Golden Gate Park at its front door, the Stanyan provides wonderful access to all of the park's cultural and natural attractions. Visitors to nearby hospitals and the University of San Francisco will find this hotel particularly convenient. While hardly hip, the Stanyan affords a comfortable stay at a reasonable price.

Archbishop's Mansion

001

1000 Fulton St. (at Steiner St.)

Phone:	415-563-7872
Fax:	415-885-3193
Web:	www.thearchbishopsmansion.com
Prices:	rooms: $159 – $279 suites: $289 – $599

10
Rooms
5
Suites

Joie de Vivre Hospitality

San Francisco City Civic Center

Built in 1904 and occupied by the Archbishop of San Francisco until 1945, this bed-and-breakfast inn today caters largely to guests sharing a romantic weekend or celebrating a special occasion. Each of its 15 guestrooms, including 5 spacious suites, is named for an opera and is individually decorated befitting its theme with lush fabrics, antiques and ornately carved bedsteads. Some rooms have working fireplaces, claw-foot tubs or Jacuzzis. Traditional in style, bathrooms tend to be rather small. Large, lofty public spaces, warmed by dark redwood and mahogany trim, feature high coffered or lavishly painted ceilings.

Every morning, a complimentary continental breakfast and a newspaper can be delivered to your room upon request, and wine and cheese are served in the parlor each evening. Electronic amenities include VCR and CD players, as well as wireless Internet access for a small fee. The hotel is located on historic Alamo Square Park not far from the grand Beaux-Arts government offices and theaters of Civic Center.

Inn at the Opera

002

333 Fulton St. (at Franklin St.)

Phone:	415-863-8400
Fax:	415-861-0821
Web:	www.innattheopera.com
Prices:	rooms: $149 – $185 suites: $199 – $249 Restaurant: **$$$**

35
Rooms
12
Suites
&

Inn at the Opera

At the heart of San Francisco's arts district, within a couple of blocks of the Opera House, Symphony Hall and the San Francisco Ballet, this small hotel has been popular with musicians, stage performers and audience members alike since 1927. Its 35 guestrooms are plain in their old-fashioned styling and furnishings, and they are on the small side. They do include microwaves, wet bars and small refrigerators, CD players and bathrobes. The Ballet Studio, Concerto and Symphony suites offer lounge or living room areas, bigger bathrooms and kitchenettes. Ovation at the Opera, the hotel's fine-dining restaurant, puts up traditional French cuisine nightly, and a continental breakfast buffet comes gratis with your room.

The Inn at the Opera is also convenient to business and government offices in the Civic Center, while just a stone's throw away, funky Hayes Street is a good place to dine or shop. Boutiques sell unique glassware, pottery and other crafts; eclectic restaurants and cafes provide a variety of lunch and nightlife options.

San Francisco City Civic Center

Phoenix

003

601 Eddy St. (at Larkin St.)

Phone:	415-776-1380
Fax:	415-885-3109
Web:	www.thephoenixhotel.com
Prices:	rooms: $109 - $179 suites: $199 - $329

41
Rooms

3
Suites

♿

🏊

heated

Joie de Vivre Hospitality

Hip and vibrant, the Phoenix bills itself as the city's "rock and roll hotel," and indeed it is popular with entertainers in the industry as well as a cool young clientele. The building retains its 1956 motel atmosphere, though updated with high-volume color and styling. Once inside, guests will feel miles away from the seedy Tenderloin district that surrounds the hotel.

The 41 guestrooms are done up in tropical bungalow décor, aglow in bright hues, bamboo furnishings and works by local artists. Though the guestrooms are ample in size, the bathrooms can be tiny (renovated bathrooms are larger). Three modern one-bedroom suites are also available. In true motel style, the rooms face—and open onto—a lushly planted courtyard where funky sculptures, Indonesian-style lounging areas and a heated swimming pool that is itself a work of art (check out the underwater mural) offer a boisterous oasis for schmoozing or sunning.

Amenities include complimentary poolside breakfast and free parking, and hotel-wide wireless Internet access. Nearby clubs and concert halls offer guests a variety of nightlife choices, from cutting edge to classical.

San Francisco City Civic Center

Hotel Adagio

001

550 Geary St. (bet. Jones & Taylor Sts.)

Phone: 415-775-5000
Fax: 415-775-9388
Web: www.thehoteladagio.com
Prices: rooms: $179 – $279 suites: $799 – $899

171
Rooms
2
Suites
&

Joie de Vivre Hospitality

Catering to the Internet cafe set, the Adagio displays a modern minimalist décor that appeals to young travelers from the U.S. and abroad. The impressive Spanish Colonial Revival structure was built in 1929 as the El Cortez, and knew several different names and owners before it was refurbished and reopened in 2003 by the Joie de Vivre Hospitality group (whose other properties include the Commodore, the Carlton and the new Hotel Vitale).

Rooms are dressed in a contemporary and sober style with earthy tones and clean lines; many of the rooms have city views. All guests enjoy complimentary high-speed Internet access, CD players, 24-inch Sony TVs and Egyptian cotton linens, plus double-paned windows to screen out the street noise. On the Executive Level, rooms boast downtown views, Frette bathrobes, hookups for iPod/MP3 players, and DVD libraries. You won't need to miss your workout here; the on-site fitness center offers Cybex equipment.

Off the lobby, Cortez restaurant *(see Financial District restaurant listings)* delights diners with Mediterranean-inspired small plates.

Hotel Bijou

002

111 Mason St. (at Eddy St.)

Phone: 415-771-1200
Fax: 415-346-3196
Web: www.hotelbijou.com
Prices: rooms: $99 - $149

65
Rooms
&

Joie de Vivre Hospitality

Hollywood comes to San Francisco at the Hotel Bijou, where Art-Deco inspired décor and a jewel-tone palette recall the golden years of the silver screen. Movies shot in San Francisco take center stage, and each of 65 small and simple guestrooms is named for one. Still photographs from the films decorate the boldly colorful walls, done up in rich reds and yellows. Bathrooms with full tubs and showers are utilitarian and well maintained; well-kept rooms offer dataports and two-line phones, with wireless high-speed Internet access available throughout the hotel. Although rooms at the back of the five-story building have no view, they are quieter than those at the front. Pastries, coffee and tea are served gratis each morning.

Just off the handsome purple and red lobby, the Petit (and it is) Bijou Theatre screens two locally set movies each evening; each guestroom is named for one such film, from *48 Hours* to *Lady from Shanghai*. The hotel is convenient to cable-car stops and the streets around Union Square, the neighborhood's posh retail district, as well as to the business center of the city.

Clift

003

495 Geary St. (at Taylor St.)

Phone:	415-775-4700
Fax:	415-441-4621
Web:	www.clifthotel.com
Prices:	rooms: $235 - $390 suites: $600 - $800

338
Rooms
25
Suites

Clift

Dark meets light, antique goes modern, and eccentric cajoles conservative at this high-style hostelry. Built in 1913 and reconceived for the 21st century by Philippe Starck, the Clift surprises at every turn. Dramatic lighting, soaring ceilings, a cacophony of textures and eclectic furnishings dress the public areas in a sleek elegance that takes equal cues from Surrealism, Art Deco and a style uniquely Californian. The legendary Redwood Room, with its original 1933 redwood paneling and huge bar (said to be carved from one tree) may be the ne plus ultra, especially as reinterpreted during the renovation.

By contrast, the guestrooms are swathed in quiet tones of foggy gray, beige and lavender. Acrylic orange nightstands and wooden wheelbarrow armchairs add whimsy to the minimalist sophistication. Standard rooms measure only 260 square feet, but more expensive chambers are larger, with a deluxe one-bedroom suite topping out at 925 square feet. All of them feature luxuries from Egyptian cotton 400-thread-count sheets to DVD and CD players with an in-room disc library.

Off the lobby, glamorous Asia de Cuba serves tasty fusion fare *(see Financial District restaurant listings).*

Hotel Diva

004

440 Geary St. (bet. Mason & Taylor Sts.)

Phone: 415-885-0200
Fax: 415-346-6613
Web: www.hoteldiva.com
Prices: rooms: $129 - $259 suites: $359

113
Rooms
2
Suites

Hotel Diva

Edgy Euro-tech style pervades the Diva, where stainless steel and cobalt blue set the tone. Renovated rooms feature wired and wireless high-speed Internet access, and CD and VCR players; you can even rent iPods at the front desk. Streamlined furnishings of metal and blond wood, and rolled-steel headboards furnish the rooms, which are done in a hip black-and-gray color scheme. Bathrooms are small but complete. Kids will love the Little Diva suites, tailored to the young traveler with pop art colors, bunk beds, kid-friendly movies and a microwave oven stocked with popcorn.

No buffet breakfast is offered, though guests can order a breakfast box in their rooms or visit the Starbucks located in the same building. PCs and laser printers are available in the business center, where copy and fax services come with a fee. The hotel occupies a favorable location facing two of the city's main playhouses, the Curran Theatre and the American Conservatory Theater (ACT), and steps from the city's fashionable Union Square shopping district.

Out front, the Diva Sidewalk of Fame displays the signatures of celebrity guests like Tony Curtis, Stevie Wonder and Lily Tomlin.

San Francisco City Financial District

Handlery Union Square

005

351 Geary St. (bet. Mason & Powell Sts.)

Phone:	415-781-7800
Fax:	415-781-0216
Web:	www.handlery.com
Prices:	rooms: $159 – $269 Restaurant: **$$**

377
Rooms
&
heated

Handlery Union Square

A three-generation family operation that opened in 1948, the Handlery is a gracious inn centrally located on Union Square. The facility comprises two buildings, the earliest erected in 1908 as the Hotel Stewart and today housing 284 rooms. They are comfortable, pleasant and clean if unremarkable in style. In-room refrigerators, coffeemakers, and Internet access number among the amenities.

In the mid-1960s, the motor inn next door was connected to the main building, adding 93 rooms. Accommodations in this "Club Section" are more spacious and comfortable; some have balconies overlooking the connecting courtyard and pool (the best choice); others face the street. Additional amenities, including bathrobes, balconies, and separate vanity areas with lighted make-up mirrors, make these rooms attractive to those who prefer a bit more luxury.

The Daily Grill Restaurant and Bar off the lobby serves breakfast, lunch and dinner and provides room service. Perhaps the hotel's more noteworthy features, the heated swimming pool and sauna are mid-city rarities.

The Inn at Union Square

440 Post St. (bet. Mason & Powell Sts.)

Phone: 415-397-3510
Fax: 415-989-0529
Web: www.unionsquare.com
Prices: rooms: $179 - $209 suites: $209 - $299

24
Rooms
6
Suites

The Inn at Union Square

San Francisco City Financial District

Perfectly located within a few feet of Union Square, this inn tucks away behind its narrow and discreet façade. Inside, a tiny lobby sporting country inn décor greets guests. Its 30 rooms, including 6 suites and 2 executive rooms with fireplaces, are undergoing major overhaul (scheduled to be completed by the end of 2006) in warm and inviting shades of red and yellow. Though bathrooms are small, they come completely equipped.

Each floor includes a small suite facing the street, while all the other guestrooms are located on the back side of the building without any views. The latter are tranquil, a real plus in such a busy, central location. In the two-room penthouse suite, a sauna and whirlpool, a fireplace, a flat-screen television and a wet bar cater to sybarites. Standard rooms are stocked with terry robes, goose-down pillows and fresh flowers, as well as high-speed Internet access. A complimentary breakfast buffet is served in tiny foyers, complete with fireplaces, on each floor. In the evenings, guests can enjoy wine and cheese there as well.

Outside, the theaters, shopping and dining of Union Square are only steps away.

JW Marriott

007

500 Post St. (at Mason St.)

Phone:	415-771-8600
Fax:	415-398-0267
Web:	www.jwmarriottunionsquare.com
Prices:	rooms: $229 - $479 suites: $679 Restaurant: **$$$**

330
Rooms
9
Suites

J. W. Marriott

Twenty-one stories soar up around the impressive atrium lobby at this hotel recently reincarnated as a high-end Marriott. Built in 1987 and occupied until 2006 by the Pan Pacific, the property retains its sleek contemporary looks, enhanced by cool Italian marble trimmings and Asian accents. Throughout, an arch motif gives windows and other architectural elements a distinctive flair. Glass elevators whisk guests up and down the atrium interior. The hotel's Pacific restaurant serves breakfast, lunch and dinner, and evening drinks and nibbles can be had at the Pacific Bar.

Spacious guestrooms, simply done in serene tones of beige and brown with dark wood furniture, feature high-speed Internet, flat-screen TVs and Bose Wave radios. Separate showers and oversize tubs make the marbled, well-equipped bathrooms particularly comfortable, and robes are provided. Rooms on the upper floors offer lovely views through the handsome eyebrow-style windows. Conveniently located in Union Square, the hotel is easily accessible to shopping, theaters and the heart of downtown San Francisco.

King George

008

334 Mason St. (bet. Geary & O'Farrell Sts.)

Phone: 415-781-5050
Fax: 415-391-6976
Web: www.kinggeorge.com
Prices: rooms: $109 – $205 suites: $189 – $219

151
Rooms
2
Suites
♿
🚶

King George Hotel

The charmingly painted façade of the 1912 King George adds a bit of fun to this Anglophile's hideaway. Inside, the lobby welcomes with its warm yellow, beige and gold color scheme, and, of course, a full-size portrait of King George. Most of the guestrooms have been recently renovated with pleasing fabrics, inviting green walls, classic wood furniture and new bedspreads to create a European feel; all include high-speed Internet access, safes, and irons and ironing boards. Executive rooms on the second floor are larger than the rest. Count on the concierge to arrange airport shuttles, restaurant reservations and theater tickets.

Enjoy breakfast on-site at the Windsor Tearoom, which also serves tea on Saturdays and Sundays. Winston's Bar and Lounge specializes in wines, champagnes, specialty beers and appetizers. For a small fee, guests can enjoy access to a nearby health club. The hotel is highly accessible to Union Square and the theater district, as well as the Moscone Convention Center and the San Francisco Museum of Modern Art.

San Francisco City Financial District

Mandarin Oriental

222 Sansome St. (bet. California & Pine Sts.)

Phone: 415-276-9888
Fax: 415-433-0289
Web: www.mandarinoriental.com
Prices: rooms: $515 - $725 suites: $1,400 - $3,000

151
Rooms
7
Suites

Mandarin Oriental

From this superb hotel's ground-floor entry, high-speed elevators whisk guests to their aeries, located in the towers of the city's third-tallest building between the 38th and 48th stories. Glass-enclosed sky bridges connect the two towers on each floor, offering spectacular views of the city and beyond. Guestroom views dazzle as well (binoculars are provided), from every angle, though corner rooms and those with a "bridge to bridge" perspective take top honors. Choose a city or bay view, and if tub-to-ceiling bathroom windows delight, reserve a Mandarin King room. Handsome Asian design elements, elegant fabrics and warm colors lend a refined air to the recently refreshed rooms and suites; spacious marble bathrooms are perfectly equipped.

Spacious and comfortable, the lobby includes a pleasant lounge area, a sushi bar and live piano music beginning at 5pm daily. The hotel features its own fitness center, and passes can be purchased for a nearby health club. In-room high-speed Internet access is available, with WiFi in the hotel's public areas.

On the second floor, Silks *(See Financial District restaurant listings)* restaurant features contemporary cuisine with pan-Asian influences.

Hotel Monaco

501 Geary St. (at Taylor St.)

Phone: 415-292-0100
Fax: 415-292-0111
Web: www.monaco-sf.com
Prices: rooms: $219 - $399 suites: $299 - $459

176
Rooms
25
Suites

Hotel Monaco/Fred Licht

This renovated 1910 Beaux-Arts beauty offers signature Kimpton high style in a great location, two blocks from Union Square in the midst of the theater district. Luxury describes the lobby, with its two-story fireplace, cozy club chairs, marble staircase, and ceiling domes hand-painted with whimsical skyscapes of hot-air balloons and planes.

In the guestrooms, bright fabrics drape over canopy beds, cheery striped paper covers the walls, and Chinese-inspired furnishings lend an exotic look. Flat-screen TVs, animal-print robes and Aveda bath amenities make staying here a treat. And don't overlook the spa and fitness room on the lower level, or the on-site business center.

Coffee and tea come complimentary each morning in the quiet living room off the lobby; every evening this same space hosts a wine and cheese reception for hotel guests. Breakfast, lunch and dinner are served in the stunning Art Deco-style Grand Café *(see Financial District restaurant listings)*, the building's former ballroom.

Your four-legged friends are welcome here, but if you can't bring Fido or Fifi along, the hotel will gladly supply a goldfish in your room to keep you company.

San Francisco City **Financial District**

Hotel Nikko

222 Mason St. (bet. Ellis & O'Farrell Sts.)

Phone:	415-394-1111
Fax:	415-394-1106
Web:	www.hotelnikkosf.com
Prices:	rooms: $179 – $269 suites: $299 – $2,700 Restaurant: **$$**

510
Rooms
22
Suites

Hotel Nikko

Though large, the Nikko offers a comfortable and convenient stay, with a choice of 12 different types of rooms and suites in various sizes. At 280 square feet, the Petite Queens are best for single occupancy but may also be of interest to two people in search of a good deal. Deluxe rooms, both king and double/doubles, occupy floors 6 through 21. The Nikko Floors (22, 23 and 24) offer more services and amenities, including restricted access, complimentary high-speed Internet, and breakfast served in a private lounge. At the top end, the two-bedroom, two-bath Imperial Suite measures in at 2,635 square feet. City views are divine, especially from the higher floors. Public areas showcase changing exhibitions of paintings, sculpture and media arts curated by the Baxter Chang Patri Gallery.

A lovely swimming pool, together with a fitness room and sauna, occupy the large and very bright fifth-floor atrium. For your business needs, the well-equipped business center can arrange printing, binding, faxing, translation and secretarial services, along with other office functions. Stop by the Nikko's fine-dining restaurant, Anzu, for sushi, Prime midwestern cuts of beef, and a sake martini.

San Francisco City Financial District

320 - San Francisco City

Omni

012

500 California St. (at Montgomery St.)

Phone:	415-677-9494
Fax:	415-273-3038
Web:	www.omnisanfrancisco.com
Prices:	rooms: $350 – $410 suites: $600 Restaurant: **$$$**

347
Rooms
15
Suites

Omni Hotel, San Francisco

Located in the heart of the Financial District with a cable-car stop right outside, this Omni opened in 2002 in an elegant 1926 bank building after a major renovation. Though only the original stone and brick façade has been preserved, the spacious wood-paneled lobby, floored in rosy marble, takes its cue and its stylishness from a bygone era.

Spread over 17 stories, the 347 rooms and 15 suites follow suit. They are large and classic in style, with details to match, including Egyptian cotton sheets and well-equipped bathrooms decorated in marble and granite. Most guestrooms feature T-1 high-speed Internet access and three phones; one is cordless. For upgraded amenities, reserve on the 16th "signature" floor, where rooms come with a Bose Wave radio and CD player, DVD player, wireless Internet and a color copier/printer. Specialty accommodations such as Get Fit rooms (furnished with a treadmill and healthy snacks) and a Kids Fantasy Suite, where bunk beds and kids rule in the second bedroom, are also available. Bob's Steak and Chop House will appeal to meat-loving guests.

Every Saturday at 10am, a guided walking tour departs from the hotel for an overview of city history.

San Francisco City Financial District

Prescott

013 545 Post St. (bet. Mason & Taylor Sts.)

Phone:	415-563-0303
Fax:	415-563-6831
Web:	www.prescotthotel.com
Prices:	rooms: $169 - $299 suites: $319 - $399

132
Rooms
32
Suites
&
♿

Prescott Hotel/David Phelps

This boutique hotel blends old and new, whimsy and tradition into an attractive whole. Especially in the comfortable lobby, playful designs and colors create a welcoming space that includes cozy armchairs and a fireplace. Guestrooms are situated in two separate but connected older buildings, one featuring Deluxe rooms and the other, known as the Club Level, offering rooms with upgraded amenities, including access to a private lounge, express check-in and departure, and complimentary breakfast. Club Level guests also enjoy an evening cocktail party with hors d'oeuvres from Postrio *(see Financial District restaurant listings)*, the on-site restaurant.

Rooms are stylishly, if soberly, decorated with hints of the Louis XVI and French Empire styles. They feature Italian linens and Ralph Lauren fabrics, and the well-equipped bathrooms are trimmed in marble. High-speed wireless Internet access, laptop-size safes and CD-player clock radios add convenience. A 450-square-foot fitness room is located on the eighth floor, and in-room spa services offer massages, facials and hand and foot treatments. The Brown Sugar Massage might be just the ticket after a hectic day.

Serrano

405 Taylor St. (at O'Farrell St.)

Phone:	415-885-2500
Fax:	415-474-4879
Web:	www.serranohotel.com
Prices:	rooms: $149 - $279 suites: $279 - $379

217
Rooms
19
Suites

Serrano Hotel/David Phelps

Masterpiece of the Serrano is its lobby, where the majestic fireplace, beamed and elegantly decorated ceilings, and Moroccan red columns exude the feel of a Spanish Renaissance hall. Indeed, the décor perfectly fits the 1924 building's Spanish revival styling. All the guestrooms and suites—236 on 17 floors—are identically decorated with warm colors that feature bright yellow wallpaper, red-and-white-striped curtains, cherry wood furniture and Moroccan flourishes. Classic bathrooms are furnished with Aveda products and amazing leopard-pattern bathrobes. The overall effect in each room is pleasantly residential. Theatrically minded guests can reserve the American Conservatory Theatre Suite, named in honor of the nearby playhouse and adorned accordingly.

The Serrano makes a library of board games available for guests to play in the lobby or in their rooms. High-speed Internet is accessible throughout the hotel, and a 24-hour business center keeps computers, scanners, printers and fax machines at the ready. Pets are welcome here.

Hotel Triton

015

342 Grant Ave. (at Bush St.)

Phone: 415-394-0500
Fax: 415-394-0555
Web: www.hoteltriton.com
Prices: rooms: $149 – $369

140 Rooms

Hotel Triton/Markham Johnson

Awash in hipness from its in-your-face décor to its eco-friendly guestrooms, this "unhotel" will startle some and delight others. Undulating columns sheathed in gold, psychedelic murals, and funky, eclectic furniture sets the tone in the lobby. The hotel's 140 rooms offer a variety of styles. Designed for one guest, Zen Dens provide incense, a Book of Buddha and your own bamboo plant to nurture. The 7th-floor Eco rooms feature water and air filtration, energy savers and all-natural linens, as well as a restful monochromatic palette. While the Triton welcomes pets, none are allowed on this floor to keep it allergy free.

The hotel's Celebrity Suites (really just larger bedrooms) have been decorated by the likes of Carlos Santana and Woody Harrelson. Even the usual queens, kings and double/doubles are quirky, artistic and comfortable. All include eco-friendly bath products, flat-screen TVs, pillow-top mattresses and luscious linens. Next door to the hotel, Café de la Presse *(see Financial District restaurant listings)* serves breakfast and provides room service.

The Triton sits outside the Chinatown gate, within a few minutes walk from Union Square and the Financial District.

Westin St. Francis

016

335 Powell St. (at Union Square)

Phone:	415-397-7000
Fax:	415-774-0124
Web:	www.westinstfrancis.com
Prices:	rooms: $189 - $489 suites: $650 - $3,330 Restaurant: $$$

1166
Rooms
29
Suites

Westin St. Francis

This luxury hotel deserves its legendary status. Regally situated at the head of Union Square, the St. Francis, opened in 1904, was modeled on the grand European hotels of the period. Barely surviving the earthquake and fire in 1906, the hotel went on to build two more wings, and in 1972 a 32-story tower was added behind the main structure. Today the St. Francis remains the grand dame of West Coast hotels; visitors and residents alike rendezvous in its lobby as they have for generations.

For full effect, you may want to reserve a room in the main building, where historic materials decorate the large hallways. Rooms here are decorated in a charmingly old-fashioned Empire style, and many have good views of Union Square. More contemporary tower rooms all have bay windows for sweeping city and bay vistas. Westin's signature Heavenly Bed™ and Heavenly Bath™ come in every room. A spa and the acclaimed Michael Mina restaurant *(see Financial District restaurant listings)* round out the amenities.

The stately 10,700-square-foot Grand Ballroom lends itself equally to society galas and business functions.

Hotel Drisco

2901 Pacific Ave. (at Broderick St.)

Phone: 415-346-2880
Fax: 415-567-5537
Web: www.hoteldrisco.com
Prices: rooms: $199 – $239 suites: $319 – $559

29
Rooms
19
Suites

Joie de Vivre Hospitality

Comfortably at home in tony Pacific Heights, this 1903 hotel offers elegant accommodations surrounded by beautiful residences and quiet streets, removed from the bustle of downtown. Well dressed throughout in shades of beige accented by rich wood tones and mellow colors, this member of the Joie de Vivre group possesses a charming atmosphere that permeates each of its rooms. Accommodations, including 19 suites, vary in size but are consistently graceful in style, and well furnished with robes and slippers, VCR and CD players, and wireless high-speed Internet access. Some rooms offer nice city views; others overlook the building's tiny courtyard.

Guests can enjoy a complimentary breakfast buffet in the sunny first-floor dining room, and coffee, tea and newspapers are available 24 hours in the hotel's lovely lobby. Each evening, wine and hors d'oeuvres come compliments of the house. An on-site workout room and complimentary access to the Presidio YMCA will appeal to fitness fiends, while the small business center provides basic services for business travelers.

Laurel Inn

002

444 Presidio Ave. (at California St.)

Phone: 415-567-8467
Fax: 415-928-1866
Web: www.thelaurelinn.com
Prices: rooms: $169 – $209

49
Rooms
&

Joie de Vivre Hospitality

The Laurel Inn, built in 1963, embraces its mid-century pedigree with gusto and good taste. Bold strokes of color enliven the interior, particularly in the artist-inspired area rugs that decorate the rooms and public spaces. Furnishings throughout are sleek and not fussy. Large windows grace the newly renovated guestrooms, which include 18 larger units with kitchenettes, much in demand by guests planning extended stays. Each room offers wireless high-speed Internet, CD and VCR players, a two-line phone with dataports, and an iron and ironing board. Rooms on the back side of the hotel feature pleasant city panoramas and are quieter than those facing the street, though all are efficiently soundproofed.

Guests traveling with cars and pets will appreciate the free indoor parking and pet-friendliness of the Laurel. A small continental breakfast is served in the attractive lobby each morning. If you're content not to be in the center of downtown action, the Laurel Inn, located in residential Pacific Heights, offers good value.

Hotel Majestic

San Francisco City *Marina District*

1500 Sutter St. (at Gough St.)

Phone:	415-441-1100
Fax:	415-673-7331
Web:	www.thehotelmajestic.com
Prices:	rooms: $120 - $195 suites: $200 - $250 Restaurant: **$$**

49 Rooms 9 Suites ♿ 🛎

Hotel Majestic

The Edwardian elegance of the Majestic dates from 1902, when it was built as a private residence. Already a hotel by 1906 when the earthquake struck, the building survived to become San Francisco's oldest continuously operated hotel. Lavish public areas, set about with French and English antiques, marble columns and wrought-iron balustrades, recall a bygone era of domestic luxury which extends to the 58 rooms and suites.

Though the standard rooms are on the small side, the suites are large, pleasant and reasonably priced for their size. Sumptuously swagged canopy beds furnish each room, and bathrooms are completely equipped and beautifully tiled and marbled. All rooms come with Turkish robes and turndown service featuring cookies before bed. Though old-fashioned in style, the hotel offers modern electronic amenities, including wireless high-speed Internet and a laptop computer for guests' use.

A complimentary continental breakfast and afternoon wine and hors d'oeuvres are served in the dining room. Check out the butterfly collection in the Avalon Room off the lobby.

Hotel Carlton

1075 Sutter St. (bet. Hyde & Larkin Sts.)

Phone:	415-673-0242
Fax:	415-673-4904
Web:	www.hotelcarltonsf.com
Prices:	rooms: $99 – $189 Restaurant: $$

161 Rooms

Joie de Vivre Hospitality/Scott Brooks

The unassuming exterior of this 1927 hotel belies the charming and cheerful atmosphere that awaits inside. Renovated and reopened in 2004, the Carlton now features a globetrotting theme realized through furniture, photographs and objects from around the world. The eclectic result is colorful and eccentric though not overdone.

Rooms are neat and tasteful, decorated in soft colors splashed with exotic accents, and the higher of the building's seven stories afford unobstructed views of the city. Though they lack air-conditioning, each room features a large ceiling fan for those rare hot days. Those on the top three floors, for a higher price, provide complimentary high-speed Internet access.

Hotel employees—an international team that speaks more than a dozen languages—are singularly dedicated to the comfort of their guests. The convenience, friendliness and style of this hotel make it a good value for the money.

The Commodore

825 Sutter St. (at Jones St.)

Phone: 415-923-6800
Fax: 415-923-6804
Web: www.thecommodorehotel.com
Prices: rooms: $89 - $179

102
Rooms

San Francisco City **Nob Hill**

Joie de Vivre Hospitality

Located at the foot of Nob Hill, three blocks west of Union Square, the Commodore offers an offbeat urban oasis of neo-Deco styling built originally as a hotel for merchant sailors in 1928. Today, whimsical custom furnishings, crazy colors, 1920s luxury-liner design elements and dramatic murals create an air of the unexpected. A young and friendly staff eager to provide personalized service further enlivens the casual and cool atmosphere.

The Commodore's rooms are good sized and well maintained but spare in their décor (except for the color-block bedspreads), with something of a streamlined, cruise-ship feel. Each features a walk-in closet, new Serta plush mattresses, and full bathroom with shower and tub.

Topping the list of hot local nightspots for late-night drinks and canoodling, the hip Red Room lounge serves a mean Cosmopolitan. The landmarks and attractions of downtown San Francisco, including the theater district, are easily accessible from this lively hotel.

The Fairmont

950 Mason St. (at California St.)

Phone:	415-772-5000
Fax:	415-772-5013
Web:	www.fairmont.com
Prices:	rooms: $289 – $499 suites: $500 – $750 Restaurant: **$$$**

528
Rooms
63
Suites

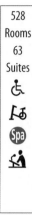

The Fairmont Hotel, San Francisco

San Francisco City **Nob Hill**

Flagship of the Fairmont hotel group, this Gilded Age palace overlooks the city from atop Nob Hill as it has since construction began in 1902, despite earthquake and fire. Recently returned to their past glory, the hotel's public spaces sparkle with turn-of-the-century splendor. The lobby alone is worth a visit, especially to see the restoration of architect Julia Morgan's original Corinthian columns, alabaster walls, marble floors, and vaulted ceilings lusciously trimmed in gold. Guests can soak up the atmosphere over a meal in Laurel Court, the hotel's original dining room. Or, for a different kind of nostalgia, visit the Tonga Room, a tiki hideaway, complete with thatched umbrellas and live music.

Rooms have been refurbished in pale yellows, refined fabrics and dark wood furnishings. With their 14-foot vaulted ceilings, those around the exterior of the original seven-story structure are particularly spacious and boast nice views of city and bay. For panoramic skyline views, choose a room in the 23-story tower, opened in 1961. All guestrooms include extra-long mattresses and have been updated with modern business amenities, though high-speed Internet comes with a fee.

Nob Hill Hotel

004

835 Hyde St. (bet. Sutter & Bush Sts.)

Phone:	415-885-2987
Fax:	415-921-1648
Web:	www.nobhillhotel.com
Prices:	rooms: $129 - $365

52 Rooms

Nob Hill Hotel

Decorated in a plush crush of Victoriana, the elegant Nob Hill Hotel combines stained glass, velvety fabrics and ornate furnishings to create a cozy turn-of-the-century hideaway. The hotel was built in 1906 and restored in 1998; its 52 rooms are generally small but nicely kept and well appointed with marble baths, brass bedsteads and richly colored wallpapers. Each is romantic and intimate, and some rooms, including two penthouse suites, have beautiful private terraces. Several suites feature whirlpool tubs. Small refrigerators and microwaves are provided, along with CD players, hairdryers and coffeemakers. Not to mention the reassuring teddy bear on each bed. The atmosphere is hushed and the rooms are quiet, whether they face the courtyard or the street.

Rates include an evening wine tasting, access to a 24-hour fitness center, and a continental breakfast. Outside, all the attractions of Nob Hill await, from historic buildings to glorious views.

San Francisco City Nob Hill

The Ritz-Carlton

600 Stockton St. (bet. California & Pine Sts.)

Phone:	415-296-7465
Fax:	415-291-0288
Web:	www.ritzcarlton.com
Prices:	rooms: $495 - $645 suites: $845 - $995 Restaurant: **$$$**

277
Rooms
59
Suites

The Ritz-Carlton Hotel

This imposing Neoclassical building began life as an insurance company in 1909, and since 1991 it has housed San Francisco's finest hotel. For pure class, luxury and service, the Ritz-Carlton reigns supreme. A multimillion-dollar renovation in 2006 enhanced its cachet with upgraded technology, guestroom amenities, and new personal services for travelers with children, pets and computers.

Decorated with a rich collection of 18th- and 19th-century antiques and paintings, the hotel's lobby includes a gracious lounge that serves afternoon tea, cocktails and sushi. On the second level, the Terrace Restaurant offers breakfast and lunch, and dining alfresco in the courtyard is among the hotel's great pleasures. For elegant suppers, the Dining Room *(see Nob Hill restaurant listings)* serves contemporary cuisine in a lavish setting.

Each of the guestrooms has been carefully restored with European charm and luxury in mind. All include wireless Internet access and high-definition flat-screen TVs, while marble bathrooms come with rain showerheads, double sinks and separate water closets. On the upper floors, the amenities of the Club Level provide unexcelled ambience, privacy and pampering.

San Francisco City **Nob Hill**

Argonaut

001

495 Jefferson St. (at Hyde St.)

Phone: 415-563-0800
Fax: 415-563-2800
Web: www.argonauthotel.com
Prices: rooms: $169 - $379 suites: $689 - $829

239
Rooms
13
Suites

Argonaut/David Phelps

There's no doubt about which hotel has the most character in this part of the city. Perfectly located near Ghirardelli Square, the cable-car turnaround and Fisherman's Wharf, the Argonaut occupies a 1907 waterfront warehouse at The Cannery. It shares the space with the Maritime National Historic Park visitor center.

There's no doubt, either, about the theme of this pet-friendly hotel: its solid, primary colors, maritime artifacts, and nautical design motifs give it away, beginning in the lobby where a lovely celestial clock hangs over the fireplace. Exposed brick walls and massive wooden beams and columns also reflect the hardworking heritage of the historic building.

Rooms and suites remain solidly in character: bold stripes and stars decorate walls, furniture and carpets. The rooms are well soundproofed and have modern amenities including flat-screen TVs, CD-DVD players and complimentary high-speed Internet access. Some of them offer views of the bay and Alcatraz. A Kimpton Group signature, six "Tall Rooms" come with extra-long beds and raised showerheads for tall guests.

Hotel Bohème

444 Columbus Ave. (bet. Green & Vallejo Sts.)

Phone:	415-433-9111
Fax:	415-362-6292
Web:	www.hotelboheme.com
Prices:	rooms: $159 - $179

15
Rooms

Candra Scott & Anderson

This quaint boutique hotel at the foot of Telegraph Hill in the heart of North Beach takes its inspiration from the bohemian Beat Generation of the 1950s. And well it might, as poet Allen Ginsberg once slept here. Next door you'll find Vesuvio Cafe and City Lights Bookstore (founded by poet Lawrence Ferlinghetti), two hangouts still haunted by Beat spirits.

Built in the 1880s and rebuilt after the earthquake, the Victorian structure has been nicely adapted to its current role. Its 15 rooms reflect a certain 1950s countercultural style in their bright colors and eclectic furniture; they are small, romantic and meticulously clean. Each has a private bath, and all the rooms offer wireless Internet access. About half face Columbus Avenue, which makes for good people-watching, but not much peace and quiet. The surrounding neighborhood is great for strolling and sipping coffee; from here you can walk up Telegraph Hill to Coit Tower and explore up and down the Filbert Steps.

The courteous staff at the Hotel Bohème is glad to help make reservations for restaurants, theater performances and tours.

San Francisco City

North Beach Area

The Argent

001

50 Third St. (bet. Market & Mission Sts.)

Phone: 415-974-6400
Fax: 415-495-6152
Web: www.argenthotel.com
Prices: rooms: $189 – $329 suites: $595 – $1,500 Restaurant: **$$**

641
Rooms
26
Suites

The Argent Hotel

With 667 rooms spread over 36 floors, the Argent definitely qualifies as a large corporate hotel; indeed, it caters to many meetings and groups. However, despite its size, the hotel cultivates a stylish and comfortable atmosphere. Its excellent location, just south of Market and convenient to downtown attractions, is another reason to stay here.

Dramatic marble floors, rich woodwork and a gold-leaf dome characterize the elegantly appointed lobby, and the Argent's art collection, including works by David Hockney and Roy Lichtenstein, adds sophisticated personality. In the rooms, floor-to-ceiling windows drench each space in natural light and afford increasingly impressive views the higher you go. Dressed in fine fabrics, the décor is warm and modern, though the bathrooms could use a facelift. Each room provides feather-filled comforters, high-speed Internet access and three phones including one cordless speakerphone.

Hotel service is friendly and efficient, and guests are invited to use the on-site business and fitness centers. Family packages, including complementary toys and games for the kids, are available, and runners should ask about guided weekday morning runs.

Four Seasons

757 Market St. (bet. Third & Fourth Sts.)

Phone: 415-633-3000
Fax: 415-633-3001
Web: www.fourseasons.com
Prices: rooms: $375 – $525 suites: $750 – $2,200 Restaurant: **$$$**

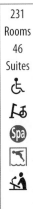

231
Rooms
46
Suites

Four Seasons Hotel, San Francisco

A testament to the burgeoning neighborhood south of Market Street, this sophisticated, modern luxury hotel opened in 2001. Occupying the first 12 stories of a residential high rise in the Yerba Buena Arts District, the Four Seasons is convenient to Union Square, the Moscone Convention Center and the San Francisco Museum of Modern Art.

The lobby, on the 5th floor, balances modern and classic design, blending golden wood tones with artwork for a quiet contemporary effect. Art, in fact, is everywhere, as the hotel showcases throughout its public spaces a considerable collection of paintings, sculpture and ceramics by Bay Area artists.

Rooms, as they ascend from the 6th to the 17th floor, offer more and more stunning views of the city. Restful tones and residential touches decorate each one, the smallest of which measures a generous 450 square feet. All rooms feature large baths with a deep soaking tub and separate shower. In-room amenities include fluffy terrycloth robes, down pillows, high-speed Internet access, a CD sound system and Playstation. Guests have complementary access to the on-site Sports Club/LA, with its junior Olympic-size pool and full-service spa.

San Francisco City SoMa

The Mosser

54 4th St. (bet. Market & Mission Sts.)

Phone:	415-986-4400
Fax:	415-495-4091
Web:	www.themosser.com
Prices:	rooms: $89 – $189

166 Rooms

The Mosser

The Mosser successfully overlays a fresh modern look against the backdrop of its historic building, originally opened as a hotel in 1913. It offers a good price in a great location accessible to destinations north and south of Market Street. Best of all, the helpful, friendly staff really sets this economical property apart.

Though they are small and lack a view, the rooms on the courtyard are quiet (all have double-pane windows) and less expensive. The clean, crisp décor includes platform beds, white-washed walls and geometrically patterned carpet for a comfortable Danish-modern effect. Some rooms feature lovely bay windows with window seats that overlook the street.

For a particular bargain, 54 of the hotel's 166 rooms share well-kept bathrooms—no more than three rooms per bath—though sinks, vanities and bath amenities furnish all the rooms. Extras include CD players, cable TV, ceiling fans, dataports and voice mail. Wireless Internet access is available for a fee. The hotel even has its own professional recording studio, in case you need help mixing your new CD.

San Francisco City SoMa

Palace

004

2 New Montgomery St. (at Market St.)

Phone: 415-512-1111
Fax: 415-543-0671
Web: www.sfpalace.com
Prices: rooms: $299 - $629 suites: $775 - $1,125 Restaurant: **$$$**

518
Rooms
34
Suites

Palace Hotel

Another of downtown San Francisco's grand dames, the Palace symbolized the city's meteoric rise from boomtown to world-class metropolis when it opened in 1875. Today, through earthquake, fire and 130-plus years, the hotel withstands the test of time. Its centerpiece is the sumptuous Garden Court, beautifully restored to its 1909 condition. Here, guests can have breakfast, lunch or brunch under a stunning canopy of intricately leaded art glass hung with Austrian glass chandeliers. In a different mood, the Pied Piper Bar displays a mural painted especially for the Palace by American illustrator Maxfield Parrish in 1909.

Classically elegant guestrooms and suites underwent a refreshment in 2002 and are now done up in pale sunny tones with broad accents of color. With 14-foot ceilings and windows that open, they are spacious and airy. For business travelers, work areas are ample and well lit, with high-speed Internet access (wireless is available in meeting spaces), two-line phones and laptop safes. The fitness center features a beautiful skylit lap pool, workout room and spa services.

Palomar

005

12 4th St. (at Market St.)

Phone:	415-348-1111
Fax:	415-348-0302
Web:	www.hotelpalomar.com
Prices:	rooms: $299 - $499 suites: $499 - $899

182
Rooms
16
Suites

Hotel Palomar/Mark Leet

Edgy, urban, artful, tranquil: this downtown addition to the Kimpton family of properties offers just enough of each in a great location. At home on the 5th through the 8th floors of a landmark 1908 building, Hotel Palomar comprises 198 guestrooms, including 16 one- and two-bedroom suites.

Some of the rooms overlook Fourth and Market streets (they are well soundproofed) while the rest face the interior courtyard. Rooms are quite spacious and strike a good balance between contemporary style and restful atmosphere, though every one sports a sassy leopard-print carpet. Rooms provide complimentary Aveda bath amenities, two plush robes, wireless Internet access, CD and DVD players and an expanded work area. Suites and luxury rooms feature Fuji spa tubs and turreted windows with circular seating areas.

Guests can enjoy the on-site fitness center on the 5th floor 24 hours a day, and complimentary yoga baskets are available upon request. Morning coffee is served in the lobby, and the stylish Fifth Floor Restaurant *(see SoMa restaurant listings)*—acclaimed for its contemporary French cuisine—is open for breakfast and dinner.

St. Regis

006

125 3rd St. (at Mission St.)

Phone:	415-284-4000
Fax:	415-442-0385
Web:	www.stregis.com
Prices:	rooms: $409 - $529 suites: $650 - $1,350

214
Rooms
46
Suites
♿
Spa
heated

St. Regis/Joe Fletcher Photography

The historic St. Regis' first incarnation in the City by the Bay is anything but stuffy. Occupying the first 20 floors of a handsome new high rise designed by Skidmore, Owings, and Merrill, the new hotel epitomizes the look and feel of classic contemporary. The oxymoron works, and it doesn't stop there. The complex also includes 102 condos on the upper floors, a 1907 building and the Museum of the African Diaspora. Next door is the San Francisco Museum of Modern Art.

Throughout, the hotel cultivates neutral colors, from the striated Zebrano wood of the lobby to the rich cocoa and foggy gray tones of the guestrooms. A striking 16-foot open fireplace greets guests as they enter the lobby, which also features a sleek lounge area. Cool, comfortable and spacious rooms and suites overlook Yerba Buena Park or have expansive city views. On the ground level, Ame *(see SoMa restaurant listings)* serves Hiro Sone's modern fusion cuisine.

Plasma-screen TVs are standard, and a touchscreen on the nightstand controls the room's temperature, curtains and lighting. Those familiar with St. Regis service will be cheered to know that the signature personal butlers are alive and well here.

Vitale

8 Mission St. (bet. Steuart St. & The Embarcadero)

Phone: 415-278-3700
Fax: 415-278-3750
Web: www.hotelvitale.com
Prices: rooms: $279 - $399 suites: $599 - $1,500

179
Rooms
20
Suites

Hotel Vitale

A San Francisco newcomer, the self-proclaimed "post-hip" Vitale occupies a prime location on the city's waterfront in the revitalized Embarcadero. Across the street, the Ferry Building Marketplace offers a panoply of gourmet delights, and San Francisco Bay laps at the front yard.

A fresh and natural luxury permeates public spaces and guestrooms. Rich wood paneling, rough-hewn stone columns, large softly curtained windows and simply designed furniture in muted hues give the lobby a modern Scandinavian look. Natural light streams into the airy guestrooms, where all the details have been carefully planned with a sumptuous touch: luxurious linens, flat-screen TVs, CD players and complimentary wireless Internet access. About half the 199 rooms on the hotel's eight floors have waterfront views; suites in the circular tower offer 180-degree panoramas of city and bay.

Among the offerings at the dog-friendly Vitale are free yoga classes for guests, and an on-site spa with rooftop soaking tubs for soaking up fabulous views. Americano restaurant *(see SoMa restaurant listings)* serves breakfast, lunch, dinner and weekend brunch; the circular bar makes a comfortable place to hang out.

San Francisco City SoMa

Claremont Resort & Spa

41 Tunnel Rd., Berkeley

Phone: 510-843-3000
Fax: 510-843-6239
Web: www.claremontresort.com
Prices: rooms: $200 – $630 suites: $600 – $1,500 Restaurant: **$$$**

263 Rooms
16 Suites

heated

Claremont Resort & Spa

Conceived in the grand tradition of 19th-century resort spas, the Claremont in its present configuration opened for business in 1915. For over 90 years, it has pampered guests with comfort, cuisine and spa services par excellence. Today the gleaming white castle-like edifice houses 279 luxurious rooms, three restaurants, a world-renowned spa, and a spectacular health club open to all guests. Surrounded by 22 beautifully landscaped acres in the hills overlooking San Francisco Bay, the Claremont promises classic resort indulgence and luxury.

Rooms offer three degrees of comfort (all sumptuous); about half of them face the stunning skyline vista of San Francisco and the Bay Bridge. Amenities include Internet access and in-room entertainment centers; some bathrooms feature whirlpool tubs.

With so much to do around the resort, however, you may not spend much time in your room. At the on-site private health club, 10 tennis courts (6 lit for evening play), 2 outdoor heated pools, fitness equipment and 65 weekly classes from yoga to hula will keep you busy. Relaxing treatments, wraps and massages at the 20,000-square-foot Spa Claremont ice the cake.

Washington Inn

002

495 10th St., Oakland (at Washington St.)

Phone: 510-452-1776
Fax: 510-452-4436
Web: www.thewashingtoninn.com
Prices: rooms: $109 – $159 suites: $149 – $169 Restaurant: **$$**

41
Rooms
6
Suites

Washington Inn

This hotel occupies a central location in a historic building in the heart of downtown Oakland. Just across the street from the Convention Center and not far from the waterfront, Jack London Square, and restaurants and shops, the Washington Inn offers convenient lodging at reasonable rates. Service, while limited, is unpretentious.

Renovated in a straightforward contemporary style in 2001, the 41 small rooms offer simple comfort. Bathrooms are standard, without any particular luxury, and pedestal sinks are located, European-style, in a corner of the bedrooms. If you're interested in larger accommodations, six suites include an additional parlor with a couch and built-in bar; these quarters also come equipped with a microwave, two televisions, a refrigerator and bar, and cotton bathrobes for a touch of class. All rooms provide wireless Internet access.

At Twist Restaurant and Bar, guests can enjoy nightly dinner and weekend lunches in a rustic, white-linen setting with live piano music several nights of the week.

Casa Madrona

001

801 Bridgeway, Sausalito

Phone: 415-332-0532
Fax: 415-332-2537
Web: www.casamadrona.com
Prices: rooms: $159 – $459

63
Rooms
&

Spa

Casa Madrona Hotel & Spa

Whether you prefer contemporary or historic surroundings, Casa Madrona has a room for you. Tucked into a hillside rising from the Sausalito waterfront, the complex includes a 19th-century mansion, a covey of quaint cottages and a modern hotel building. From its elevated vantage point, the Victorian Mansion, built in 1885, offers lovely bay views.

Nineteenth-century atmosphere pervades its small but charming guestrooms, each decorated individually with antique furniture and period wallpaper. Cottage-style accommodations built into the hillside since 1976 include the mid-size Garden Court rooms (decorated in contemporary or historic styles), and the Bayview rooms, each of which features a distinctive decorating theme—from the Rose Chalet to the exotic Katmandu room. Most of these offer fireplaces and large private balconies. Brick pathways and outdoor stair steps set about with gardens and scented plantings connect these chambers. California contemporary-style rooms occupy the most recently opened addition to the hotel in a building perched on the waterfront.

Downstairs, Poggio *(see North of San Francisco restaurant listings)* dishes up authentic Italian fare.

The Inn Above Tide

002

30 El Portal, Sausalito (at Bridgeway)

Phone:	415-332-9535
Fax:	415-332-6714
Web:	www.innabovetide.com
Prices:	rooms: $285 – $895

29 Rooms

©Marco Ricca, NY

You can't get much closer to the bay than at The Inn Above Tide, where balconies extend out over the lapping water. Also nearby the attractive shingled building is the San Francisco ferry landing and the Sausalito visitor center kiosk.

The hotel's small lobby accommodates only the reception desk; complimentary continental breakfast is served in the adjacent small guest lounge—or the staff will deliver it to your room, if you prefer. Each of the 29 newly renovated rooms faces the water and offers stunning views of San Francisco, Sausalito and Angel Island. Floor-to-ceiling windows bring the outdoors in, and binoculars come standard in each room.

Small superior rooms offer no deck, but deluxe rooms feature terraces and wood- or gas-burning fireplaces, and a host of amenities that increase as you upgrade from queen to king to grand. All rooms offer wireless Internet access. Interiors are styled in sober but soothing beige tones, with nature providing a vivid blue accent just outside.

Hotel De Anza

001

233 W. Santa Clara St., San Jose
(bet. Almaden Blvd. & Notre Dame Ave.)

Phone: 408-286-1000
Fax: 408-286-2087
Web: www.hoteldeanza.com
Prices: rooms: $129 - $399 suites: $375 - $475 Restaurant: $$

80
Rooms
20
Suites
♿
🚲
🧖

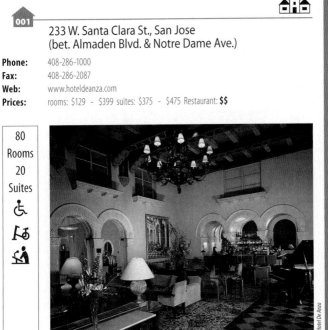

Hotel De Anza

A complete renovation in 1990 brought this Art Deco gem back to life, where it most decidedly remains. Behind its unmistakable pink façade, the Hotel De Anza exudes a genuine period charm, from its spacious and comfortable lobby to its pleasant guestrooms and suites. Its ideal location in downtown San Jose makes it convenient for business or pleasure.

Neutral taupes and browns with blond wood furniture warm the bedrooms without overdoing it. And though most rooms face a busy street, they are adequately soundproofed. Bathrooms are decorated in green marble. High-speed Internet (with wireless in the public areas), two TVs, and a VCR with complimentary videos furnish each room, along with three phones.

Check out La Pastaia restaurant for Italian cuisine served in a colorful taverna atmosphere. Late-night snackers can "Raid Our Pantry" for free deli sandwiches between 10pm and 5am. In the morning, a full buffet featuring cold and hot items is served in the brightly hand-painted breakfast room. Don't miss sipping a cocktail at the Hedley Club lounge, accented by an exotic Moorish-Spanish décor.

Hotel Montgomery

002

211 S. 1st St., San Jose (at San Carlos St.)

Phone: 408-282-8800
Fax: 408-282-8850
Web: www.hotelmontgomerysj.com
Prices: rooms: $109 – $309 suites: $169 – $339 Restaurant: **$$**

80
Rooms
6
Suites

♿

South of San Francisco

Jose de Vivre Hospitality

With some subtle modern stylings, well-placed accents and warm undertones of color, this 1911 landmark hotel has been made new again. The entire Renaissance Revival building was moved 186 feet from its original location in 2002, in order to save it from the wrecking ball. Refreshed by a renovation in 2004, today's Montgomery offers an attractive and reasonably priced stay in downtown San Jose.

Pleasant and tastefully decorated, the 86 rooms and suites feature Egyptian cotton linens and down comforters. The unpretentious furniture was specially designed for the hotel in keeping with its timeless atmosphere, and bathrooms are elegantly appointed with lovely beige marble. Conveniences, including high-speed Internet and laptop-size safes, make the rooms thoroughly modern.

A 24-hour business center and a fitness room are available for guests, who are also welcome to enjoy a free beverage weeknights at the Paragon Restaurant and Bar (famous for its expansive choice of vodkas). If the spirit moves, you can enjoy a friendly game of bocce ball in the outdoor plaza.

Hotel Valencia

003

355 Santana Row, San Jose (bet. Olin Ave. & Tatum Lane)

Phone:	408-551-0010
Fax:	408-551-0550
Web:	www.hotelvalencia.com
Prices:	rooms: $169 – $500 suites: $400 – $1,500 Restaurant: **$$$**

195
Rooms
16
Suites

Hotel Valencia

This charming hacienda, punctuated with Asian accents, is located in Santana Row, San Jose's new upscale "urban oasis" where shopping, dining, living and entertainment venues share 42 acres near downtown. The hotel spans an entire block, and, inside and out, evokes a gracious Old World atmosphere done up in chic California style.

Visitors enter through the large main lobby and take an elevator to the third-floor reception area, warmly decorated in rich tones of red and ochre. Outside, the hotel floors rise around a charming courtyard, complete with a central fountain and an open fireplace. Dine on this cozy patio at Citrus, the hotel's sleek, contemporary steakhouse. Or, for a spectacular view with your Shiraz, ascend to the seventh-floor terrace of the Cielo Bar.

Accommodations are generously sized; deluxe rooms feature balconies overlooking Santana Row or the hotel's courtyard. Deep yellow walls and dark wood furniture and trim give rooms a European feel. Perfectly equipped bathrooms include robes and oversized plush towels. High-speed and wireless Internet access are complimentary. For relaxing, Valencia offers an Ayurvedic spa and a lovely outdoor pool on the fifth floor.

Auberge du Soleil

180 Rutherford Hill Rd., Rutherford (off the Silverado Trail)

Phone:	707-963-1211
Fax:	707-963-8764
Web:	www.aubergedusoleil.com
Prices:	rooms: $550 – $925 suites: $950 – $1,750

40
Rooms
19
Suites
♿
🛏
Spa
🎿
heated
🛎

Auberge du Soleil

The quintessential Wine Country hideaway, the "Inn of the Sun" tucks into 33 hilly acres overlooking the Napa Valley. It was the valley's first luxury hotel when it opened its rooms to guests in 1985. More than 20 years later, silvery olive trees and sunny colors still create a rustic Mediterranean feel, while flat-screen TVs, DVD players and complimentary wireless Internet access provide all the modern amenities you could wish for.

Scrambling down the hillsides, newly renovated rooms and suites, all housed in "sun and earth" cottages, feature Italian linens, down pillows and duvets, robes and slippers, private terraces and mini-bars stocked with beverages and snacks—compliments of the house. Spacious bathrooms are equipped with skylights, separate showers, and LCD flat-panel TVs to watch while you soak in the tub.

Be sure to savor a meal at The Restaurant at Auberge du Soleil *(see Napa Valley restaurant listings)*, which is renowned as much for its breezy terrace and sweeping views as for its excellent Mediterranean cuisine. And pamper yourself with a Napa-themed treatment (a warm grapeseed-oil massage or the Vineyard Head to Toe) at the 7,000-square-foot Spa du Soleil.

Lavender

2020 Webber St., Yountville (bet. Yount & Jefferson Sts.)

Phone:	707-944-1388
Fax:	707-944-1579
Web:	www.lavendernapa.com
Prices:	rooms: $200 – $250

8
Rooms
♿

Four Sisters Inn

Nested in a profusion of lavender and roses, this country inn offers a comfortable, rustic stay in the heart of Napa. A wraparound porch embraces the main farmhouse, and inside, the small entry parlor and sunny breakfast room welcome guests. A full complimentary meal is served each morning, to be enjoyed here or in the lovely terrace garden.

Two guestrooms also occupy the main house, one with a private spa tub tucked onto an enclosed outdoor deck. Six cottage rooms surround the house and garden, each with its own private entrance and patio. All the accommodations are spacious and decorated with warmth and sophisticated country charm in the Provençal style; they include king beds and fireplaces. Glazed tile glistens in the gracious bathrooms, set off pleasingly by brightly painted walls. Double sinks and a generous-size tub make these baths particularly pleasant, though soaking tubs have no showers. Wireless Internet access is available throughout the hotel.

Guests at Lavender can borrow house bicycles for a spin, and enjoy pool privileges (for a fee) at nearby Maison Fleurie. Or, try your hand at *boules*, the French version of lawn bowling.

Wine Country Napa Valley

Maison Fleurie

003

6529 Yount St., Yountville (at Washington St.)

Phone:	707-944-2056
Fax:	707-944-9342
Web:	www.maisonfleurienapa.com
Prices:	rooms: $200 – $250

13
Rooms
♿
⛷
heated

Four Sisters Inn

The "flowering house" has given itself over to a lush French country style, with Provençal-inspired fabrics, furnishings and atmosphere. Located in three buildings set amid beautifully landscaped gardens and overlooking vineyards, the 13 rooms of the Maison Fleurie spell charm and comfort.

A homey lobby/lounge complete with a fireplace welcomes visitors in the main building, where seven of the guestrooms are located. These include king and queen rooms, along with two very small rooms without televisions. The two Carriage House rooms have private entrances, and those in the Bakery Building all include fireplaces, king beds and whirlpool spa tubs. Breakfast (with home-baked muffins and bread) and evening wine and hors d'oeuvres are complimentary for all guests, and every room features wireless Internet access.

On the grounds, the small heated swimming pool and outdoor hot tub are pleasant, and the vistas delightful. Guests can borrow bicycles for a spin in the countryside or an exploration of the surrounding town of Yountville, known for its trendy boutiques and excellent eateries.

Meadowood

004

900 Meadowood Lane, St. Helena (off the Silverado Trail)

Phone: 707-963-3646
Fax: 707-963-3532
Web: www.meadowood.com
Prices: rooms: $525 - $825 suites: $750 - $1,450 Restaurant: **$$$**

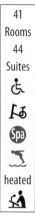

41
Rooms
44
Suites

heated

Meadowood Napa

Set on 250 exquisite acres a mile east of downtown St. Helena, this world-class resort off the Silverado Trail nestles amid wooded hills, where accommodations take the form of individual cottages. A country-club ambience pervades this Relais & Châteaux property, and white wainscoting, stone fireplaces, French doors and private terraces highlight the room décor. (The resort doubles as a private country club for Napa Valley residents.)

While Meadowood makes the perfect perch for Wine Country adventures, between the 9-hole golf course, 7 tennis courts, 2 croquet lawns, 2 lap pools, the fitness center and the full-service spa, you may never want to leave the grounds. There's even a wine center (ask the staff to arrange vineyard picnics), where the resort's wine tutor holds tastings and seminars for guests. Meals can be either casual, at The Grill, or more formal, at The Restaurant at Meadowood (jackets required) with its refined California cuisine.

An ambitious renovation is currently under way here; the restoration is scheduled to end in 2008 with the completion of a brand new spa.

Wine Country Napa Valley

Napa River Inn

Napa River Inn

005

500 Main St., Napa (at 5th St.)

Phone: 707-251-8550
Fax: 707-251-8504
Web: www.napariverinn.com
Prices: rooms: $179 - $399

68 Rooms

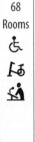

The Historic Napa Mill (1884), with its present-day complex of shops and restaurants, forms a wonderfully convenient setting for this downtown boutique hotel. Rooms at the Napa River Inn are divided among three structures and are distinguished by three different design themes. Full of vintage charm, eight rooms in the 1884 Hatt Building are done in Victorian style with canopy beds, fireplaces, and old-fashioned slipper tubs. In the Plaza Building, 34 rooms sport a rustic Wine Country décor and creature comforts such as marble bathrooms and balconies with river views. The remaining guestrooms are housed in the 1862 Embarcadero Building, where they are decked out in a maritime motif, complete with cherry wood wainscoting, porthole mirrors and carved-rope frames.

All rooms offer amenities such as complimentary daily newspaper, bottled water, irons and ironing boards, terrycloth robes, and nightlights and make-up mirrors. Grapeseed-oil-based bath products are de rigueur for this Wine Country inn.

Napa city's points of interest lie close by, and if you don't feel like walking, the city trolley stops in front of the hotel every 15 minutes to transport you around the downtown area.

Rancho Caymus Inn

1140 Rutherford Rd., Rutherford (off Hwy. 29)

Phone: 707-963-1777
Fax: 707-963-5387
Web: www.ranchocaymus.com
Prices: rooms: $155 - $320 suites: $215 - $450

23
Rooms
3
Suites
♿

Rancho Caymus Inn

Wine Country Napa Valley

Nicely located between St. Helena and Yountville, Rancho Caymus Inn blends a bit of old California with Wine Country convenience and unpretentious western hospitality. All the rooms and suites are housed in the rambling hacienda-style building. Each bears the name of a Napa Valley personality, from Lillie Langtry to Black Bart.

Mexican-style wooden furniture, hand-carved walnut bedsteads, wrought-iron details and colorful woolen rugs impart a genuine Old West ranch feeling to the spacious rooms. Massive century-old oak ceiling beams and trim of walnut, fir and redwood add a natural warmth. Designed as "split levels," the sleeping areas are set up a step in each room. Standard amenities include televisions, air conditioning, wet bar and refrigerator, and some rooms have mission-style fireplaces and private outdoor balconies or sitting areas. More elaborate Master Suites feature whirlpool tubs against a stained-glass backdrop in their bathrooms. All the rooms are quiet, well maintained and clean, and breakfast is included in the room rate.

In the evening, dine in style at La Toque *(see Napa Valley restaurant listings)*, which is adjacent to the inn.

Villagio Inn & Spa

007

6481 Washington St., Yountville

Phone: 707-944-8877
Fax: 707-944-8855
Web: www.villagio.com
Prices: rooms: $295 – $505 suites: $490 – $610

86 Rooms 26 Suites

♿ ♿ Spa ♿ heated ♿

M. Linda Lee/MICHELIN

Villagio brings to mind a Tuscan village; two-story villas range through lush gardens and vineyards that share a 23-acre family-owned estate with the Vintage Inn. A stroll around the grounds here reveals tranquil pools and fountains, vivid flowers, and cypress, olive, and Meyer lemon trees.

Accommodations are done in Tuscan style with warm tones, wrought-iron accents, plantation shutters and wood-burning fireplaces. Rooms on the upper levels have domed ceilings and furnished balconies (ground-level rooms have patios). Villagio accommodates business functions with 10,000 square feet of meeting space. In the morning, breakfast takes the form of a complimentary gourmet buffet (complete with champagne) served in the lobby. Also included in the room rate is the afternoon tea and Friday evening wine tastings, sponsored by local vineyards.

At the end of a long day spent cycling or visiting wineries, a Napa River stone massage at the Spa at Villagio is a great way to unwind. (A new expanded spa is in the planning stages.) Weddings are memorable events at Villagio, especially with the addition of the new outdoor pavilion surrounded by grassy lawns and bright plantings.

Vintage Inn

008

6541 Washington St., Yountville

Phone: 707-944-1112
Fax: 707-944-1617
Web: www.vintageinn.com
Prices: rooms: $230 - $485 suites: $385 - $610

72
Rooms
8
Suites

heated

Vintage Inn

Wine Country Napa Valley

Opened in 1985, this lovely property lines Yountville's main street with French Country charm. Paths and footbridges connect the two-story buildings, where French antiques, toile de Jouy fabrics, plush robes and down duvets set the tone for luxurious comfort. Each room features a wood-burning fireplace, and bathrooms are equipped with dual sinks and an oversize whirlpool tub; suites add wet bars and eating areas.

Rates include a bottle of wine in your room, a gourmet breakfast buffet and afternoon tea. If you tire of touring wineries, the inn offers an outdoor heated lap pool, tennis courts and bicycle rentals. Not to mention the fact that guests have equal access to the spa at sibling Villagio and to the Yountville Fitness Center (at no charge). Pets are welcomed here with their own goodies (no wine, but some yummy treats).

Shoppers can stroll next door to explore Vintage 1870. Once the Groezinger Winery, this brick complex now houses shops, galleries and eateries. Foodies will love the fact that some of Napa Valley's most renowned restaurants—Bouchon, Bistro Jeanty, Redd, The French Laundry *(see Napa Valley restaurant listings)*—lie within easy walking distance of the resort.

Duchamp

421 Foss St., Healdsburg (at North St.)

Phone: 707-431-1300
Fax: 707-431-1333
Web: www.duchamphotel.com
Prices: rooms: $325 - $385

6
Rooms
♿
🏊
heated

Duchamp Hotel/David Livingston

This unusual small hotel is located within minutes of Healdsburg's downtown plaza, convenient to the wineries of the Russian River, Dry Creek and Alexander Valley. The owners also run a small winery of the same name. Their affection for French Dada artist Marcel Duchamp manifests itself in wonderful, whimsical ways at both locations.

The hotel comprises seven small bungalows: one for reception and six housing one guestroom each. The grouping surrounds a heated swimming pool equipped with sundeck and Jacuzzi. Each room is large, but minimalist in style, with whitewashed walls and decorative murals to add just a touch of color. Floors are polished concrete, the furniture contemporary. French doors let in the light, and each cottage features a private patio. King beds furnish the rooms, along with a high-definition flat-screen TV, a CD player and free wireless Internet access. White walls and tiles dress the very large bathrooms, which include two washbasins and a roomy shower.

Guests are treated to a continental breakfast buffet in the reception cottage, and the hotel staff will gladly arrange for private tours and tastings at Duchamp Estate Winery.

Hotel Healdsburg

25 Matheson St., Healdsburg (at Healdsburg Ave.)

Phone: 707-431-2800
Fax: 707-431-0414
Web: www.hotelhealdsburg.com
Prices: rooms: $260 - $545 suites: $547 - $790

51
Rooms
4
Suites

Hotel Healdsburg

Facing Healdsburg's century-old town plaza, Hotel Healdsburg fills two connecting buildings with a warm, contemporary décor. Start in the lobby, with its clean lines, comfy seating and adjacent screened porch for refreshments. Then it's off to your spacious room, where you'll be greeted by Tibetan rugs, teak furniture, fine linens, and French doors leading to your own private balcony.

Oversize bathrooms are outfitted with walk-in showers and separate soaking tubs. Outside, the pool beckons from its olive- and cypress-tree-shrouded nook.

Pamper yourself at the hotel's spa, where you can unwind with a Thai massage or a wine and honey wrap. For an amorous afternoon, indulge yourself and a loved one in a massage and soak à deux, complete with sparkling wine and chocolates. After your spa treatment, finish off the day right by savoring refined contemporary cuisine at Charlie Palmer's Dry Creek Kitchen *(see Russian River Valley restaurant listings)*. A kicked-up continental breakfast is included in the room rate.

Wine Country Russian River Valley

Honor Mansion

14891 Grove St., Healdsburg
(bet. Dry Creek Rd. & Grand St.)

Phone:	707-433-4277
Fax:	707-431-7173
Web:	www.honormansion.com
Prices:	rooms: $225 – $575

13 Rooms

♿

The Honor Mansion

Romance awaits behind the unassuming façade of this restored 1883 house, located less than 1 mile away from the tony boutiques, tasting rooms and fine restaurants lining Healdsburg's downtown plaza. Owners Cathi and Steve Fowler have anticipated guests' every need in the 13 individually decorated rooms and suites. Rooms in the main house vary in size and style, while four separate Vineyard Suites (the priciest accommodations) foster *amore* with king-size beds, gas fireplaces, and private patios complete with your own whirlpool (robes and rubber ducky included). On the four-acre grounds, landscaped with rose gardens and Zinfandel vines, you'll find a lap pool, a PGA putting green, bocce and tennis courts, a croquet lawn, and a half-basketball court.

The multicourse gourmet breakfast, which will steel your stomach for a day of sampling wine at area vineyards, is included in the room rate. Following the Fowlers' hospitable lead, the staff will pack you a picnic lunch, and make arrangements for everything from private winery visits to poolside massages, all with equal aplomb.

On weekends, count on a minimum stay of two nights in low season, and four nights in high season.

Les Mars

27 North St., Healdsburg
(bet. Foss St. & Healdsburg Ave.)

Phone: 707-433-4211
Fax: 707-433-4611
Web: www.lesmarshotel.com
Prices: rooms: $425 – $1,025

16
Rooms
&
[bike]
[pool]

Les Mars Hotel

Picture the limestone façade of a 19th-century French chateau just off Healdsburg's plaza, and you've got Les Mars. Step inside and you'll be instantly awash in luxury, from the 17th-century Flemish tapestry that hangs in the lobby to the hand-carved walnut panels and leather-bound books that line the library.

Sumptuous antiques fill the 16 individually designed rooms with the likes of Louis XV armoires, draped four-poster beds, and chaise longues. Italian linens, reading lights and switch-operated fireplaces provide extra thoughtful touches. In the bathrooms, lined with salt and pepper marble, you can pamper yourself with deep soaking tubs, lavender bath salts and Bulgari amenities. Third-floor rooms boast high ceilings with exposed wood beams. Yes, the prices are steep, but this level of luxury doesn't come cheap.

The adjoining Cyrus restaurant (a separate venture; *see Russian River Valley restaurant listings*) makes an equally elegant setting in which to linger over chef Douglas Keane's contemporary cooking.

Note that there's a minimum stay of two nights on weekends, and this family-owned hotel is not recommended for children under 12 years of age.

Vintners Inn

005

4350 Barnes Rd., Santa Rosa (at River Rd.)

Phone: 707-575-7350
Fax: 707-575-1426
Web: www.vintnersinn.com
Prices: rooms: $215 - $350

44 Rooms

Vintners Inn

Nestled in 92 acres of vineyards, Vintners Inn welcomes guests with a bottle of wine. The inn, owned by Dan and Rhonda Carano of Ferrari-Carano Winery, is located just north of Santa Rosa and convenient to Highway 101.

Four two-story Tuscan-style buildings with red-tile roofs range around a landscaped courtyard. Each room enjoys its own private balcony or small patio. Country décor is rustic and refined, and Internet access and a copy of the local newspaper come compliments of the house. Rooms on the second floor boast vaulted ceilings with exposed wood beams; some are equipped with fireplaces. If you want a bit more space, reserve a Junior Suite, outfitted with a king-size featherbed, a fireplace, and a sitting area with sleeper sofa. A 32-inch television with VCR and CD player, two-line phones and dataport add to the modern amenities.

Rates include a buffet breakfast each morning; for lunch or dinner, you need only walk next door to John Ash and Co. *(see Russian River Valley restaurant listings)* for a meal that highlights Sonoma County products.

In June 2006, the inn opened its new Event and Conference Center, with more than 6,000 square feet of meeting space.

Wine Country **Russian River Valley**

El Dorado

001

405 First St. West, Sonoma (at W. Spain St.)

Phone: 707-996-3220
Fax: 707-996-3148
Web: www.eldoradosonoma.com
Prices: rooms: $145 - $195

27
Rooms
&
heated

El Dorado Hotel

Wine Country Sonoma Valley

The El Dorado occupies a spot at the heart of historic Sonoma, located directly on Spanish Plaza in a recently renovated historic building. Laid out by Mariano Vallejo in 1835, the eight-acre site is the largest Mexican-era plaza in California.

Light and color set the hotel's 27 rooms aglow, while cool tile floors suggest the town's Spanish origins and four-poster beds made up with fine linens add romance. French doors open onto private balconies or terraces and admit a wash of sunlight into the rooms. Some look over the historic plaza; others face the restaurant terrace, which is shaded by a fig tree. Though most bathrooms offer only showers, they are well appointed. Electronics include a flat-screen TV, along with DVD and CD players, cordless phone and dataport.

If you don't mind casual service, the El Dorado presents good value for the money, as well as an alternative to the Provençal or Tuscany style that predominate in other Wine Country hostelries. Savor seasonal California cuisine at El Dorado Kitchen *(see Sonoma restaurant listings)*.

The Fairmont Sonoma Mission Inn & Spa

002

100 Boyes Blvd., Sonoma (bet. Arnold Dr. & Hwy. 12)

Phone:	707-938-9000
Fax:	707-938-4250
Web:	www.fairmont.com
Prices:	rooms: $299 - $499 suites: $499 - $899 Restaurant: **$$$**

166
Rooms
60
Suites

heated

Fairmont Sonoma Mission Inn & Spa

Tile roofs, adobe walls and the historic character of a Sonoma Valley mission create the perfect backdrop for a relaxing weekend getaway or a visit to Wine Country. Originally built around an ancient hot springs in 1895, the resort was rebuilt in 1927 after fire destroyed the property. Renovated and greatly expanded since then, the facility retains its gracious 1920s atmosphere with all the comforts of a modern hotel and spa.

Nowadays, guests can still "take the waters," and enjoy the services of the modern 40,000-square-foot spa as well. They can also play the private 18-hole championship golf course, hike the countryside, lounge by the pool, take fitness classes or join bike tours. The sprawling resort comprises a central "living room" with a variety of accommodations spread among an assortment of buildings. Done up in French country décor, standard rooms tend to be small; wood-burning fireplaces furnish about half of them. Signature Mission Suites, the most recent additions to the property, foster romance with two-person Jacuzzi tubs and private patios or balconies.

Gaige House Inn

13540 Arnold Dr., Glen Ellen (at Railroad St.)

Phone: 707-935-0237
Fax: 707-935-6411
Web: www.gaige.com
Prices: rooms: $300 - $450 suites: $500 - $595

12
Rooms
11
Suites

heated

Gaige House Inn

The Gaige House Inn offers a complete departure from typical Wine Country accommodations. Here, serenity trumps country or western charm; Japanese influences replace French and Spanish inside an 1890 Queen Anne Victorian. Tucked away on three wooded creekside acres, this intimate inn features a full menu of spa services, a particularly fine breakfast and a lovely swimming pool.

Guests can reserve a room in the main house or a garden or creek suite in separate cottage settings. Though all 23 rooms and suites share a similar palette of earthy browns and grays with design details inspired by nature, each one has been thoughtfully furnished, decorated and arranged individually. In some, tatami mats cover hardwood floors, and rice paper screens decorate the walls; others feature fireplaces. In eight new spa suites, beautifully hewn granite soaking tubs and Japanese tsubo gardens for massage services turn your room into a spa. All cottage rooms feature private terraces or a little garden by the creek. This secluded inn promises quiet nights and peaceful days.

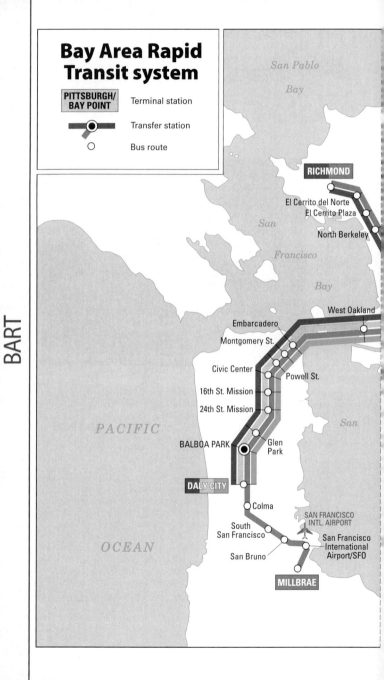

Bay Area Rapid Transit system

PITTSBURGH/ BAY POINT — Terminal station

Transfer station

Bus route

RICHMOND
El Cerrito del Norte
El Cerrito Plaza
North Berkeley

West Oakland
Embarcadero
Montgomery St.
Civic Center
Powell St.
16th St. Mission
24th St. Mission
BALBOA PARK — Glen Park
DALY CITY
Colma
South San Francisco
San Bruno
SAN FRANCISCO INTL. AIRPORT
San Francisco International Airport/SFO
MILLBRAE

San Pablo Bay
San Francisco Bay
PACIFIC OCEAN

BART

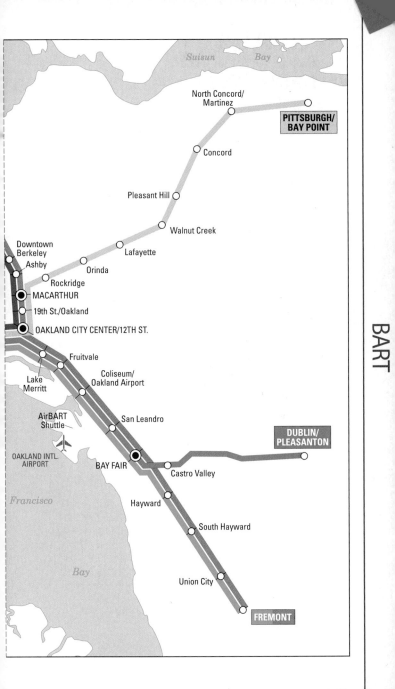

Notes

Notes

Notes

Notes

Notes

Notes

Notes

Notes

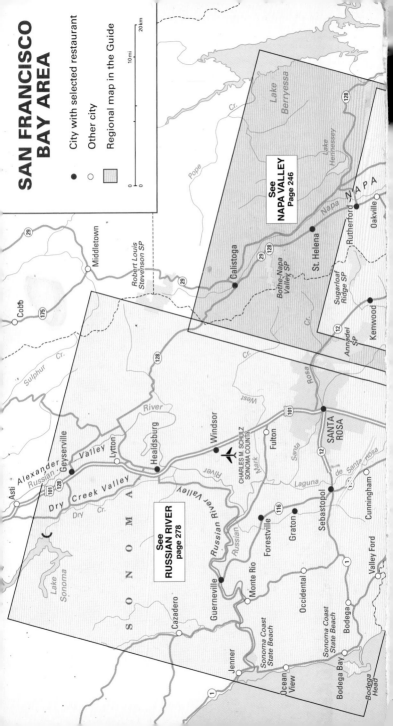